D1595837

The Human Cost of Welfare

The Human Cost of Welfare

How the System Hurts the People It's Supposed to Help

Phil Harvey and Lisa Conyers

Foreword by Jonathan Rauch

 PRAEGER™

An Imprint of ABC-CLIO, LLC

Santa Barbara. California • Denver. Colorado

Library of Congress Cataloging-in-Publication Data

Names: Harvey, Philip D., 1938- author. | Conyers, Lisa, author.
Title: The human cost of welfare : how the system hurts the people it's supposed to help /
    Phil Harvey and Lisa Conyers ; foreword by Jonathan Rauch
Description: Santa Barbara, California : Praeger, [2016] | Includes bibliographical references
    and index.
Identifiers: LCCN 2015039114 | ISBN 9781440845345 (alk. paper) | ISBN 9781440845352 (ebook)
Subjects: LCSH: Public welfare—United States. | Welfare recipients—United States. | Poor—United
    States. | United States—Social policy.
Classification: LCC HV95 .H327 2016 | DDC 362.5/8—dc23 LC record available at
    http://lccn.loc.gov/2015039114

ISBN: 978-1-4408-4534-5
EISBN: 978-1-4408-4535-2

20 19 18 17 16   2 3 4 5

This book is also available on the World Wide Web as an eBook.
Visit www.abc-clio.com for details.

Praeger
An Imprint of ABC-CLIO, LLC

ABC-CLIO, LLC
130 Cremona Drive, P.O. Box 1911
Santa Barbara, California 93116-1911

This book is printed on acid-free paper ∞

Manufactured in the United States of America

For those who work, or will.

Contents

Figures, Tables, and Appendices   ix
Foreword *by Jonathan Rauch*   xi
Acknowledgments   xv

Introduction: Welfare Reforms Need Reforming   xvii

Part I. The Welfare Conflict

Chapter 1.   What Does Work Have to Do with Happiness?   3

Chapter 2.   The War Between Welfare and Work   9

Part II. The Counterproductive Qualifications for Welfare

Chapter 3.   What Counts as Poverty   19

Chapter 4.   Marriage, Childbearing, and Teen Pregnancy   25

Part III. Welfare Programs in Theory and in Fact

Chapter 5.   TANF: The Changing Face of Cash Assistance   41

Chapter 6.   A Housing System Leaves the Needy Out in the Cold   49

Chapter 7.   Who Gets Food Stamps?   53

Chapter 8.   WIC: Missteps with Women and Children   65

Chapter 9.   How We Disable the Disabled   71

Chapter 10.   Medicaid and the Affordable Care Act   93

Chapter 11.   The Earned Income Tax Credit: Welfare Done
(Almost) Right   109

Part IV. Building Blocks for a Better Welfare System

Chapter 12.   Patterns of Dependence and Independence:
American Indians on Reservations, Barterers,
and Immigrants   127

Chapter 13.   What Should Be Done: From Incentives to
Special Savings Accounts, Solutions Abound to
Get Americans Back to Work   145

Notes   169

Bibliography   193

Index   199

Figures, Tables, and Appendices

FIGURES

3.1 Amenities in Poor Households   22
4.1 Child Poverty Rates by Living Arrangement, 1975–2009   26
4.2 Percentage of Total Births to Unmarried Women, 1940–2013   27
5.1 TANF Case Loads   42
5.2 MOE and Block Grant Spending   43
5.3 Estimated Number of TANF Recipients by Poverty Status, 2010   44
6.1 Median Asking Rent, 1988–2013   50
6.2 Federal Housing Assistance   51
7.1 SNAP: Costs and Participation Rates   55
7.2 Food Stamp Recipients by Poverty Status, 2010   57
8.1 Average Monthly Participation in WIC, FY 1980–2013   66
8.2 WIC Expenditures per Year   66
8.3 Savings from Infant Formula Rebates   68
9.1 SSDI and SSI Recipients, by Year   73
9.2 Diagnostic Causes of New SSDI Awards   74
9.3 Labor Force Participation Rate   83
9.4 Trends in the Number of Veterans Receiving VA Disability Payments and in Spending on VA Disability Compensation   87
10.1 Where the States Stand on Medicaid Expansion   94
10.2 Maximum Annual Income to Retain Medicaid Eligibility   95
10.3 Medicaid Participation by Year   98
10.4 Federal, State, and Local Medicaid Expenditures, 1980–2010   99

11.1   Real Federal Spending on EITC, CTC, and TANF, 1975–2011   111
11.2   Percentage of Filers Receiving EITC, by State, 2010   112

TABLES

2.1   The Negative Value of a Gift: Ryan's Income   14
4.1   Value of Federal Public Assistance Programs, Georgia   29
7.1   SNAP Eligibility Levels, 2013   54
8.1   Maximum Monthly Allowances of Supplemental Foods   67
9.1   SSI Red Book Calculation of SSI Payment   79
9.2   Milestone Outcome Payment Method   91
10.1   Medicaid Benefits under the ACA   100
11.1   Earned Income Credit and Child Tax Credit
       Calculation, 2013   113
13.1   Suggested Scale for Supplementing the Wages of
       Low-Income Workers   149

APPENDICES

1   TANF Total Number of Recipients and Percent Change,
    1996–2011   47
2   USDA Survey Questions to Assess Household Food Security   63
3   SSDI Eligibility   88
4   SSI Eligibility   88
5   The Nine-Month Rule   89
6   VRAs and ENs   89
7   Medical Qualifications for Disability Benefits   92
8   Opt-In and Opt-Out States and the District of
    Columbia, 2014   105
9   The Cost of Serving Medicaid Enrollees by State   107
10   EITC and CTC Calculations: Single Taxpayers   119
11   EITC and CTC Calculations: Married Taxpayers   122

Foreword

Although transportation deregulation in the 1970s and Obamacare in 2010 have their supporters (and detractors), the 1996 recasting of welfare has a compelling claim to being the single most important federal reform of our time. By promising to end welfare as we knew it, Bill Clinton changed the Democratic Party, at least for a while; by forcing Clinton to accept changes that his party mostly loathed, Newt Gingrich's Republicans held him to his promise. By succeeding beyond almost everybody's hopes, the reform itself created a durable, bipartisan consensus around what had been a controversial idea: the best way to help people out of poverty is not to give them money but to help them work.

Today it is easy to forget the world before welfare reform, perhaps because that world is painful to remember. Aid to Families with Dependent Children (AFDC), the income-support program first designed during the New Deal for a very different country, was riddled with perverse incentives and outmoded provisions whose effect was to discourage work and family formation. By the Clinton era, even AFDC's supporters were exasperated with it, though they feared the consequences of replacing it. The 1996 reform required beneficiaries to work or seek job training, and it encouraged welfare agencies to move people off the dole and into jobs. The welfare rolls shrank, work effort increased, and the country learned some things. First, the emphasis on work was well founded: jobs confer not just income but also life skills, community standing, self-esteem, and a sense of vocation. Second, incentives matter. People really do respond to the rules. Third, the government can change incentives, and if it gets the changes right instead of wrong, a lot of people will be better off.

Those lessons are still important and relevant, which is why *The Human Cost of Welfare* is a book to read and ponder now. Although no one would exchange today's welfare programs for those of the 1980s, over the past couple of decades work requirements have eroded and new problems have arisen. If today there is a case of systemic failure equivalent to yesteryear's broken AFDC, it would be the federal disability program, which analysts from across the political spectrum agree has not only grown beyond its intended mission but also actively discourages reintegration into the labor force. Participation in what used to be called food stamps (now called SNAP) has soared, partly because of the economy but also partly as a result of loosened eligibility and work requirements. By common consent, wage subsidies, another successful innovation of the Clinton era, need changing so that low-income workers without children can get them. And the cost of Medicaid, the health program for the needy—like the cost of its big sister, Medicare—is rising. Where will the money come from?

Meanwhile, looming in the background is today's most worrisome economic trend: working-class men's flight from work. Through the late 1960s, more than 95% of American men in their prime working years (that is, between 25 and 54) were in the workforce; beginning in the 1970s, male workforce participation declined steadily through times good and bad, falling to 88% by 2013 and showing no sign of bottoming out. Eighty-eight percent workforce participation may still seem pretty high, but there is more to the story. Men with four-year college degrees, about a third of the total, are still working at high rates. But the lower you go on the education ladder, the higher the labor force dropout rate becomes. According to the Hamilton Project at the Brookings Institution, fully a quarter of men with only high school degrees were out of the workforce in 2011, and a third of men without high school degrees had dropped out.

Why? No one is sure, but probably for several mutually reinforcing reasons. Well-paying jobs for less-skilled workers, the factory and farm jobs of days past, have grown more scarce. The low-skilled jobs that are around have moved away from traditionally masculine venues like construction sites and toward traditionally feminine ones like nursing homes, and so blue-collar men seem reluctant to take them. As women have streamed into the workforce and become breadwinners, it has become both more affordable and more socially acceptable for men to let women support them, and for women to dispense with men altogether. As more children are raised by single mothers, more grow up without strong male role models, which research suggests disadvantages boys more than girls—repeating the cycle. And men, for reasons unknown, are not keeping up with women in the acquisition of education and skills.

All those and other variables figure in the equation, but here is the point: working-class men in the United States are in a tailspin. They are migrating out of the world of work and marriage, which for so many years defined masculine dignity, and they are entering—well, some other world, one whose terrain is uncertain but probably not very attractive. What will these people do for money and dignity in an increasingly postindustrial, white-collar economy? How can public policy generally, and welfare policy specifically, help to reverse the cycle of nonwork, rather than exacerbating it? We don't have answers yet, but to find them we will need to ask the right questions, which Phil Harvey and Lisa Conyers do here.

Their book is valuable for many reasons. Although the authors have a point of view, they are careful with the evidence, offering an accurate and comprehensive account that leaves the reader to make the hard policy judgments. And the choices *are* hard, which the book acknowledges— another virtue. Unlike many diatribes from both left and right, *The Human Cost of Welfare* is sophisticated about the inherent trade-offs, paradoxes, and dilemmas of welfare policy. For example, if you cut off relief above a given income threshold, you do a better job of targeting aid to the truly needy—but you also create a "benefits cliff," so that welfare recipients are punished, often severely, for getting jobs. You can address that problem by phasing out benefits gradually as income rises above the poverty level— but then you wind up with a lot of nonpoor people on welfare (and a higher price tag). Or again: we want welfare programs to encourage skills training, the road to self-improvement and better jobs; but allowing people to go to school while on welfare carves loopholes in work requirements. To be sure, there are win-wins in the world of welfare, and the authors point to them: bringing common sense to the disability program; strengthening wage subsidies for the childless. But the authors also show why so many of these problems are so tough.

Another virtue of *The Human Cost of Welfare* is that it lets us hear the voices of the people welfare serves. Often those voices are strikingly clear and candid. No expert could explain as well as this mother in Oregon how Medicaid's benefits cliff pushes her into the gray economy: "I just do baby-sitting out of my house, for cash, for neighbors, and I rent out my garage to a guy who works on motorcycles on the side. That is all cash I don't declare, so I have some income, but I don't have to report it and lose my benefits."

Or Holly, of Oregon, on marriage penalties: "We have thought about getting divorced to increase our benefits, but that would be hard to explain to our family and friends. I admit, I have friends who chose not to marry because they knew they'd lose money in the process."

A Latino immigrant, collecting recyclables with his two children: "I am the father of these children. I show them there are many ways to make money here, if you just try. This is what I want them to learn. Some day they will be American citizens, and they will get good jobs, but until then, they know we can find ways to eat and live, from our own hands."

A teenage boy the authors encounter in a parking lot on the Navajo reservation: "A lot of the kids here, they know they aren't going anywhere. Some might try and leave for a while, but they always come back. And here we are, with nothing to do. There's a big meth problem and a big drinking problem. We're bored. Nothing is happening, nothing is going to happen, our chances of ever leaving are low, our chances of finding work are even lower. So, why not get high, get drunk, and forget about it?"

Some of these people are on welfare, some are working; some are downtrodden, others undaunted. But all speak with dignity. Too much writing on the subject of poverty and welfare dwells in the ether of data and analysis. It is to the authors' credit that they have gone out on the streets and talked to the people who matter most.

One other strength of this book about welfare is that it is not just about welfare. In the senescent days of AFDC, welfare's biggest injuries were self-inflicted, the result of a policy at war with itself. Today, by contrast, although some problems can be alleviated by tinkering with the income-support system, many of the best ideas lie outside the four corners of TANF and SNAP and the rest of the federal alphabet soup. Private-sector apprenticeship programs, for example, can provide new paths into the workplace for people without baccalaureates. Repealing pointless licensing requirements can help people of modest means and education start businesses or use their skills. Reducing unnecessary arrest and incarceration, particularly of the nonviolent, can bring many people back from economic purgatory and into employability.

The Human Cost of Welfare thus tees up the debate about the next version of welfare. Call it Welfare 3.0. Version 1.0, the old AFDC regime, was about welfare. Version 2.0, the 1996 overhaul, was about workfare. Version 3.0 will be about *work*: rescuing and restoring it for those drifting dangerously away.

Jonathan Rauch
Washington, DC
September 2015

Acknowledgments

We are especially grateful to all the people we met and interviewed across the country who have bravely shared their stories. This book would not be the book it is without their insights.

We thank Jonathan Rauch for his thoughtful foreword and Judith Appelbaum for her valuable editing and guidance. We are grateful to the Cato Institute's David Boaz, Michael Tanner, and John Samples and Atlas Network's Tom Palmer, who all provided important support and advice. Thanks to Kitty Thuermer, Solveig Eggerz, Bob Gibson, Susan Clark, Catherine Flanagan, Frank Joseph, Alice Leaderman, Linda Morefield, and Leslie Rollins for editorial advice.

Help in manuscript preparation was provided by Michele Thorburn, Ankur Singh, Phoebe Chastain, and Meagan Banks. Chris Rosato provided graphic design, and Paul Mayson technical savvy. Mark Halloran, Eileen Winnick, Kevin Floria, and Kenn Bell provided videography for the book's publicity and our accompanying Web site, humancostofwelfare.com.

Kudos to Free to Choose Network's Bob Chitester, Tom Skinner, and Carmine Camillo for bringing the book to life in their upcoming documentary.

Introduction: Welfare Reforms Need Reforming

Nothing will work, unless you do—Maya Angelou

This book fills an important gap in the national debate about welfare. There is a great deal of material from the conservative perspective about the failures of welfare, and a great deal from the liberal perspective about the moral imperatives of a safety net for America's vulnerable citizens. But little has been written about how welfare impacts the lives and happiness of welfare recipients themselves.

The fact that welfare might actually be harmful to those it is meant to benefit dawned gradually on us. Living and working with the poor in many parts of the world, we found it easy enough to see that humans everywhere were happier when they were self-sufficient. Only over time we realized that people receiving welfare payments in the United States often seemed less satisfied with their lives than many people in developing nations who were getting no financial aid and who were doing backbreaking work to survive. Given such enormous expenditures and such minimal results, we started wondering how the richest nation in the world could better address the issue of work—indeed the *necessity* of work—as a component of human happiness, even while providing significant help to its neediest citizens.

To find answers, we visited with more than 100 men and women around the country whose lives are, or were, sustained by welfare programs. They told us about what life is like when you rely on the government safety net for sustenance, about what work means to them, and about how satisfied they are, or are not, with their lives. We spoke with people in homeless tent cities in Seattle and public housing in New York's Harlem. We went to Washington State and Washington, DC, from South Dakota to Arizona and Colorado, and from Louisiana to Georgia. We visited Native American reservations and workfare programs for single moms, asking the same questions everywhere we went: What is it like living on welfare? Is it possible to be happy on welfare? Would you rather be working?

As it turns out, work matters not just because working is the way we earn the money to pay for the things we need and want, but also because—as you will see in the following chapters—our happiness often depends on it.

While we were learning about the lives of welfare recipients, we found it helpful to remind ourselves from time to time that they live in a world quite different from that of most Americans. If you haven't had to make the decision between putting gas in the car to get to work or paying the electric bill, it can be hard to understand why a drop in income of $300 or $400 a month is a big deal. But understanding that level of financial insecurity is the key to understanding why our system is so harmful. The value of welfare benefits, scant as they may be, often puts enormous pressure on recipients to stay on welfare, not because they think it is the right thing to do, or the best way to live a life, but because they will lose money for necessities if they work.

What do welfare beneficiaries themselves think about these programs? What we learned from our interviewees is that—whether they were grateful for the help or not—they all felt the system was broken. We did not meet a single recipient who had anything positive to say about the programs they were on, aside from the fact of the assistance itself. The stories people told us were rife with examples of redundancy, incompetence, fraud, and general decay and disarray, reflecting programs that are unresponsive, inflexible, and illogical. Surely, we thought, we can do better than this.

Today, there are more than 100 means-tested federal assistance programs. Our interviews and our other research focused primarily on the ones generally recognized as "welfare programs"—those involving government payments for food, housing, medical care, and cash assistance—which are the ones that serve the most people. These programs have all expanded since the 2008 recession because of the American Recovery and Reinvestment Act, passed in 2009,[1] a response to the financial crisis that injected an additional $150 billion into the welfare system,[2] but, surprisingly, not by giving more help to the poorest citizens. Instead the changes expanded the rolls of the welfare programs by raising the level of income recipients could earn and still qualify for benefits. Many of these programs now accept applicants who earn 150%–300% of the poverty line income, and these higher earnings limits have not been rolled back with the post-recession recovery.[3] And those welfare expenditures are rising fast. The Organisation for Economic Co-operation and Development (OECD) calculates that the United States has increased public social expenditures (as a percentage of GDP) from 7% in 1965 when we launched our War on Poverty to close to 22% percent of GDP today. Strikingly, defense spending is now considerably less than expenditures on welfare programs.

A hopeful note relates to the Earned Income Tax Credit (EITC), which is targeted at low-income working families. The EITC and its accompanying Child Tax Credit are nearly the only welfare programs that reward work and, while they need fixing, they are aimed in the right direction and provide a basis for steps to improve our welfare system generally.

Although we found that many people abuse today's welfare programs, it is important to remember that the great majority of welfare recipients need the help, and that most do not abuse the rules. Rather, they feel trapped. Most want to work, but the system can be stultifying. It deadens the spirit, undermines morale, and takes participants down a path that leads away from work and away from the chance for a satisfying life. What a waste of a major national resource! Tens of millions of Americans who want to work are not working because they are stuck in a system that discourages work and leads our most enterprising welfare recipients to hide their part-time, off-the-books income from the authorities as though work for pay was some sort of crime. What a boon to America's economy and spirit, we thought, if our welfare system instead paved the pathway to good jobs. We believe that is possible, and as noted below, we suggest how it can be done.

This book's thirteen chapters explore what has gone wrong with our current welfare programs and how they actually work before outlining many ways to improve the welfare system. Each chapter includes stories we gathered along the road, and the wisdom we gleaned from interviewing more than 100 welfare beneficiaries has shaped our recommendations for change.

PART I. THE WELFARE CONFLICT

Chapter 1. What Does Work Have to Do with Happiness?

Happiness and work have been closely linked for many centuries, and they are linked for today's welfare participants. When welfare undermines the pathway to work, it undermines happiness.

Chapter 2. The War Between Welfare and Work

Whatever the good intentions behind welfare programs as originally created and as amended over the years, people in these programs can't stop being scared of "the welfare cliff" when all payments are cut. That goes a long way toward explaining why our current welfare programs continue to impede employment goals, break up households, and encourage out-of-wedlock births.

PART II. THE COUNTERPRODUCTIVE QUALIFICATIONS FOR WELFARE

Chapter 3. What Counts as Poverty

An analysis of who really qualifies for federal welfare programs reveals that people who are not poor are collecting staggering sums in benefits, with unfortunate consequences for people truly in need.

Chapter 4. Marriage, Childbearing, and Teen Pregnancy

We discuss how the welfare system encourages single parenthood and discourages marriage, exacerbating the trend toward a two-class society as marriage rates fall and poverty increases for single-parent families, especially the children.

PART III. WELFARE PROGRAMS IN THEORY AND IN FACT

Chapter 5. TANF: The Changing Face of Cash Assistance

Temporary Assistance for Needy Families (TANF) provides cash assistance for families in need, but the time limitations and workfare requirements imposed by the 1996 welfare reforms are becoming unraveled.

Chapter 6. A Housing System Leaves the Needy Out in the Cold

The supply of subsidized housing is limited and when beneficiaries continue to occupy housing they no longer qualify for, the more deserving are left out.

Chapter 7. Who Gets Food Stamps?

The Supplemental Nutrition Assistance Program, commonly known as SNAP or "food stamps," is now the largest American welfare program, with

47 million beneficiaries. While the food it provides has alleviated widespread hunger, many SNAP benefits go to people who freely admit they do not really need them.

Chapter 8. WIC: Missteps with Women and Children

WIC (Women, Infants and Children) is a popular program that helps boost the nutritional health of pregnant and nursing mothers and young children, but critics note that it encourages formula feeding at the expense of breastfeeding.

Chapter 9. How We Disable the Disabled

Social Security disability programs are stacked against the disabled. Keeping people out of the workforce and out of the public eye, they run directly counter to the intent of the Americans with Disabilities Act, which seeks to empower the disabled to join the workforce. Even physically fit children are placed on disability, with some condemned to illiteracy as a result.

Chapter 10. Medicaid and the Affordable Care Act

We describe what did and didn't change with the passage of the ACA and how people on welfare are affected.

Chapter 11. The Earned Income Tax Credit: Welfare Done (Almost) Right

Despite some fixable flaws, the EITC has become the most effective government program for the poor. It rewards work and helps people get on, and stay on, the path to self-sufficiency.

PART IV. BUILDING BLOCKS FOR A BETTER WELFARE SYSTEM

Chapter 12. Drivers of Dependence and Independence: American Indians on Reservations, Barterers, and Immigrants

Insights about avoiding welfare dependency come from the stories of people who are victims of generational dependence on government money and from the stories of people who have gotten off welfare or managed to avoid getting on it.

Chapter 13: What Should Be Done: From Incentives to Special Savings Accounts, Solutions Abound to Get Americans Back to Work

Recommendations from social scientists and scholars along with recommendations distilled from our talks with men and women on welfare show that there are many ways to make welfare programs far less costly for our country and far more helpful to the people they are hurting now.

PART I

The Welfare Conflict

Chapter 1

What Does Work Have to Do with Happiness?

Happiness belongs to the self-sufficient—Aristotle

"I don't know if it's happiness," said Cora*, a teacher and tribal member we met on the Pine Ridge Reservation in South Dakota. "I just know that something happens to people when they get a job. They sit up straighter. Their chin comes up. They carry themselves with pride. They say hello to me in the supermarket. I know everyone on this reservation, and I can tell when someone is working, because they'll greet me at the store, and brag on what they are doing with their lives."

The links between happiness and work came up often in our conversations with people on welfare across the country. For example, when we met Marta in New York City, she told us: "I have to work or I'd go crazy." Homeless and living on the streets of Brooklyn, she continues to string jobs together under the table. "As long as I can keep busy, then I'm happy," she said. And Terry, who currently lives in a homeless tent city in Seattle, offered these observations: "When I worked I definitely looked down on all those people on welfare with their food stamps and their hand-me-downs. Then I became that person in the checkout line with the food stamps. I'm the one who is homeless. I'm the one who is taking socks from

---

*Interviewees' names have been changed to protect their privacy.

the church ladies that stop by. Self-esteem? Gone. I would much rather be working, at any job, than living the way I live right now. I know I'll never be a medical tech again, but I'd be happy working at McDonald's. Happy to be working."

As they pointed to the relationship between working and being happy, Cora, Marta, and Terry didn't stop to define happiness, probably because they know it when they feel it and they assumed correctly that we do too. Still, some definition is useful in this context. Although happiness can mean different things to different people, we have followed many philosophers, religious thinkers, and psychologists by defining it in terms of living a good life, not just in terms of emotion. Accordingly, what we mean by happiness is a long-term, overarching condition. Like "a long and happy life" and "a happy marriage," "happiness" as defined here does not entail the absence of pain and problems. It entails engagement with people and projects geared toward accomplishment and the tangible and psychological rewards of getting things done. While happiness is subjective and often idiosyncratic, it almost always involves effort, whether we embrace the effort or have it thrust upon us.

Like Cora, Marta, and Terry, other welfare recipients across the country reflected this broad understanding of happiness, as did people interviewed on National Public Radio (NPR). Shortly after the 1996 welfare reforms, which mandated workfare and a five-year time limit, NPR ran a series of interviews with single mothers who had left the welfare rolls for work.[1] Many of the mothers dwelt on the hardships of arranging transportation to work, the cost of day care, and the fact that working limited options in their lives. But not one of them wanted to go back on welfare.

First-person testimony about connections between happiness and work is not the only available evidence. Several recent investigations have explored the connection. Studies at Santa Clara University's Center for Applied Ethics (2012)[2] and Arizona State University's School of Public Affairs (2011)[3] came to similar and strong conclusions concerning welfare dependence, work, and happiness based on their findings about what happened to the subjective well-being (SWB) of single mothers after the 1996 welfare reforms.

Those sweeping reforms, as you may remember, were agreed upon by President Clinton and Congress and were supposed to "end welfare as we know it." Back then, the Aid to Families with Dependent Children (AFDC) program had enabled increasing numbers of young single mothers (and others) to slide easily into a life of welfare without working, and the reforms addressed that problem. The new Temporary Assistance for Needy Families (TANF) program that replaced AFDC required everybody receiving cash assistance to work or train for work; its benefits had a lifetime limit of five years and it resulted in millions of women moving into work and out of poverty.

Comparing data from the years before and after such "workfare" reforms, both studies found that single mothers reported higher levels of subjective well-being after they entered the workforce. Chris Herbst's study at Arizona State concluded that the reforms had mostly positive effects: "These women experienced an increase in life satisfaction, greater optimism about the future, and more financial satisfaction."[4] Herbst also provides indirect evidence that "the mothers' employment after welfare reform can plausibly explain the gains in subjective well-being."[5] Similarly, John Ifcher's report on the Santa Clara University study concludes that results "appear to indicate that the package of welfare and tax policy changes [requiring work] increased happiness."[6] Even relatively menial work, it seems, made these single mothers happier.

These two studies are important because they were rigorously executed and because they addressed the most notably dependent members of our society—single mothers on Temporary Assistance for Needy Families (TANF). By definition these women need financial help to meet life's basic needs for themselves and their children. If they are happier adding the demands of working to their lives, it seems likely that other economically dependent Americans will be happier working as well.

A comprehensive study using the German Socio-Economic Panel,[7] quoted in the *World Happiness Report*,[8] reached a similar conclusion: "Our main result is that we cannot identify a single job feature, nor a combination of such features that constitute such low quality jobs that remaining unemployed would be a better choice for the individual. On the contrary the bulk of our evidence shows that even low quality jobs are associated with higher life satisfaction, and this effect is statistically significant for most specifications of 'bad' jobs."

Whether the jobs are low quality or high quality, working can be arduous. But dealing with its difficulties is essentially a plus because the happiness that flows from a successful accomplishment correlates strongly with the effort required to achieve it. For a homespun example, imagine that someone has now created a pill that will instantly give any child all the skills needed to ride a bicycle. Then think back to the days when you learned to ride a bicycle, and remember the pleasure and satisfaction you felt when you could finally pedal away on your own without wobbling the bike or tipping over. There would be no "I did it!" moment for any child who could acquire those skills with a pill instead of doing all that work.

The joy of dealing with difficulty also stimulates some people to add extra challenges to a routine job. A waitress quoted in Studs Turkel's *Working* provides a striking example:

I want my hand to be right when I serve. I pick up a glass, I want it to be just right. I get to be almost Oriental in the serving. I like it to look nice all the way. To be a waitress, it's an art. I feel like a ballerina, too. I have to go between those tables, between those chairs. . . . Maybe that's the reason I always stayed slim. It is a certain way I can go through a chair no one else can do. I do it with an air.

If I drop a fork, there is a certain way I pick it up.[9]

Of course, paid employment—a particular category of effort—offers an additional reward: the paycheck. A job, whatever its shortcomings, contains the seeds of self-sufficiency. Bringing the paycheck home lets us enjoy the feeling "I did that."

Work can sometimes be very hard to find, as we were reminded in the 2008–2009 recession. At the time of this writing the U.S. unemployment rate was still somewhat higher than normal. But while economic swings impact the availability of work, they do not detract from its intrinsic value as a contributor to happiness. "[Work] allows us to create value in an easily measurable way," notes author Arthur Brooks. "It is something that makes us feel like our lives are worth living."[10]

A dramatic reminder of the power of employment on people's well-being is the rise in suicide rates during recessions as people lose their jobs. As reported in a recent study in the *British Journal of Psychiatry*, suicide rates in Europe and the United States during the most recent recession increased by 6.5% between 2007 and 2009, a rate that was sustained until 2011. During this period the United States lost an additional 4,750 residents to suicide compared to prerecession numbers. Some countries, including Austria, Sweden, and Finland, bucked this trend by focusing their policy efforts during the recession on providing training and employment so that their citizens could stay engaged in the workforce.[11]

Here are quick takes on a few of the reasons that work is so important for happiness:

Self-respect requires achievement. If we don't accomplish anything, it is nearly impossible to think highly of ourselves. One Southern Ute tribal member remembers losing his job. "We went on the assistance for a few months, but I told my wife we either find jobs here on the reservation or we leave. And we left, moved away, got jobs, and later started our own business. I could feel my pride go, and I didn't want to become *that* person. I'm a worker, I have to be able to look back on my life and be proud of the life I built for my wife and my family."

Having no work to do means boredom, and often depression, alcohol, and drugs. While many of those on welfare keep busy, many do not. Several mothers we met at a local park in Harlem described what they do all day. "We hang out with our friends. We eat. We drink," one said. "Then we hang out some more." Added another, "I'd rather be working, I know that. I get so bored sometimes I start making work for myself, washing clothes that don't need washing, doing my babies' hair up into silly hairdos." Working at a job means, at the very least, doing things that need doing.

Being needed gives us stature and importance. Parents of young children are needed, for sure, and we may be faced with imperative demands to fulfill needs of other family members or friends. But work also means we are needed. That paycheck is proof of it. One Decatur mother put it this way: "I remember that first paycheck when I went back to work like it was yesterday. One hundred seventy-seven dollars. Not much, right? But it was mine, and I took it home and showed it to the kids and it made me feel good inside. My kids, they need so many things, diapers, toys, shoes, clothes. And they need me to provide for them, and it gives me a lot of pride to do that instead of them seeing momma cashing welfare checks."

Independence is important to self-respect. If we depend on others for our sustenance, we are incurring a debt that diminishes us and makes us feel patronized, undermining happiness. Work allows us to contribute to our own self-sufficiency.

"I'd rather be able to find enough work to pay my own way all the way. What man wouldn't?" said Ken in Atlanta. "Pay the rent, pay the bills, *and* buy food. But I can't find a full-time job so I'm stuck with the food stamps. Every time I go into that welfare office I get treated like dirt by those old ladies in there and I can't say nothing back to them. I can't wait till I can pay all my bills all on my own."

Given the extent to which our welfare system discourages work, Ken's wait is likely to be a long one, further crippling his chance at happiness. And of course he is far from alone. As you will see, the current welfare system is undermining happiness for millions of Americans on welfare by placing obstacles between them and employment.

Chapter 2

The War Between Welfare and Work

It cannot too often be stated that the issue of welfare is not what it costs those who provide it, but what it costs those who receive it—Daniel Patrick Moynihan

As long as there have been economists, they have told us that when you pay for something, you will get more of it. Today we are, in effect, paying people to stay poor and we should not be surprised that the number of poor people keeps creeping up. Charles Murray warned us about this in 1984 when he defined the Law of Unintended Rewards: "Any social transfer increases the net value of being in the condition that prompted the transfer."[1] If we pay people for having a condition, the value of having that condition goes up.

Thus, if we reward people for staying unemployed and poor, and remove those rewards when they take steps to begin earning a living, we should not be surprised that they arrange their lives so that they keep getting the rewards.

Our current welfare system has several ways—some of them subtle—of keeping its beneficiaries poor.

ASSET DEPLETION

The first thing an applicant for any welfare benefits must do is divulge all personal assets. Anyone with any assets of serious value must get rid of them.[2] In some states applicants must not even own a car, unless it is a low-value clunker. In theory, insistence on asset depletion guarantees that welfare programs serve only the needy. In practice, it deepens the hole recipients are in to begin with. If we're going to help you, the system says, you have to be poor. So, as a first step, we're going to make you poorer than you were before.

Jane, a young woman we met in Harlem, was offered her grandfather's car when he died. With the car, Jane could have driven to the job interviews and training classes required by the work requirements in the Temporary Assistance for Needy Families (TANF) program; she could have dropped her children at day care and taken her mother to doctors' appointments. But the car was valued at $8,000, roughly four times TANF's allowed asset limit, and Jane's benefits would have been reduced if she accepted it. So the family sold the car at a loss and split the proceeds among Jane and her three siblings. She got to keep her benefits but lost a tool for getting to work and moving off welfare.

James, a married construction manager and father of two in Seattle, applied for Social Security Disability Insurance (SSDI) disability benefits* after a work-related truck accident that left him disabled. At the time of his accident James owned his own home, two cars, and a small boat. Once he was no longer able to hold a full-time job, he knew he would not be able to afford his mortgage payments on disability, so he sold his home. He and his family moved into a small rental house. During the application process he was informed that his SSDI income would be low enough so that he would also qualify for the more generous Supplemental Security Income (SSI) disability benefits, but that he would not meet the asset tests for SSI benefits if he owned the second car and the boat. So he sold both of them and lived on the proceeds. When the proceeds ran out he qualified for SSDI and SSI, but no longer had assets he could fall back on. The system had just made him poorer.

INCOME LIMITS

A welfare applicant's income is also scrutinized.[†] All income and savings must be declared.[3] Income must fall within federal poverty guidelines, and savings must be minimal.[4]

---

*SSDI is not a welfare program because it is not means tested and is paid from payroll deductions from workers' salaries. See chapter 9.

†Note that welfare benefits are never counted in the poverty calculation. When assessing a person's eligibility for food stamps, for example, the cash or medical benefits that person may already be receiving are not counted.

Time and again we met people who had made decisions to turn down extra working hours, or even a pay raise, because the welfare benefits they would lose were worth more than the increased income being offered. For most low-wage earners, raises are small, perhaps a few hundred or a thousand dollars a year, not enough, in most cases, to compensate for the value of the benefits they would have to give up. And welfare inertia can be powerful, making many beneficiaries reluctant to risk change.

Karen is a nurse who works in a low-income migrant farmworker's clinic in rural Washington State. "I was offered a promotion in my clinic last year," she told us. "I would have become the nursing supervisor, which paid about $15,000 a year more than I earn now. Unfortunately, between my Section 8 HUD [Department of Housing and Urban Development] housing voucher, Medicaid for me and my kids, and our food benefits, I would have lost money if I'd taken the raise, because the raise would have taken me above the limit. I really wanted that job—offers like that don't come around very often out here—but I couldn't afford to take it."

Karen reveals a mindset we encountered often in our talks with welfare recipients. Whether their benefits are small or, like Karen's, relatively generous, welfare payments are reliable and steady. Beneficiaries quickly come to fear losing those payments even if they dislike the welfare lifestyle. The many pluses of working in the more unpredictable (and taxed) job market take a back seat to the importance of keeping regular funds coming in.

The prospect of losing most or all benefits as a result of crossing an income line is often described as the welfare cliff. Many welfare recipients approach this line cautiously, keeping their earnings—at least their declared earnings—low. Others are so concerned about the "cliff" that they choose not to work at all. In Pennsylvania, a single mother of two could theoretically put together an earned income and welfare package well in excess of the median U.S. income of $46,000 per household, according to calculations by Gary Smith, Pennsylvania's former secretary of public welfare. Smith notes that this hypothetical woman can earn $19,000 a year (the poverty level figure for a family of three) without losing any benefits. Having qualified, she can get TANF (cash assistance) benefits of $407 per month, Supplemental Nutrition Assistance Program (SNAP food stamps) benefits of $526 per month, housing and energy assistance valued at $1,084 a month, and medical assistance valued at $833 per month. She also gets free child care through her TANF program, valued at $700 per month per child.[5]

These benefits, taken together, are worth more than $40,000. Add this to her net annual salary of $19,000, and she and her children would be living on the equivalent of $59,000, a middle-class income in excess of the U.S. average. Because she will lose all of those benefits if her earnings take her over the poverty threshold, she would be worse off, especially after taxes, with a raise of anything less than $40,000.[6]

While we have not encountered anyone who has managed to put together this "ideal" package, the example illustrates a fundamental point: earning money is economically dangerous for low-earning families with substantial welfare income.

THE FOOD STAMP TRAP

Frank, a long-term resident of a Seattle tent city, lives mostly on his $200 a month in food stamp benefits. Frank also gets a daily free round-trip bus pass to any location served by the Seattle Metro Bus system.[7] He lives at the tent city for free in exchange for doing chores, and the tent city has a kitchen tent with free food stocked by local charities. Local churches also deliver hot meals every night. There are several locations in Seattle that give out free clothing to the homeless.[8] Frank gets by.

While Frank has his basic needs met, he dreams of living better, having a little cash for emergencies, and maybe someday living in an apartment. But he is well aware of what will happen if he starts earning money—the income caps will kick in and he will lose the $200 in SNAP food stamps he has come to rely on. (He sometimes trades in part of his food stamps for cash, a disallowed but common practice, as detailed in chapter 7.) Frank has some social and behavioral issues, so the types of jobs he is qualified for are low-wage, seasonal, or temporary, which means that from month to month, if he were to work, his income could fluctuate dramatically. And that is part of the problem. If he does land a job and declares his earnings to his social worker during his semiannual requalification for SNAP, they may exceed the allowable income threshold. He can earn up to $500 a month without losing anything; but if he earns more, he gradually loses the SNAP income.[9] With sporadic earnings, he may earn more than $500 in a particular month, and if that happens, his benefits will be terminated for that month, and he'll have to start from scratch to requalify when the temporary job ends. In any given year, Frank could get bounced on and off the food stamp list multiple times as temporary jobs come and go, and he might well end the year having had less money than if he had simply not worked at all. Earning money is thus a threat to his well-being.

People all want some stability in their lives, and people on welfare can count on their welfare benefits, month after month, if they keep their income and assets below the threshold level. They thus have a powerful incentive to remain poor. Working means risking the benefit—perhaps just for one month, but it's a risk all the same, especially if reinstating the benefit is iffy or complex (see Ryan's story in the next section). One way out of this trap, and one that a great many welfare recipients resort to, is working off the books and concealing the earnings from case workers. If Frank works off the books, he, like many others, will have to keep his earnings in cash; he can't put them in the bank, because he must declare the value of his bank accounts. But by keeping them in cash, he risks theft and loses the ability to amass savings that would earn interest and build credit, all steps that could pave the path to financial independence.

While visiting with Frank we met Willis and Tim, two young men who had previously been residents of the tent city but had found jobs and moved out of their tents and into apartments. They now return regularly as volunteers, helping current tent city residents with job searches, résumés, and welfare program applications.

Both Willis and Tim had run up against their food stamp income limits once they got jobs, so they had to choose between keeping their incomes low enough to continue to qualify for food stamps and earning enough to buy their own food. Willis chose to forgo the food stamps and pay his own way. He was proud of the fact that he was no longer on welfare. His demeanor was relaxed and confident: "I'm doing good. I can't believe I used to live here and now I'm here helping out. I've got my own apartment, a couple roommates. We're making ends meet, and even have money for a beer on Friday night. Don't get me wrong, it's not luxury living, but it is a good start, and that paycheck is all mine and I can spend it however I want."

Tim chose to keep doing part-time work rather than take a full-time offer, so that he could continue to get the benefit. He realized that his employers had little incentive to pay him well for his part-time work, and his demeanor reflected the fact that he felt frustrated, trapped, and unhappy with his options. He agreed that, in the long run, he would be happier if he dropped the food stamp benefit and took a full-time job, but he wasn't ready to make that leap. "Look, I'm at the bottom of the employment heap," he said. "I'm making minimum wage doing labor work, I could be let go at any time. There's just no security, and I'm afraid of losing that food money—it doesn't seem like much, but it's the difference between hungry and not hungry. And, at 20 hours a week, I have some cash in hand *and* the food stamps—hard to let that go."

THE NEGATIVE VALUE OF A GIFT

In Georgia we met Ryan, a part-time waiter who also receives SNAP benefits. He had his benefits cancelled when he reported a gift from two of

Table 2.1   The Negative Value of a Gift: Ryan's Income

Monthly	November	December	January	February	March
Earned income	$500	$500	$500	$500	$500
SNAP benefits	$200	$200	−$200	$0	$200
Gift from aunts		$500			
Total Income According to SNAP	$700	$1,200	$300	$500	$700

his aunts at Christmas time. Ryan had told his aunts he needed help with his utility bills when the power company threatened to cut off electricity to his apartment. His aunts gave him a check, which he deposited in his checking account. When it came time for his food stamp benefit review, he showed his bank statement to his caseworker, along with the payment to his utility company. The caseworker told Ryan that the gift had to be counted as income for the month of December, and adding it to his earnings for the month took him over SNAP's monthly income limit.

Furthermore, it meant that he had received SNAP benefits in December that he technically didn't qualify for, so he had to repay his December SNAP benefit of $200 before he could reapply. And since he couldn't reapply until February, he couldn't start receiving benefits again until March. Table 2.1 shows what happened.

By Ryan's calculation, the gift from his aunts was mostly wiped out. He got the $500 and kept his lights on, but lost three months of benefits, or $600.

FROM WELFARE TO WORK: OBSTACLES

TANF, the only welfare program that requires training or work,* was created as part of the welfare reform package of 1996.[10] When it was implemented, its advocates envisioned that participants would be placed in training programs, which would lead them to good jobs that would allow them to move off the welfare rolls, or at least place them in jobs that would give them a path out of poverty.

---

*SNAP theoretically has work or work activity requirements, but they are rarely enforced, and in many states they are waived. See chapter 7.

TANF's workfare component means that participants must enroll in a work training and job placement program to qualify for cash assistance, although each state is free to design and implement programs best suited to its own residents.[11]

The workfare requirement has succeeded in many respects. Literally millions of young mothers have been moved off welfare and into employment, and that is real progress (see chapter 5). However, as TANF beneficiaries have decreased, other programs have moved up. There are several other programs available to impoverished young mothers, and many women turn to them when TANF runs out. Further, the jobs that most TANF beneficiaries can get pay very little and provide few prospects for growth.

Kate and her son and daughter are in the TANF program in the Bronx, in New York City, where they live in a shelter for single mothers and children. The children attend a local charter school. Kate is interested in becoming a beautician and has done some work for off-Broadway shows, doing hair and makeup for cast members. She also volunteers at the local children's theater, where her daughter participates.

Because she is in the TANF program, when she applies for jobs, she has to tell her social worker where she has interviewed, and the social worker calls to see if there was in fact a job interview and/or a job offer. As a result, employers learn of Kate's status as a welfare recipient, and that information often leads them to rescind job offers or offer work at lower hourly rates.

Tammy, a young mother in Everett, Washington, told us that she had applied at every store in her local mall, walking the halls with her résumé in one hand and her other hand on her baby's stroller. "You'd think these employers would give people on welfare a little extra consideration," she said. "I don't want to live on welfare but I have to 'til I get a job. If people on welfare were given a fair shot at jobs, they could get out faster, but instead when employers find out you're on welfare, they think less of you, give you their crappiest jobs, and pay you as little as possible. And you have to take it, because with TANF you have to be looking for work and accepting work if it comes your way."

Kate and Tammy are ambitious mothers of small children and they are not averse to hard work. But the workfare system often pushes these mothers into very low-wage jobs, with the stigma of TANF dependency clouding their chances for promotion.

Several large national employers employ most of the participants in workfare programs. Goodwill, Walmart, and Maximus Inc. (a nationwide temporary services agency) are some of the largest TANF employers. A Maximus Inc. case management director is quoted by authors Jane Collins and Victoria Mayer[12] discussing Maximus's experience with the workfare system: "I think there's two ways to look at the [workfare] program. One is as an economic program designed to allow participants to become more part of the economic fabric of the community. The second—maybe just as motivating—is to get a low-cost workforce into the economy so that employers don't have to pay ever-increasing wages."[13] It seems unlikely that such employers will provide workers with meaningful jobs and a way up the economic ladder. It can certainly be argued that getting welfare should not be easy and that work requirements must be enforced. But putting people into the lowest-wage jobs and making it hard for them to move up makes it more likely that many will stay on their other welfare programs, or seek new ones, when their TANF benefits end.

Work that pays less than the legally required minimum wage is likely to have similar effects, and this happens in some states when workfare employers are allowed to designate some of the TANF recipients' work hours as unpaid training hours. In Wisconsin, for example, ten hours per workweek can be designated as "training," which workfare participants must provide for free.[14] The workweek for these participants is actually a fulltime 40 hours, but because of the training portion, they are usually classified as part-time workers and thus get no benefits.

In Georgia we visited a private organization that contracts with the state to provide TANF participants with job training and placement. Participants receive six months of training—thirty hours per week with no salary—before they are placed in paid positions. To the extent they are "earning" their TANF cash assistance ($464 a month for a family of three), they do so at $3.86/hour, far below the federal minimum wage.[15] When their TANF benefit expires, they have little on their résumé that would impress potential employers.

PART II

The Counterproductive Qualifications for Welfare

Chapter 3

What Counts as Poverty

Continued dependence upon relief induces a spiritual disintegration fundamentally destructive to the national fiber. To dole out relief in this way is to administer a narcotic, a subtle destroyer of the human spirit—Franklin Delano Roosevelt

Only a few years ago worldwide poverty was defined by a very simple number: $1 a day. People who had to live on this amount were held to be extremely poor. As the world, including much of the less developed world, has gotten richer, the worldwide poverty line has been increased a bit to $1.25 per day. Approximately 1.2 billion people live on that amount or less in the second decade of the twenty-first century.[1]

In the United States, the official poverty level is $32 per day.[2] You can be poor in the United States at 25 times the income level of the UN poverty standard. Even adjusting for purchasing power, the U.S. standard is munificent from a world perspective.

The United States, like most industrialized countries, has steadily increased welfare benefits even as the need for these benefits, at least ostensibly, decreases. Writer William Voegeli notes that 60 years ago the entire American middle class was poor by today's standards, yet reaching that standard for the poor today has not meant a leveling off in benefits. For the industrialized Organisation for Economic Co-operation and Development (OECD) countries:

The years 1980 to 2003 were a period of vigorous economic growth, one that began at a time when the citizens of industrial democracies were already the most prosperous people in human history.

What's notable is that all these democratic nations chose to regard growing prosperity over a quarter-century as an opportunity to expand the welfare state rather than an opportunity to reduce it. Public Social Expenditures grew, in absolute terms, in all 13 countries during these years, and grew relative to the size of the economy in 12 of them. No serious consideration—or at any rate, no consequential consideration—seems to have been given to the idea that greater prosperity had significantly increased the number of households who could provide for their medical care, education, economic security and retirement largely by relying on their own resources, thereby reducing the need and justification for the government to provide for these needs by transferring wealth from some people to others.[3]

Is there a limit to taxpayers' willingness to improve living standards for the poor? Probably, but we don't appear to have reached it yet. The continuing American concern with income inequality reminds us that *relative* poverty is still considered cause for concern, and welfare benefits for the poor will likely continue to grow as long as some in society have much less than others, probably an indefinite condition.

The current U.S. definition of poverty is based on three times the amount of money needed to purchase food.[4] If it costs an average of $333 a month to purchase food for one person, then the poverty rate is $1,000 a month for a single person; earn less than that and you are defined as poor. The generally accepted level of income that defines poverty in the United States was between $900 and $1,100 per month for an individual in 2015.

In our visits around the country, we found that the poor are not particularly conspicuous; most are living in houses and driving cars; most own TV sets and computers. Destitution is rare, though it would surely be less so without the existing programs.

PAYMENTS TO THE NONPOOR

One worrying aspect of today's welfare system is the extent to which benefits are provided to those who do not meet the federal definition of poverty. A major push in this direction was provided by the American Recovery and Reinvestment Act introduced by Congress in 2009 in response to the financial crisis and subsequent recession. As mentioned, that act allowed states and implementing agencies the flexibility to push the qualifying income level for several of the major welfare programs up to 200% of the poverty line (and in the case of the Temporary Assistance to

Needy Families program, or TANF, as high as 250% of the poverty line).[5] This means that a single person who might previously have been able to qualify for welfare only with income below $12,000 might now, depending on state-level discretion, qualify for several programs at income levels up to more than $20,000, and a family of four, previously limited to a poverty line of $23,000, could earn as much as $41,000 and still get benefits (the most common limit is 180%).[6] These expanded eligibility levels were a reasonable response to a prolonged recession, but there has been no move to reset the levels and they now appear to be permanent. This has set the stage for a substantial expansion of our welfare state.

According to authors David Armor and Sonia Sousa, writing for *National Affairs* magazine, "Today more than half of the benefits allocated through programs we think of as 'anti-poverty' efforts actually go to people above the poverty line as defined by the U.S. Census Bureau. As a result, our poverty programs—once justified and defended as a safety net for Americans truly in need—exist, increasingly, to make life more comfortable for the middle class."[7]

Given the fact that America's federal welfare budget, at nearly $700 billion, now exceeds the defense budget ($595 billion), the expansion of our welfare state to include so many nonpoor is cause for serious concern.

Over the years, each program and each state has taken the poverty benchmark and tweaked it to meet its own needs, creating a working definition that applies to its constituency. Not surprisingly, welfare benefits vary widely from state to state. Under the Temporary Assistance for Needy Families (TANF) program, for example, a mother of three in Massachusetts can be allotted $600 per month in benefits, while she would get just $170 living in Mississippi.[8]

During our interviews we found that this patchwork of welfare standards caused a good deal of moving from state to state. "I was living in Montana," Tracy told us, sitting in her tent in Seattle's Tent City #3, "but Washington State has a lot better benefits so I moved here and I just drive home every so often to see my family."

In Hawaii we met several men living in a private campground on the beach in Maui. None was from Hawaii. "I realized I was going to run out of money, and I was living in New York City," Jim said. "I knew I was probably going to end up homeless, so I figured I'd come here to Hawaii. If I'm going to be homeless, I might as well be homeless on the beach, in the most generous welfare state in the USA." All the beaches in Hawaii are public, and camping is common. Food stamp benefits average over $200 per person per month and monthly TANF benefits average $750, high by national standards.[9]

Economist Nicholas Eberstadt of the American Enterprise Institute argues that our current poverty definition fails to measure poverty accurately

Figure 3.1

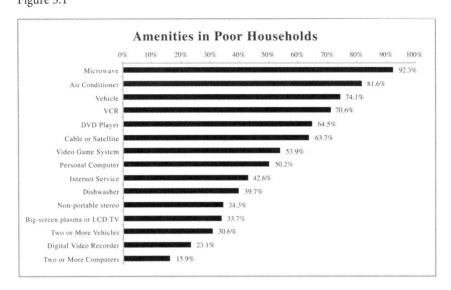

Sources: U.S. Energy Information Administration, Residential Energy Consumption Survey (RECS): 2009 RECS Survey Data and U.S. Census Bureau, American Housing Survey for the United States: 2009.

because food stamps, housing vouchers, medical care, and other welfare benefits are not factored in to calculations of income.[10] When a mother is being considered for TANF benefits, for example, the value of food stamps she is already receiving is not counted as part of her income, even if she has been receiving those benefits for some years.

Also not counted are earnings in the underground economy. In our travels we were heartened to see the extent to which welfare recipients work "off the books." Even though this is usually against the rules, it shows a willingness—in many cases even a determination—to work. More than half the people we talked with had unofficial jobs, belying the image of welfare sloth. Because such work is unlawful, payment is normally in cash or in kind and hidden from the welfare staff. We wondered repeatedly: Why should work be a crime?

Like payment off the books, payment by barter and trade—a haircut in exchange for a basket of vegetables, an oil change in exchange for child care—leaves no income trail. People who barter and trade manage to fulfill many of their needs while having very little earned income to declare when applying for welfare benefits. In addition, many Americans have consumption rates far beyond their declared income and many are better situated financially than they seem according to the relationship of their earnings to the 2014 national poverty threshold of $973 a month.[11] The *New York Times* noted in a 2014 analysis, for example, that "the differences in what poor and middle-class families consume on a day-to-day basis are much smaller than the differences in what they earn."[12] The amenities available in most households that have been assessed as poor bear this out. See Figure 3.1.

"[The] official yardstick that informs and guides our antipoverty efforts is broken," says Eberstadt. "We . . . need a replacement for it."[13]

The yardstick is not the only misleading aspect of antipoverty efforts. The way several major welfare programs are supposed to operate in theory is often very different from the ways they actually work, as the chapters in Part Three explain.

Chapter 4

Marriage, Childbearing, and Teen Pregnancy

I remember leaving the hospital thinking "Wait, they're just going to let me walk out of here with my baby? I don't know beans about babies. I don't have a license to do this"—Anne Tyler

During our interviews, many young women we met were carrying babies. Most were single and had had a first child while still in high school. They know the welfare mathematics. Mothers we talked with could cite the exact dollar amount in increased benefits each of their children had brought in to their households.

Tanya, a high school dropout and mother of five in Georgia, explained that when she got pregnant with her first child, she was under 18, still in high school, and living at home. The child was simply added to her mother's welfare case file as another member of her mother's household, which meant an increase of $155 per month in her mother's food stamp benefits.[1] By the time Tanya had her third child, she was still unmarried but old enough to "graduate" to a social service case file of her own.

Julie, a single mother in Decatur, Georgia, described her own childhood as fluctuating between a stable, almost middle-class lifestyle with two sporadically employed parents, and a chaotic, welfare-dependent lifestyle linked to her parents' inability to hold their jobs. The one constant was the dependence on welfare—her family always managed to qualify for food stamp benefits, so she grew up within Georgia's welfare system. Julie got pregnant in high school. Eventually she married the father of her child and moved in with him, but he soon disappeared, leaving her with a daughter to raise and no means of support. She quite naturally turned to welfare.

While teen pregnancy rates overall have fallen, there are still more than 300,000 babies born to teens every year.[2] More than 90% of these teen births are to single moms, and 80% of teenage girls who have babies end up on welfare.[3] Having a baby frequently prevents a girl from finishing school, making it less likely that she will be able to get a job. Further, many teen mothers have inherited their welfare status; their mothers received welfare and it seems the natural choice for them as well.

Single parenthood and poverty rates are strongly linked. It is no surprise, then, that child poverty rates have been creeping upward for the last decade; the poverty rate among mothers-only families is disturbingly high at 42%.[4] Revealingly, the most significant decline in child poverty rates occurred in the early years after the 1996 welfare reforms, as Figure 4.1 shows. During the initial implementation of those reforms many mothers left welfare for work, increasing their earnings and decreasing poverty. More recently, as the changing rules for Temporary Assistance for Needy Families (TANF) continue to erode the return-to-work pattern, recipients have been staying on welfare for longer periods, and child poverty rates have been increasing.

Figure 4.1

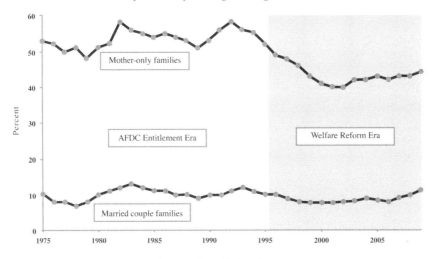

Child Poverty Rates by Living Arrangement: 1975–2009

Source: U.S. Census Bureau, Current Population Reports.

Figure 4.1 also shows the dramatic difference in poverty rates for single-mother families and married-couple families.

UNMARRIED MOTHERS

The percentage of U.S. babies born out of wedlock has been moving steadily upward since 1970 and has remained at around 40% since 2008. See Figure 4.2.

Twenty-nine percent of single white mothers have children out of wedlock, as do 53.3% of Hispanic single mothers and 72.5% of African American single mothers.[5] The implications of this radical change in family structure, which is overwhelmingly concentrated among America's lower income groups, are staggering. Commentators of all political stripes have begun sounding the alarm. Fifty years ago Senator Daniel Patrick Moynihan warned that "a community that allows large numbers of young men to grow up in broken families . . . never acquiring any stable relationship to male authority—that community asks for and gets chaos."[6]

In 2015, columnist George Will quotes political scientist Lawrence Mead who wrote, "The inequalities that stem from the workplace are now trivial in comparison to those stemming from family structure. What matters for

Figure 4.2

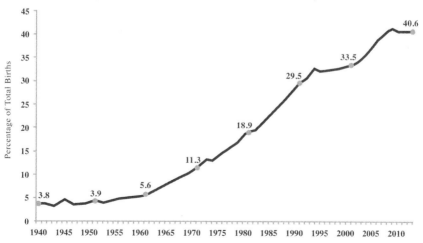

Source: Centers for Disease Control and Prevention National Vital Statistics Reports

success is less whether your father was rich or poor than whether you knew your father at all."[7]

Liberal columnist Nicholas Kristof adds that the strong and consistent correlation between one-parent families and persistent poverty "suggest that growing up with just one biological parent reduces the chances that a child will graduate from high school by 40%."[8] We will return to this issue in chapter 13.

WELFARE AND CHILDBIRTH

Do welfare benefits cause unmarried girls and women to have more babies? There is some evidence that they do,[9] but the data are not conclusive. Clearly, however, the rewards for childbirth provided by the system are compelling. More kids equals more assistance.

In order to receive benefits under the Temporary Assistance for Needy Families (TANF) and the Women, Infants and Children (WIC) programs, applicants must have at least one child. Mothers who get TANF and Supplemental Nutrition Assistance Program (SNAP) food stamp benefits and housing vouchers receive between $322 and $454 per month for each additional child.[10] For those on SSI (SSI is Supplemental Security Income for the low-income disabled who are not covered by government insurance. See chapter 9), the payoff is even greater. See Table 4.1. All welfare programs—including SNAP, TANF, Medicaid, Section 8 subsidized housing, disability benefits, and the Earned Income Tax Credit—tie their benefits to household size. The data in Table 4.1 are for Georgia, a state whose benefits are about average for the country (since each state is responsible for welfare payments to residents, there are large differences state to state).

While we seem to have created a system that virtually begs indigent young women to get pregnant, this by itself does not appear to be the most compelling reason young single women have children. Their reasons are, of course, more complex. Trish and Renata provide good examples.

Trish, reuniting with her homeless husband after a separation, deliberately became pregnant after learning he had been prostituting himself to earn money for drugs. Getting pregnant was her last-ditch effort (if unconscious at the time) to get him to rejoin his family and clean up his act. Now she is a single, homeless mother of a two-year-old boy.

Renata, whose husband joined the military and served in Iraq, got married and pregnant before graduating from high school. At the time she said it was an accident, but now she feels she must have wanted to have her husband's baby in case he didn't come home.

Table 4.1   Value of Federal Public Assistance Programs, Georgia

Benefit	Number of People in Household								
	1	2	3	4	5	6	7	8	More than 8
SNAP	$200.00	$367.00	$526.00	$668.00	$793.00	$952.00	$1,052.00	$1,202.00	$150/per person
TANF	$154.80	$309.60	$464.40	$619.20	$774.00	$928.80	$1,083.60	$1,238.40	$154.8/per person
Section 8 House Voucher	$505.00	$505.00	$599.00	$599.00	$773.00	$773.00	$801.00	$801.00	No information available
SSI	$674.00	$1,348.00	$2,022.00	$2,696.00	$3,370.00	$4,044.00	$4,718.00	$5,392.00	
SSI recipient's spouse	$287.00	$287.00							
SSI recipient's dependents	$318.00	$318.00	$636.00	$954.00	$1,272.00	$1,590.00	$1,908.00	$2,226.00	$318/per person

Notes

Household members do not have to be related.

Mothers may have to leave the program and re-enroll after child is born—some states do not pay for additional children born while on TANF.

Housing vouchers are calculated by multiplying the income of the household by 70%; 30% of the rent is the responsibility of the recipient.

Vouchers are determined by number of bedrooms, 2 people per bedroom.

SSI recipient's spouses receive a cash benefit of $287/month.

SSI recipient's dependents (children or other dependent on them for support) receive $318/month.

All of these numbers are maximums; benefits decrease on a sliding scale as income increases.

Sources: U.S. Department of Health and Human Services, and State of Georgia, 2013 Guidelines.

Several authors have suggested that girls from deprived backgrounds have babies to provide a focus in their lives, to give them "something to love," something to give their lives meaning.[11] Pregnancy and childbirth may even be seen "as a path to redemption in an otherwise violent, unpredictable, hopeless world," says *New York Times* reporter Annie Lowery.[12] Robert Pondiscio of *Time* magazine interviewed several teenage parents in the South Bronx in 2013, asking why they got pregnant and how they felt about being parents. One young mother replied, "I love that they will always love me no matter what."[13] Tanya, who was on welfare with five children by the time she was 28, told us, "I love babies, I just love my babies, I can't get enough of my babies, and I want to give them everything and be everything to them."

Birth control is often simply overlooked. While a significant number of low-income women take advantage of state health and Planned Parenthood clinics, they usually do so after they already have one or two children. "A lot of my patients don't give birth control a thought, even though it's free," says Dr. Ann James, director of medical services for a community college in Eugene, Oregon. "Those who do say they don't like the side effects, though the side effects of a pregnancy are far more unpleasant. There's also the issue of sex education. Patients report that their high school teachers were often scared of their conservative school boards, which demand emphasis on abstinence in spite of ample evidence that teenagers are sexually active."

A notably thoughtful and incisive analysis of early childbearing by poor women is provided by Kathryn Edin and Maria Kefalas in their book *Promises I Can Keep*. For two and a half years in the early 2000s the authors lived in low-income neighborhoods in the Philadelphia area, chronicling the lives of 162 low-income women. Their conclusion: poor women, including single women, have much to gain and little to lose by having babies early in life. A child doesn't interrupt their career paths or plans for college, as these prospects are extremely bleak to begin with. "[F]amily background, cognitive ability, school performance, mental health status, and so on . . . have already diminished their life chances so much that an early birth does little to reduce them much further."[14] The arrival of a child, on the other hand, is a "magic moment" seen as a major step to a better, more fulfilling life. For most impoverished young women, life prior to parenthood is dominated by failures, low expectations, "and the general sense that life has spun completely out of control." Into this void "comes a pregnancy and then a baby, bringing the purpose, the validation, the companionship, and the order that young women feel have been so sorely lacking. In some profound sense, these young women believe, a baby has the power to solve everything."[15]

Subsequent events rarely change their perception. Most young mothers Edin and Kefalas encountered believed that they are good mothers, that they will always "be there" for their children, and that even if their children's lives turn out badly, they will have done their best by them. To these women and their male partners, it is childlessness that represents the greatest failure. "The poor view childlessness as one of the greatest tragedies in life," these authors say; "female high school dropouts are more than five times as likely and male high school dropouts are more than four times as likely as their college-educated counterparts to say they think childless people lead empty lives. . . . For most women living in impoverished, inner-city communities, remaining childless is inconceivable."[16]

On the other hand, young mothers who give up their own youth by becoming single parents also give up employment, education, and training prospects, and they struggle to house and feed themselves and their children. Refrains we often heard from single mothers included, "I didn't know it was going to be so hard," "I wish I hadn't had to drop out of school," and "I wish I had waited 'til I was older." Camilla, a young mother in Georgia, told us: "I didn't want kids. I had no idea how to take care of a kid. I'm just a kid myself. Let's be blunt—getting pregnant is a really stupid idea if you're a teenager. Who's gonna feed that kid, raise that kid? Well, I'm finding out— me. And I was gonna go to school, get me a job. There go those dreams."

THE PROMISE OF LONG-ACTING REVERSIBLE CONTRACEPTION

In 2009, the state of Colorado, using funds from an anonymous donor, ran a pilot study to see what would happen if young girls were given access to long-acting reversible contraceptives (LARCs), primarily the IUD and implanted hormonal devices. The results were significant: a 26% reduction in teen pregnancies, which, in turn, resulted in a measurable reduction in welfare dependence, including a 23% reduction in participation in WIC, the nutritional supplement program for poor mothers and infants.[17] It is estimated that for every dollar spent on such long-acting contraceptive services, the state could save nearly six dollars in welfare costs.[18] In a second Colorado study, the results were even more promising for those mothers who used the devices *after* having their first child. Only 2.6% of these mothers had a repeat pregnancy within a year versus 19% of the control group whose members did not get a LARC inserted after their delivery.[19]

Long-acting reversible contraceptives are safe and effective. The only downsides are their costs, averaging $1,000 for the device and insertion, and the fact that they do not prevent STDs.[20] Condom use should be encouraged for the prevention of STDs, and a combination of the two methods deals with both issues. Another challenge is that it is hard to get young women to start on LARCs because they require a visit to a clinic—you can't simply purchase them off the shelf. Nevertheless, the results appear unequivocal. When young women are given access to long-acting reversible contraceptives, there is a marked drop in single motherhood and their resultant poverty.[21] LARCs, like all FDA-approved contraceptives, are eligible for payment under the health insurance policies purchased on state or federal exchanges under the Affordable Care Act, so they should be increasingly accessible.

STAYING SINGLE

Although each additional child results in a substantial gain in welfare benefits for single mothers, any household that combines two adults into a family unit may well end up with reduced or eliminated benefits. As a result many couples who would prefer to set up a family unit instead remain in separate households, usually their parents'.

Rosie, a young woman we met in the Bronx, is a good example. Rosie continued to live with her mother during the first three years of her marriage, even after she and her husband had a child, because it made more sense financially for her to live in her mother's subsidized public housing and have her husband live with his mother in *her* subsidized public housing than for the two of them to live together in an unsubsidized unit. Rosie's husband had a part-time job at modest pay, but his wages were high enough to disqualify his family of three from receiving HUD (Department of Housing and Urban Development) housing benefits. Rosie had a better chance of qualifying as a single mother, but if she had applied it is likely the marriage would have been discovered and would have disqualified her, because her husband's income exceeded the housing unit limit for a married couple. If they had moved in together and reported their marriage, they would no longer have received separate food stamp benefits either. Instead of SNAP benefits of $277 a month for Rosie and her child plus SNAP benefits of $152 for her husband, the household of three would have gotten $401 a month, a drop of $28 a month, just for living together. Luckily for them both, Rosie's husband found a better paying job, and three years into the marriage the three of them got off welfare and began living together as a family.

Many welfare recipients we spoke to do benefits math on a regular basis, comparing different benefit levels based on where they live and whom they live with. They keep track of all available programs and of the rules for qualifying. They calculate each dollar of welfare benefits as equal or better than dollars they might earn at a job, recognizing that private-sector salaries are taxed (at sometimes unpredictable rates) and welfare payments are not. Captured by this arithmetic, people who have been dependent on welfare programs for a year or two often lose sight of the benefits of non-dependence, including living together as a family unit and joining the above-ground economy, among the many other pluses of life outside the dependency network. Welfare inertia sets in.

PROMOTING MARRIAGE

Recognizing that single mothers and their children are the most likely group to be on welfare, the welfare reforms of 1996 created programs meant to increase marriage rates and decrease out-of-wedlock births, which, it was assumed, would lower the number of welfare recipients.[22] States were encouraged to come up with marriage promotion and teen pregnancy prevention programs. Almost 20 years on, it appears that marriage promotion hasn't worked very well despite significant effort and expenditures of more than $800 million.[23] As early as 2002 the Welfare Reform and Family Formation Project (a collaborative research project at the University of California at Berkeley) issued a report on welfare recipients' attitudes toward marriage and childbearing after participation in various programs designed to increase marriage rates and decrease out-of-wedlock births. The report concluded that "policies of persuasion alone are unlikely to substantially reduce single parenting among people who rely on welfare. . . . it thus seems unadvisable to undertake further efforts to persuade welfare recipients to marry and desist from out-of-wedlock childbearing. . . . Policies that focus on educating women about the value of marriage are . . . unlikely to have much effect."[24]

This finding was graphically illustrated by Annette, a mother of three in Bend, Oregon. "Marriage? Nah," she said. "The social workers give you these flyers every time you go in, for 'marriage enhancement workshops' and 'healthy marriage training,' that kind of stuff, but we just throw them away. None of my friends are married, I have my girlfriends who have kids and we hang out together, we have our mom club, we don't need guys around. In my high school all we got was abstinence lectures in health class—obviously that didn't work, and now they're gonna tell us to marry the fathers of our kids? No thanks."

Another attempt to encourage marriage, the Healthy Marriages Initiatives (HMI) program, was created in 2003 by the Department of Health and Human Services (DHHS). In 2013, DHHS's budget included a new $500 million Fatherhood, Marriage, and Families Innovation Fund,[25] adding parts of that program to the DHHS list of tasks and line items.

The same year a study in the *Journal of Family Relations* assessed the impact of the HMI from 2000 to 2010. The results were bleak. After a decade and billions in expenditures the HMI programs had little to no effect on marriage and out-of-wedlock births,[26] the authors concluded. Significant positive changes occurred only in Washington, DC, and that was because many welfare families there moved out of the area and were replaced by more affluent two-parent families.[27]

FAMILY CAPS

To test the impact of some of welfare's childbearing incentives on birthrates, several states instituted "family caps," starting with New Jersey in 1992. These experiments allowed states to deny additional TANF benefits to mothers who had more children while participating in TANF.[28] A mother would continue to receive benefits, as would the children she already had when she entered the program, but additional children would not be covered.

In 2004 the authors of a National Bureau of Economic Research (NBER) working paper, "Family Cap Provisions and Changes in Births and Abortions," examined whether the Family Cap Provisions in place in twenty-three states changed behavior, and found that the caps had little or no impact on birth and abortion rates.[29] States that had no caps experienced similar birth patterns to those that did have them.

At about the same time a novel experiment called the "Illegitimacy Bonus" aimed to reduce out-of-wedlock births using a system that rewarded states for reducing their out-of-wedlock birthrate without a corresponding increase in abortion rates.[30] The federal government awarded $100 million annually between 2005 and 2010 to the states that ranked best on these measures, but a recent NBER paper reported that the three states that won the bonus most often were simply states where the overall birthrate was falling. The ratio of out-of-wedlock births to in-wedlock births did not change.[31]

FINANCIAL NUDGES

To see why marriage rates continue to decline, we may not have to look further than the marriage penalties in the welfare system and the U.S. Tax Code. While the mathematics are complicated, getting married has a cost for many couples and the penalties can be substantial for those who claim the EITC (Earned Income Tax Credit) and CTC (Child Tax Credit). A 2012 paper from George Mason University's Mercatus Center states: "As an alternative to marriage, cohabitation is a common choice for low income couples facing significant fiscal penalization from the joint income filing requirement, particularly when qualifying for the Earned Income Tax Credit." The paper also notes that for the same reason, many middle-income couples are also foregoing marriage.[32]

In a 2014 article in *The Atlantic* magazine, "How Anti-Poverty Programs Marginalize Fathers," author Elizabeth Stuart noted: "Cohabitating with a boyfriend who is not biologically related to any of the household's children is the most advantageous setup in most states. The children get the benefit of government help, but still have a second adult in the house to bring in cash."[33]

The financial incentives for remaining single are complex and, depending on circumstances, can be minor or even neutral. But welfare recipients make the calculations and too often find that the figures suggest that marriage doesn't make sense. Sam, a single mother of two who works at a fabrication plant in Renton, Washington, gave us her view: "When I first got pregnant I thought we'd get married," she told us. "But we were both just getting started with working, and whenever we looked at the numbers, it just didn't make sense for us to marry. The sad thing is, now he's gone and married someone else who doesn't work, and he never sees our kids. We would've made a good couple if we had had reasons to stick together, but the whole system seems tilted towards single parents."

While financial incentives through our tax and welfare systems often work against marriage, the decoupling of marriage and childbirth in American society runs much deeper, and the reasons for this are not well understood. In *Promises I Can Keep*, Edin and Kefalas suggest that the reasons behind this sea change in American cultural norms may constitute "the biggest demographic mystery of the last half of the twentieth century."[34] They and others cite as contributing factors the sexual revolution of the 1960s, which gradually removed the stigma from nonmarital sex; the women's movement, which encouraged women to be, and to succeed, on their own; the declining pool of marriageable men in poor communities; and the expansion of welfare programs, which made single parenthood financially viable for millions.

In black communities the declining pool of marriageable men may result from a shortage of men, period. In 2015 the *New York Times* reported that national surveys have shown that there were only 83 black males in the 25–54 age group for every 100 females, nationwide. The reason: high rates of incarceration for black men and their higher mortality rate.[35]

The shortage of well-paid jobs, especially for men (and the lure of illegal drug dealing), contribute further to the decline of marriage among the poor. Real wages for American men at the lower end of the economic scale have fallen precipitously in the past twenty-five years. It has become much harder for men to hold down or find stable jobs that pay well and "that make them attractive both in their own eyes and the eyes of their partners as husbands and as providers."[36]

Men who are noncustodial parents are legally required to pay child support if they do earn money,[37] and their earnings can be garnished through payroll deductions if they refuse to cooperate or fall behind. In some states, nonpayment of child support can even lead to imprisonment.[38] But according to current law, any child support paid by a noncustodial parent (usually the father) is deducted dollar for dollar from any welfare benefits paid to the custodial parent (usually the mother) and the child.[39] So if a mother gets $500 a month in child support from an absent father, the welfare benefits for mother and child will be reduced by $500. As a result, child support practically never lifts a family out of poverty or dependency; most parents involved in the welfare system believe that any child support they provide will be paid to the state, and most balk at paying.[40]

Sociologists Maureen Waller and Robert Plotnick, reporting on their research into child support policies, note that "low-income, unmarried parents hold strong, collective beliefs about paternal responsibility and endorse the principle of child support,"[41] but "parents experiencing persistent economic insecurity believe that non-custodial parents' contributions should further increase their children's standard of living. In contrast, the practice of retaining child support payments to recoup welfare payments . . . [is] viewed as a way to offset public welfare spending." They quote one father saying, "The money doesn't go to the kid. It's not like you're buying the kids something." This logic leads to maternity ward negotiations over whether or not to put fathers on birth certificates. Because birth certificates are legal documents used to enforce child support, it is not uncommon for fathers to try to avoid being listed. The fathers often promise to give informal cash gifts to the mother and child in exchange for not being claimed as the fathers, believing that the money will go right to the child that way, not to the state. Sadly, these informal cash payments often drop off rapidly, leaving the mothers with children to raise but no legal rights to collect child support, and leaving the children with no proof of paternity.[42]

Tanya, the young mother we met in Decatur, does not get support from any of the five different fathers of her five children, not even the ones who promised gifts. She had chosen not to have the fathers named on the children's birth certificates, and her reasoning had its own logic, born of her experiences both with the fathers and with the system she was stuck in. "Why hassle my 'baby daddies' for child support when welfare will give me the same amount of money without the hassle? It's not like I'm going to see the child support they pay in anyways, so why bother? Just take the welfare."

The alternative of marriage often seems sadly irrelevant. It's certainly not a solution for Tanya: "Marry my baby daddies? No. Oh, no, no, no. . . . I don't want them around, they are nothing but trouble. They just want to 'have fun' and get in trouble with the law, they're always in and out of jail, causing trouble. No way. I'd rather be on my own."

If society accepts nonmarital sex and childbearing, as American society clearly does; if welfare benefits are provided directly to single mothers and structured to rise with each child, as they overwhelmingly are; if welfare rules discourage marriage, which they usually do; if women work nearly as often as men, as they do; and if young men in the lower socioeconomic groups cannot find jobs that hold the promise of supporting a family, it is hardly surprising that out-of-wedlock birthrates keep rising and marriage rates keep falling among the poor.

PART III

Welfare Programs in Theory and in Fact

Chapter 5

TANF: The Changing Face of Cash Assistance

No woman can call herself free until she can choose consciously whether she will or will not be a mother—Margaret Sanger

The 1996 welfare reforms were designed to replace lifetime public assistance with a welfare-to-work pathway for the nation's poor. No longer would people live and die on the dole. Instead, we would help our poor get trained for and placed in jobs, allowing them to escape poverty and lead a life of self-sufficiency. But this pathway, notably successful in its first decade, is slowly being eroded.

Consider the 1996 overhaul of cash assistance to the needy. In response to public pressure, Aid to Families with Dependent Children (AFDC) was replaced with the Temporary (cash) Assistance for Needy Families (TANF) program.[1] The key word was *temporary*. TANF participants would have to train for work, seek employment, and move off welfare within five years. This was "the end of welfare as we know it," and it was expected to end the most flagrant abuses.

The changes instituted in 1996 have been remarkably successful in reducing TANF welfare caseloads. As Figure 5.1 shows, the number of people receiving benefits under the program plummeted from 12.2 million that year to 4.4 million in 2010 (see Appendix 1 for a state-by-state breakdown). In addition, as discussed in chapter 1, former AFDC/TANF recipients

Figure 5.1

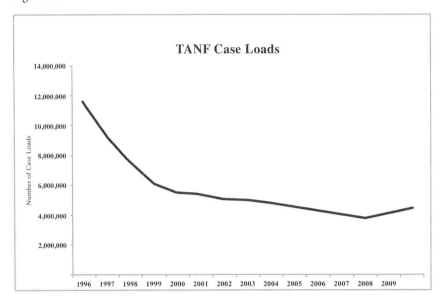

Source: U.S. Department of Health and Human Services, Office of Family Service.

who have been pushed into employment generally appear happier and better off.

While this reduction in the number of beneficiaries is impressive, it has not been accompanied by a reduction in the costs associated with TANF. When Congress passed the Personal Responsibility and Work Opportunity Reform Act in 1996, it established maintenance funding for each state at levels approximating state spending during 1992–1994 on the three programs that TANF replaced (AFDC, Emergency Assistance, and JOBS).[2] These funds were made available in block grants to the states, and in almost every year since welfare reform, TANF costs have risen. Figure 5.2 shows federal funding (TANF Expenditures), the states' matching contribution (Maintenance of Effort funding), and funding that has been transferred to Social Service Block Grants and Child Development Block Grants (TANF Transfers). These block grants are one of the methods used to give the states greater flexibility in how they spend their funds, allowing them to allocate money to programs that might not otherwise qualify for federal funding. In essence, we have falling participation along with rising costs, a phenomenon that seems to epitomize government programs. TANF funds, once simply cash funding for mothers and children, are now used for a variety of programs including child care, job training, marriage support, and teen pregnancy programs.[3]

Figure 5.2

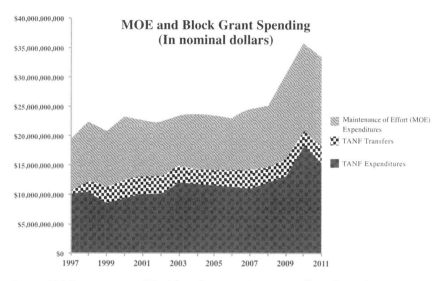

Source: U.S. Department of Health and Human Services, Office of Family Assistance.

TANF is one of the programs that reaches many people who do not meet the poverty guidelines. As *National Affairs* authors Armor and Sousa note, the states establish TANF eligibility, and "qualifying income can go as high as 250% of the federal poverty threshold"; and as Figure 5.3 shows, "more than 2 million people receiving TANF payments—about 55%—were above the federal poverty line in 2010."[4] This is a striking phenomenon in a program ostensibly tasked with helping our poorest citizens with cash assistance.

Two major changes that have taken place over the years also make the reduction in the number of TANF beneficiaries less impressive than it appears. First, there has been a major increase in the number of Americans receiving benefits from other welfare programs, especially SNAP (Supplemental Nutrition Assistance Program), disability benefits, and housing and medical subsidies. Although TANF accounts for less than 4% of the federal investment in means-tested poverty programs,[5] it often serves as a gateway; many people encounter welfare first through TANF, and once they are off TANF, they remain on, or seek to get on, other welfare programs that do not require work or training and are not time limited. Second, TANF itself has become frayed around the edges. Many states loosened the work and training requirements as jobs became

Figure 5.3

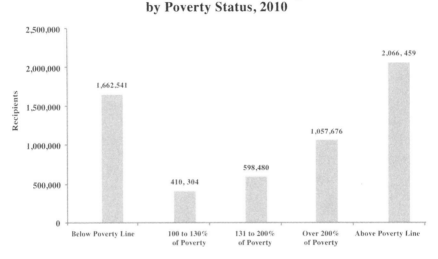

Estimated Number of TANF Recipients
by Poverty Status, 2010

Source: U.S. Census Bureau, PUMS Data.

scarce during the recession that began in 2008, on the grounds that there is little sense in training people when there are few jobs to place them in. And states have found and used loopholes in the time limit requirement as well.[6]

Every year each state receives a TANF block grant subject to a set of federal guidelines, which let the states choose among ways to spend the money. As a result, each state's TANF program is unique, and many states have found ways to allocate TANF money that do not require workfare and may not have time limits. Some states choose to focus on job training and placement services for adult TANF recipients, in accordance with the intent of the 1996 reforms. Other states choose to spend the bulk of their TANF funding on programs to benefit children, including day care and counseling. Still others use a mixed approach, allocating some resources to parents and the rest to children. All these approaches can be made to meet federal guidelines. For example, according to a 2012 Center on Budget and Policy Priorities study, Texas chooses to spend most of its TANF money on child welfare programs, including child care and counseling, which qualify as appropriate substitutes for TANF cash payments. Less than 10% of the families approved for TANF benefits in that state get cash assistance. A single mother with two children in Texas who *does* receive TANF cash assistance gets $271 per month.[7] In Michigan, one in three participating families gets cash assistance under TANF, and that single mother of two would get $478. California spends half of its TANF block grant on cash assistance, using the balance for other programs, such as those involving child care and job training. Colorado spends less than 2% of its TANF funds on work-related activities such as job training and placement, while Mississippi spends 40% on them.[8]

The basic federal rule requires states to keep 50% of their adult TANF recipients in a workfare program.[9] In theory, this means that half of TANF recipients are employed full time or in training full time. But training and placing adult beneficiaries is challenging, especially for those with no work history and limited education, who make up a sizable portion of applicants. Donna, a single mother of two, told us about a workfare training program in Georgia. "I've been to training after training after training, but it's a joke, you know, they just sit us in front of computers day after day. We're supposed to answer ads for jobs all day, and they try and help us with résumés and stuff, but we haven't worked, we don't have anything to put on a résumé. Or they just get these people up in the front of the room talking, talking, talking about how to dress for work and how to act—but the fact is, there's no jobs out there, so they just keep sending us to these trainings, and we just keep having to go, it seems like a waste of everyone's time to me, but that's how I get my TANF check."

After the 2008 recession it became more and more challenging to obey the federal requirement for having 50% of adult TANF recipients in a workfare program. Many states decided to bypass that requirement by keeping unemployed adult beneficiaries off the welfare rolls and providing benefits for their children instead. It is an appealing alternative because, for example, a state with TANF funding for 1,000,000 beneficiaries would normally have to place 500,000 of them in the workfare system. But if 300,000 of those households can be served by providing benefits exclusively for the children, the number of adult beneficiaries becomes 700,000 and the number the state has to place in the workforce system drops to 350,000. In other words, since no rule governs the number of adults versus the number of children on TANF, and since children are exempt from the work requirement, more and more states are shrinking their workfare programs for adults and simply giving cash assistance to children in the form of checks to their custodial parents. This means that an unemployed mother may be excluded from TANF participation but still receive a check as custodial parent. The check will be for less than she could receive if she were unemployed and getting assistance herself, but typically it will be $150 a month for each child under 18, with no workfare requirement and, usually, with no five-year time limit. The fewer un- and underemployed parents the states have on the rolls, the less work and training the states have to provide and the more money they have for other uses. For them, it is cheaper to pay the child-only benefit for each child than the family benefit that includes the parent with all those troublesome requirements.

As a result of these shifts, 40% of TANF cases are now "child-only." This leaves just 30% of TANF beneficiaries—half of the 60% of adult cash recipients—in workfare. If this trend continues, most TANF beneficiaries could soon be children.[10] The fact that children can become financial assets for families participating in TANF—as well as for families participating in disability programs (see chapter 9) and in the food stamp program— creates an often potent incentive for welfare mothers to have babies. Ten states have taken steps to deal with this by instituting a TANF "family cap," as discussed in chapter 4.

Although TANF benefits are only for families, a pregnant woman who does not already have a child can apply. Maryland allows women who are one month pregnant to receive TANF benefits, while Delaware will not enroll a pregnant woman in TANF until she is in her ninth month.[11] According to the Washington State TANF office, some women become pregnant, enroll in TANF, and then miscarry or decide to terminate their pregnancies, remaining on benefits until the office discovers they are ineligible.[12]

Like rules relating to workfare, rules relating to the five-year lifetime TANF limit have been vitiated. The Center on Budget and Policy Priorities study[13] points out that some states allow recipients to continue to get benefits after five years if they are still employed below the poverty threshold level, if they are cooperating with the program but unable to find employment, or if they are pregnant, ill, caring for an ill person, caring for a child, or are victims of domestic violence.[14] The study also noted that sanctions for noncompliance with the work requirement have loosened, and the average length of time recipients are sanctioned (i.e., temporarily removed from the rolls because of breaking the rules) has become shorter. In other words, sanctions are now less onerous and they last for shorter periods than they previously did.

Some beneficiaries can mount a pretty persuasive argument for exemption from the work rules. "I got me five babies," Tanya, a TANF recipient, pointed out. "I want to work, I really do, but full time? How'm I supposed to do that, *and* get my kids to school and doctor's appointments and stuff like that? I only got a year left on TANF, and then I'm supposed to suddenly be working full time—I don't see how that is going to happen. Thank god, I'll still have my food stamps, my Section 8 [subsidized] housing, and my other programs that help me, so we'll see . . . maybe I won't ever work."

Appendix 1: TANF Total Number of Recipients and Percent Change, 1996–2011

STATE	August 1996	March 2011	(1996–2011)
Alabama	100,662	55,619	−45%
Alaska	35,544	10,252	−71%
Arizona	169,442	41,406	−76%
Arkansas	56,343	18,317	−67%
California	2,581,948	1,493,754	−55%
Colorado	95,788	33,075	−65%
Connecticut	159,246	32,488	−80%
Delaware	23,654	15,437	−35%
District of Columbia	69,292	20,025	−82%
Florida	533,801	100,060	−81%
Georgia	330,302	36,464	−89%
Hawaii	66,482	26,989	−59%
Idaho	21,780	2,832	−87%
Illinois	642,644	80,650	−87%
Indiana	142,604	67,941	−52%
Iowa	86,146	44,634	−48%
Kansas	63,783	38,354	−40%
Kentucky	172,193	62,566	−64%
Louisiana	228,115	23,213	−90%
Maine	53,873	26,712	−50%
Maryland	194,127	60,001	−69%
Massachusetts	226,030	99,657	−56%
Michigan	502,354	172,111	−66%
Minnesota	169,744	50,075	−70%
Mississippi	123,828	23,765	−81%
Missouri	222,820	86,725	−61%
Montana	29,130	8,393	−71%
Nebraska	39,228	15,510	−60%
Nevada	34,261	27,542	−20%
New Hampshire	22,937	10,532	−54%
New Jersey	275,637	83,756	−70%
New Mexico	99,661	50,936	−49%
New York	1,143,962	279,552	−76%
North Carolina	267,326	43,326	−84%
North Dakota	13,146	4,625	−65%
Ohio	549,312	226,760	−59%
Oklahoma	96,201	19,765	−79%

STATE	August 1996	March 2011	(1996–2011)
Oregon	78,419	80,220	2%
Pennsylvania	531,059	140,123	−74%
Puerto Rico	151,023	41,805	−72%
Rhode Island	56,560	15,097	−73%
South Carolina	114,273	40,253	−65%
South Dakota	15,896	6,642	−58%
Tennessee	254,818	153,507	−40%
Texas	649,018	107,205	−83%
Utah	39,073	9,888	−75%
Vermont	24,331	6,176	−75%
Virginia	152,845	74,977	−54%
Washington	268,927	146,655	−45%
West Virginia	89,039	23,399	−74%
Wisconsin	148,888	60,967	−59%
Wyoming	11,398	659	−94%
U.S. Total	12,228,913	4,401,012	−64%

Chapter 6

A Housing System Leaves the Needy Out in the Cold

The American Dream. For me, it was that house with the white picket fence, the yard with room for my kids to play. That dream? Gone—Beatrice L.

Subsidized housing is a major component of the U.S. federal welfare system. While the number of beneficiaries has remained constant over recent decades, the cost of the program went from $20 billion in 1990 to $41 billion in 2010, due to rising rents, and its cost is still going up. Census data from 1988 to 2012 show monthly rent for a one-bedroom unit increasing from less than $350 a month in 1988 to more than $700 in 2013. The median monthly rental rates for the United States are graphed in Figure 6.1. Since the HUD (Department of Housing and Urban Development) Section 8 program pays for market-rate housing, these are the rental rates tenants seeking housing paid on average nationwide.

To get vouchers for Section 8 benefits, applicants must first locate housing and then apply for assistance.[1] Although the vouchers were initially valid only for public housing complexes (and 60% are still used that way[2]), they can now be used for housing in any available rental units people can find with landlords willing to take Section 8 renters.[3] Landlords are not required to do that and many refuse.

Once a unit—public or private—is located and an application is filed, the Section 8 program evaluates the applicant's income to determine how

Figure 6.1

Median Asking Rent, 1988–2013

Source: U.S. Census Bureau.

much of the rent HUD will cover and how much will be covered by the tenant. They then issue a housing voucher, which is used to pay the landlord or public housing agent. Tenants are not required to pay more than 30% of their income as their contribution to rent. Tenants with no income pay nothing (see Figure 6.2).

While costs have been escalating, the number of families who need subsidized housing and can't get it has also been rising rapidly. The Center on Budget and Policy Priorities, a nonprofit think tank in Washington, DC, estimates that 8.5 million eligible family heads are waiting for subsidized units.[4] In large part, this is because some mid- and long-time beneficiaries of Section 8 housing are hanging on to units they no longer need and aren't currently eligible for. Someone who lands a rental unit and lines up HUD funding is pretty much left alone afterwards. Unlike other programs, which require at least some periodic requalification, public housing is treated as a permanent entitlement. We do not want to be rooting up families on a regular basis, the reasoning goes. As a result, a great many units remain in the same hands for years, if not decades, regardless of whether or not the renters still qualify.[5] Some of these renters stay in their units. Others move out and rent their apartments to family and friends, thus obtaining a steady cash income. Meanwhile, the units are unavailable for people who really need them.

Figure 6.2

Source: U.S. Office of Management and Budget.

Mary, a Brooklyn mother of two, is steamed. "My aunt, she's had her Section 8 unit for over thirty years. All kinds of people have lived there, from her kids to nieces and nephews, to boyfriends. And she charges them all rent. She's got a decent income, just sitting at home, doing nothing, managing the rooms in that apartment as a rental. In all these years, not once has anyone come by to check on her to see if she is still qualified to live there, or to see who is in the unit. Meanwhile, here I am, with my husband and two kids, and we went and applied, and we were told that our kids would be out of high school before we could ever hope to get a unit. How is that fair?"

The issue has attracted some attention. The Obama administration's 2014 budget plan included a provision giving local housing authorities the power to set time limits and work requirements for public housing.[6] At this writing, the change had not become law.

Strikingly, 41% of those who receive public housing assistance have incomes above the poverty threshold.[7] This program, originally conceived as a way to aid the poor by paying for housing, has now morphed into a subsidized housing program for more than 2 million recipients who are not poor, as the costs continue to escalate.[8] A recent audit by the HUD inspector general's office discovered $37 million a month spent on rent for noncompliant participants, who by law are required to do community service or job training or education in exchange for housing. Overall, auditors estimated that in 2013 ineligible residents occupied 106,000 of the 550,000 units that are set aside for people who have compliance requirements for the Section 8 subsidy. This means those 106,000 units are not available for those who are truly eligible. The auditors also found that no sanctions are being levied for noncompliance, so residents can stay in their units even after HUD discovers they are out of compliance.[9] This further explains the ongoing shortage of public housing for those who need it most.

Chapter 7

Who Gets Food Stamps?

For even when we were with you, we would give you this command: If anyone is not willing to work, let him not eat—2 Thessalonians 3:10

Shame upon him who will not stretch out the helping hand to his brother— Theodore Roosevelt

The Supplemental Nutrition Assistance Program (SNAP), commonly referred to as food stamps, is a means-tested entitlement program administered through the United States Department of Agriculture that provides debit cards that can be used to purchase food. Unlike the paper stamps originally issued, which many recipients were embarrassed to use, the debit cards are replenished monthly and look like any other debit or credit card.

The program costs $85 billion annually, a huge increase from the $20 billion it cost as recently as 2000;[1] its costs are borne entirely by the federal government. Benefit eligibility is determined by income levels. As shown in Table 7.1, people who earn up to 130% of the poverty line qualify, and the value of other public benefits they get is not factored into calculations of their income.

As the table indicates, a household of four with a combined annual income of $30,000 or less may receive SNAP benefits. Benefits are increased or reduced as recorded earnings increase or decrease. Once an earner crosses the maximum income threshold, benefits cease altogether.

Table 7.1   SNAP Eligibility Levels, 2013

Household Size	Gross Monthly Income (130% of poverty)	Maximum Monthly Allotment
1	$1,211	$200
2	$1,640	$367
3	$2,069	$526
4	$2,498	$668
5	$2,927	$793
6	$3,356	$952
7	$3,785	$1,052
8	$4,214	$1,202
Each Additional Member	$429	$150

Source: U.S. Department of Agriculture.

For example, an applicant who is unemployed, has no income, and passes the means test can get the maximum SNAP benefit, $200 a month. If that applicant later lands a part-time job, the benefit is recalculated in accordance with earnings reported to the SNAP office. The more detailed example for a family of three that follows is from the SNAP office in Massachusetts. Each state calculates these SNAP benefits in its own way.

Example: Carl and his family have $500 in net income after allowable deductions. To determine the family's SNAP benefits, take 30% of the "net income" (30% of $500) and subtract it from the maximum benefit, as follows:

$500	Net income for Carl's family
x .30	(Multiply by 30%)
$150	Countable Income
$526	Maximum SNAP for 3 persons
− $150	Countable Income
$376	**Monthly SNAP benefits for Carl's family**

The SNAP program has expanded dramatically over the last decade. It is now the second largest welfare program in the country after Medicaid,[2] and it currently serves more than 47 million Americans. This means that nearly one-sixth of Americans are now on food stamps (Figure 7.1).[3]

Though the SNAP program has a requirement that able-bodied participants either enroll in a training program or participate in a workfare

Figure 7.1

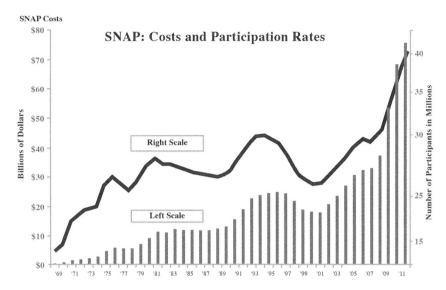

Source: U.S. Department of Agriculture.

program, states and counties are allowed to waive that requirement.[4] In our travels we did not encounter a single SNAP recipient enrolled in any training or workfare programs. As Ivan, a young SNAP recipient in Washington, DC, put it: "Yeah, there is supposedly a work requirement, but all you have to do is sign a paper saying you are looking for work. There's no money for training programs, and there's no jobs out there they can train us for, so we just jump through the loophole and get our benefits." Maine, which had previously dropped workfare requirements, reinstituted them for SNAP eligibility in 2015. In making this change Governor Paul LePage noted, "We must continue to do all that we can to eliminate generational poverty and get people back to work. We must protect our limited resources for those who are truly in need and who are doing all they can to be self-sufficient."[5]

Part of the rapid rise in the number of SNAP recipients is due to hardships resulting from the 2008 recession, but increasingly aggressive recruitment by the United States Department of Agriculture and by the states is also a major contributor. Mel, a college student in Olympia, Washington, describes his recent experience with a USDA recruiter: "I went to a local food bank with a friend who doesn't have much money, and we were waiting in line to go in and noticed this lady with a clipboard moving up the line. When she got to us, she asked us if we were on food stamps. We said no. She asked us if we were college students, and when we said yes, she said we were entitled to benefits and should sign up. I thought that was pretty weird. She didn't ask for ID or proof of income or anything. She said she could get us $200 a month this month for sure, and then we would just have to come in to her office to fill out paperwork to stay on."

Recruiting SNAP beneficiaries has become a notable feature of the program, in part because more beneficiaries means that more money flows to the states. A recent *Washington Post* article noted that one food stamp recruiter in Florida is expected to sign up 150 new recipients a month, a quota she usually manages to beat.[6] Florida has seen its food stamp rolls grow from 1.45 million to 3.35 million since 2008, partly thanks to such recruiters, who visit seniors and encourage them to sign on. "I don't want to be another person depending on the government," one reluctant senior told the recruiter, according to the *Washington Post* article. Her response was: "How about being another person getting the help you deserve?"

Though this recruiter feels she is doing a service for the eligible beneficiaries least likely to enroll in SNAP (less than 40% of eligible seniors enroll, compared to 75% of eligible Americans overall), the article notes that "the job also has a second and more controversial purpose for cash-strapped Florida, where increasing food-stamp enrollment has become a means of economic growth, bringing almost $6 billion each year into the state. The money helps to sustain communities, grocery stores and food producers."[7] Such financial benefits make many states eager to sign up eligible beneficiaries. The Rhode Island Food Bank, a nonprofit group contracted with the state to promote the federal SNAP program, recently advertised for a SNAP outreach coordinator to host SNAP-themed bingo games for the elderly. Recruiters for the SNAP program in Alabama hand out fliers that read, "Be a patriot. Bring your food stamp money home." "Three states in the Midwest throw food-stamp parties where new recipients sign up en masse," notes the *Washington Post* report.[8]

In 2011, the state of Oregon won $5 million in awards from the USDA for its "exceptional administration of the SNAP program" by ensuring that people entitled to the benefit signed up for it, and by swiftly processing their applications.[9] These are competitive awards—states compete to see which state can get the most people onto the SNAP program most quickly. Thus the federal government rewards states with taxpayer money when they arrange for more people to get money that is also, of course, from the taxpayers.

Economist Paul Krugman called the food stamp program "heroic" in a 2013 *New York Times* op-ed column,[10] in considerable part because of the economic stimulus provided by the dispersal of these federal funds. While a Department of Agriculture food program is a clumsy way to implement Keynesian economics, the states clearly want those federal dollars.

Reflecting the efforts of SNAP recruiters and the expansion of eligibility limits in 2009, SNAP increasingly serves the nonpoor, much as many other welfare programs now do. While the official rules call for a cutoff of SNAP benefits at 130% of the poverty line (roughly $16,000 a year in 2015), in 2010 nearly 8 million Americans whose incomes were over 200% of poverty (i.e., $46,000 for a family of four) were receiving SNAP benefits, as Figure 7.2 shows. A further 7 million beneficiaries were earning between 131% and 200% of the poverty line.

The SNAP program receives continuing attention from Congress. In late 2013, some lawmakers pushed for a workfare requirement and stricter means-testing, while others advocated expanding the program further. Supporting expansion, a Department of Agriculture (USDA) survey found that 49 million Americans lived in "food insecure" households in 2012,[11] with "food insecure" defined as lacking consistent access to food throughout the year. (For the questions asked in the survey, see Appendix 2.) The survey links access to adequate healthy food with access to money to buy it, but it does not ask about other food sources, or about whether respondents cook at home. Millions of children get free meals at school, for

Figure 7.2

Food Stamp Recipients by Poverty Status, 2010

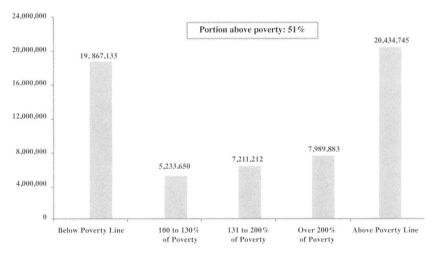

Sources: U.S. Census Bureau, 2010 American Community Survey, PUMS data.

example; many adults have access to food banks. And many rural residents hunt, fish, and grow food.

A 2013 *New York Times* article included an interview with "reluctant food stamp recipient" Dustin Rigsby, "a self described 'true Southern man' who [as] a struggling mechanic, hunts deer, doves and squirrels to help feed his family. He shops for grocery bargains, cooks budget-stretching stews and limits himself to one meal a day. . . . [He] dreams of becoming a game warden and said it irritated him to see people 'mooch off the system.'"[12] Asked what he thinks will happen if the food stamp benefits go away, he said that he would find a way to make do. "The way I was raised, it's 'Be thankful for what you've got.'" Still, Rigsby and his family count on SNAP, as the *Times* story noted: "On the refrigerator of their sparsely furnished apartment is a calendar marked with the date—the 6th—that their card is refreshed. 'Food!' it declares."[13]

THE HOME HEATING/COOLING CONNECTION

States also draw more SNAP dollars through what is known as the LIHEAP loophole. As a 2012 Senate Budget Committee report noted: "Fifteen states take advantage of a loophole by mailing small checks (less than a dollar a month) to individuals under the Low Income Home Energy Assistance Program (LIHEAP) to automatically increase recipients' food stamp allotment—even if they pay no home energy expenses."[14]

Here's how this works. As mentioned, applicants for food stamps must declare income and assets. In some states they may be allowed to deduct certain living expenses from their income, thus reducing it enough to satisfy SNAP eligibility requirements. Deductible expenses include those for home heating and cooling, but beneficiaries do not have to declare actual costs. If they can say they are receiving "home heating and cooling assistance" (even just $1), their caseworkers can provide them with the state's average home heating and cooling cost for their region. They can then deduct the average number, rather than the actual number, from their income, perhaps reducing their income enough to qualify for food stamp benefits they would not otherwise be eligible to receive.[15] Alice, a young mother we encountered in Georgia, put it this way: "I had a little bit of income from my part-time job, and that made my food stamp payment go down, but then my case worker told me about this home heating program she was going to sign me up for. The utility company would send me a check to help me with my utilities in my apartment. I said I don't have utility bills since I'm on Section 8 housing, it's already covered. Well, they sent me the check anyway, and sure enough it made my food stamps go up. I don't really understand it, but hey, I get more money, so I'm not complaining."

Use of this loophole was still increasing in 2014.[16] States encourage the practice because it brings in more food stamps, which means more income for their grocers and other merchants. Eliminating the loophole would save taxpayers more than $9 billion over 10 years.[17]

WHAT SNAP CARDS BUY

Whatever the number of SNAP participants a state has, SNAP cards can be used to purchase just about any food and any nonalcoholic beverage.[18] There is no requirement that the food meet any nutritional standards. A recent investigation by the *Washington Times* into what exactly was being purchased with food stamp debit cards[19] was stymied by federal officials who told the reporters it would be illegal to divulge such information. Even asking how much each grocer gets in food stamp income was a no-no, the paper reported: "Maryland denied *the Times'* request for data under the Freedom of Information Act, saying the information belonged to the federal government which instructed states not to release it. . . . Legislation seemingly designed to protect the industry goes so far as to say that anyone who releases the amount of food stamp dollars paid to a store can be jailed."[20] Food debit card purchases could, of course, be tracked with a few keyboard clicks, but reporters and other private citizens may not access the information about whether the food stamps are feeding the poor they were intended for, what foods are being purchased, or how much business is being done this way. The USDA argues that this data is proprietary to the grocers, and the government refuses to divulge any related information.[21]

There may be a crack in this wall of silence. The *Argus Leader*, a South Dakota newspaper, filed a Freedom of Information Act request in 2012 calling for release of food stamp redemption information by retailers in Sioux City, South Dakota. The FDA refused, and the newspaper filed a lawsuit in federal court to compel the USDA to release the data. The USDA then filed a motion for summary judgment, contending that all necessary factual issues were settled and the case need not be tried. The District Court granted the government's motion. The *Argus Leader* appealed, and the Eighth Circuit Court of Appeals reversed the District Court, shooting down the USDA's arguments. At press time the case was back at the District Court and a trial was pending.[22]

Some states have tried to pass laws limiting food stamp purchases to healthy food items, and others have tried to exclude categories of unhealthy foods (soft drinks, for example). But the only current limit is a stipulation that prevents the purchase of warm food, or food from a restaurant.[23] Many people we interviewed said grocery store delis often circumvent this rule by serving up hot meals with cold meal price stickers on them, and even this single limitation may soon be waived.[24] Several states have recently introduced a pilot program that allows some restaurants to accept food stamp cards.

MISUSE AND ABUSE

Often thought of as a necessary short-term program for people temporarily down on their luck, SNAP, for most participants, has become long-term. According to a USDA report in 2011, 56% of SNAP beneficiaries remain on the program for more than five years, with fewer than 25% leaving the program in a year or less.[25] According to Michael Tanner at the Cato Institute, "This fact suggests that SNAP is not being used as a temporary safety net, but rather as a permanent source of income."[26]

Food stamp misuse is imaginative and commonplace. News stories from all over the country tell of million-dollar profits made by retailers trading in stolen cards,[27] of ineligible recipients (including prison inmates) receiving cards,[28] and of recipients receiving multiple cards because no questions are asked if a recipient reports losing a card.[29]

Exchanging food card privileges for cash is illegal but very common among those we interviewed. Fifty cents on the dollar is the usual rate. "Sometimes I just need some cash," said Mary, a woman we chatted with in Decatur, Georgia. "Since I live at home with my mom, and my kids get fed at school, I'll just sell my card so I can have some cash for the month—we aren't going hungry; we don't really need the card every month." People in Oregon and Louisiana also reported common trades at 50 cents on the dollar.

New York is a little different. During a visit to a park in Harlem we came across a young couple playing with their two children on a jungle gym. When we brought up the subject of SNAP benefits and the trade for cash at 50 cents on the dollar, the man smiled and said, "Hey, this is New York! We get 70 cents on the dollar for our food stamps. Everyone sells their food stamp cards for cash," he added. "There's plenty of food in this city—the kids get two free meals a day at school, there's lots of food banks and churches, so if we're short on cash we just sell the card, 70 cents on the dollar. Just walk in to that grocery store over there and start filling up your cart, and soon enough someone will come up to you and offer you their food stamp card for sale. You buy a $100 card for $70, you just saved yourself 30% on your grocery bill. You're a fool if you're paying full price."

Some abuses show real entrepreneurial acumen. In 2013, the *New York Post* reported that barrels of food purchased by SNAP recipients in New York City were being shipped to their families in the Dominican Republic. The barrels were filled with cereal, baby formula, juices, olive oil, and canned soup. "Whatever I don't need, I sell," said one of the people who got the shipments in the Dominican Republic. Another said she gets barrels every few weeks from her sister, who buys everything on Prospect Avenue in Brooklyn using food stamps.

SNAP, like TANF (Temporary Assistance for Needy Families), can be a gateway to many other welfare programs for low-income Americans. The "Obama phone" provides an example. This "free phone" program was actually started under President Reagan for land lines and expanded to cell phones under President George W. Bush.[30] The idea is that cell phones can help low-income citizens find opportunities for employment or training, follow up on them, and stay connected to society. More than 14 million Americans in 38 states now use these free cell phones, which are available through various telecommunications providers. The phones are paid for by fees tacked on to the phone bills of all cell phone users (essentially a dedicated tax). The eligibility requirement is simply participation in any one of a number of welfare programs, most commonly SNAP.[31] And since the number of eligible participants in all federal programs ballooned with the American Recovery and Reinvestment Act of 2009, millions more Americans now qualify for such phones.

Danny, a young man we met in Harlem, said: "Yeah, I've got three or four of those things. When they run out of minutes I just go get me another one. It's really easy. I'm on food stamps so all I've gotta do is show my food stamp debit card and they give me another one."

Rita, a Brooklyn mother of two, agreed. "My aunt gets a bunch of them and just gives them to all the nieces and nephews so they can call her and stay in touch with each other. There's no problem asking for another one. You just show your food stamp card."

Of the people we interviewed around the country, a strong majority smoked cigarettes, alcohol use was common, and many admitted to using drugs. "I smoke cigarettes, and drink, and smoke pot, sure," said Rachel. "Why not—this living on the welfare check business is a dead-end road; this way I don't have to think about it too much. Get high, and the day goes by faster and with less stress." "I go to work high every day," said Ken, a young man on food stamps who works two part-time jobs and still can't quite make ends meet. "That way I don't stress about it."

We have some sympathy for these positions. Life on welfare can be rotten. For all of the reasons we have seen—low self-esteem, constant fear of losing benefits, resentment of a patronizing system that controls their lives—welfare recipients are often desperately unhappy. That they seek a few moments of pleasure or escape, perhaps even joy, seems not only natural but perhaps necessary. On the other hand, taxpayers should not be asked to pay for these indulgences, however important they may be to those who seek them. Surprisingly, although federal food benefit cards prohibit the purchase of alcohol and tobacco products, many state assistance programs do not. Often the state welfare rules prohibit the use of state benefit cards only at casinos, liquor stores, and adult entertainment venues. Tobacco and alcohol purchases at convenience stores are just fine.[32]

Stories of illicit drug use create backlash. At least 36 state legislatures considered laws for mandatory drug testing for welfare recipients in 2013 and 2014. Florida has gone so far as to require applicants to pay for their own drug tests; those who pass are reimbursed the $40 fee.[33] Michigan is considering legislation that would prevent people who fail employment application drug tests from collecting unemployment. Currently, job applicants who fail such a test are reported as "unavailable for work," which allows them to collect unemployment—a perverse incentive to use drugs and fail the drug test.[34] According to the *New York Times*, Ken Goike, the state representative who introduced the bill, said he had decided to propose it "after his brother-in-law tried hiring employees at a local manufacturing facility. Half of the applicants tested positive for drugs, Mr. Goike said, making them 'unavailable for work,' which is a condition for receiving unemployment compensation."[35]

These laws, and many others making their way through state legislatures, are billed as attempts to target limited resources to places where they are needed most. Proponents argue that such laws are needed to insure that money from the public coffers is used for true necessities, not luxuries. Opponents say the laws are an unfair intrusion into recipients' lives, holding the poor to a different standard than other Americans.

FOOD STAMPS AND WEIGHT

SNAP recipients on average are somewhat more overweight than the general population. A 2014 U.S. Department of Agriculture study reported that 72% of adult food stamp recipients and 38% of their children were either overweight or obese as compared to 64% and 28%, respectively, in higher income categories.[36] One reason for this disparity may be that cheap foods tend to be higher in carbohydrates and fats and lower in proteins, in addition to being more convenient to purchase and eat. Another reason may be limited access to healthy food; many inner cities have few grocery stores. Joe, the owner of a grocery store in Harlem, explained it this way:

"People come in here, they are rushed, they are tired, they don't have time or money to shop for health—they want the most bang for the buck, and that means pasta, beans, rice, chips, anything to fill up on. You can live on a food stamp card, but you won't be healthy, you'll be eating high-calorie carbs for the most part." The USDA does have programs that encourage the use of food stamps at farmers' markets, but they have had little impact.

Appendix 2: USDA Survey Questions to Assess Household Food Security

1. "We worried whether our food would run out before we got money to buy more." Was that often, sometimes, or never true for you in the last 12 months?
2. "The food that we bought just didn't last and we didn't have money to get more." Was that often, sometimes, or never true for you in the last 12 months?
3. "We couldn't afford to eat balanced meals." Was that often, sometimes, or never true for you in the last 12 months?
4. In the last 12 months, did you or other adults in the household ever cut the size of your meals or skip meals because there wasn't enough money for food? (Yes/No)
5. (If yes to question 4) How often did this happen—almost every month, some months but not every month, or in only 1 or 2 months?
6. In the last 12 months, did you ever eat less than you felt you should because there wasn't enough money for food? (Yes/No)
7. In the last 12 months, were you ever hungry, but didn't eat, because there wasn't enough money for food? (Yes/No)
8. In the last 12 months, did you lose weight because there wasn't enough money for food? (Yes/No)
9. In the last 12 months did you or other adults in your household ever not eat for a whole day because there wasn't enough money for food? (Yes/No)
10. (If yes to question 9) How often did this happen—almost every month, some months but not every month, or in only 1 or 2 months?

(Questions 11–18 were asked only if the household included children age 0–17)

11. "We relied on only a few kinds of low-cost food to feed our children because we were running out of money to buy food." Was that often, sometimes, or never true for you in the last 12 months?

12. "We couldn't feed our children a balanced meal, because we couldn't afford that." Was that often, sometimes, or never true for you in the last 12 months?
13. "The children were not eating enough because we just couldn't afford enough food." Was that often, sometimes, or never true for you in the last 12 months?
14. In the last 12 months, did you ever cut the size of any of the children's meals because there wasn't enough money for food? (Yes/No)
15. In the last 12 months, were the children ever hungry but you just couldn't afford more food? (Yes/No)
16. In the last 12 months, did any of the children ever skip a meal because there wasn't enough money for food? (Yes/No)
17. (If yes to question 16) How often did this happen—almost every month, some months but not every month, or in only 1 or 2 months?
18. In the last 12 months did any of the children ever not eat for a whole day because there wasn't enough money for food? (Yes/No)

Chapter 8

WIC: Missteps with Women and Children

If we can conquer space, we can conquer child hunger—Buzz Aldrin

Women, Infants and Children (WIC) is a special U.S. Department of Agriculture (USDA) program that provides vouchers for supplemental foods, food packages, and health care referrals as well as nutrition education for low-income pregnant women and breastfeeding and nonbreastfeeding postpartum women. The program also provides supplemental foods for infants and children up to age five who are at "nutritional risk" due to inadequate diets.[1] (Virtually all low-income mothers and children are now deemed "at nutritional risk" due to repeated broadening of the criteria for inclusion in this category, and many observers argue that the "nutritional risk" criteria should therefore be eliminated altogether; for now it remains.[2])

Unlike other welfare programs, WIC is funded through an annual appropriation from Congress, which must be reauthorized each year.[3] Although being on WIC is not the same as being on SNAP because WIC is a nutritional program specifically created to provide healthy foods and counseling to mothers and infants, WIC families usually qualify for SNAP benefits as well, and they are also likely to be on TANF and Medicaid, assuming they qualify in the states where they live.

Use of the WIC program has grown steadily over the years. See Figure 8.1. Half of all newborns in the United States, most of them not in poverty,

Figure 8.1

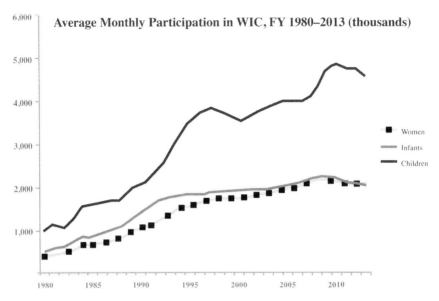

Source: U.S. Department of Agriculture Food and Nutrition Service.

Figure 8.2

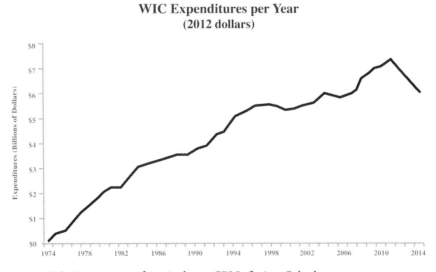

Source: U.S. Department of Agriculture, CPI Inflation Calculator.

now receive benefits from this welfare program,[4] which has more liberal criteria for inclusion than any other.

The cost of the program has also grown steadily over the years, peaking in 2010. Since the end of the latest recession, costs have been reined in to prerecession levels, but they remain high by historical standards. See Figure 8.2.

Unlike SNAP benefits, WIC benefits are limited to certain foods. Using federal guidelines and federal block grant funding, each state determines which foods will be included in the list of healthy foods available for purchase with WIC food vouchers. Participants either go to authorized retailers and choose from the items available (as shown in Table 8.1) or they receive preassembled WIC food packages provided by local health departments and authorized retailers. While the WIC vouchers are restricted to

Table 8.1   Maximum Monthly Allowances of Supplemental Foods

Foods	Children	Women		
	Food Package IV: 1 through 4 years	Food Package V: Pregnant and Partially Breastfeeding (up to 1 year postpartum)	Food Package VI: Postpartum (up to 6 months postpartum)	Food Package VII: Fully Breastfeeding (up to 1 year postpartum)
Juice, single strength	128 fl. oz.	144 fl. oz.	96 fl. oz.	144 fl. oz.
Milk	16 qt.	22 qt.	16 qt.	24 qt.
Breakfast cereal	36 oz.	36 oz.	36 oz.	36 oz.
Cheese				1 lb.
Eggs	1 dozen	1 dozen	1 dozen	2 dozen
Fruits and vegetables	$6.00 in cash value vouchers	$10.00 in cash value vouchers	$10.00 in cash value vouchers	$10.00 in cash value vouchers
Whole wheat bread	2 lb.	1 lb.		1 lb.
Fish (canned)				30 oz.
Legumes, dry or canned and/or Peanut butter	1 lb. (64 oz. canned) or 18 oz.	1 lb. (64 oz. canned) or 18 oz.	1 lb. (64 oz. canned) or 18 oz.	1 lb. (64 oz. canned) or 18 oz.

Source: U.S. Department of Agriculture, WIC.

the foods listed, the USDA authorizes a very large number of retailers so that most mothers can get these foods conveniently.

In addition, nonbreastfeeding mothers receive formula for their newborns. Purchasing of the formula products involves a quirky funding scheme that requires the state to contract with the lowest-bidding formula manufacturer, which must, in turn, rebate part of what they are paid to the state. In turn, the state normally allocates the rebate to its WIC program. See Figure 8.3. Accordingly, the more formula that is sold, the higher the rebate payments and the more money the WIC program gets, all of which adds up to an incentive for states to support formula use over breastfeeding.[5]

The WIC program is strongly criticized for this antibreastfeeding bias, as breastfeeding has consistently been shown to be better for most babies than formula. As of 2012, only 29% of WIC infants breastfed, and of those only 12% were exclusively breastfed, with the rest receiving a combination of breast milk and formula.[6] For non-WIC babies the percentage breastfed is more than 60%. With half of all infants now on WIC, this is an important public health issue.

In 2013 WIC experimented with changes in the way the program provides breastfeeding and formula packages to new mothers, eliminating the mixed package designed for mothers who wished to do both formula

Figure 8.3

Savings from Infant Formula Rebates

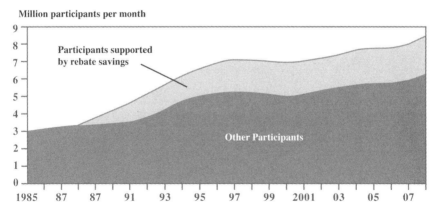

Note: WIC is the acronym for the Special Supplemental Nutrition Program for Women, Infants and Children. The WIC program started in fiscal 1974, and the infant formula rebate program started in fiscal 1988.

Source: USDA, Economic Research Service using data from USDA, Food and Nutrition Service.

feeding and breastfeeding. The result was even higher rates of formula feeding.[7]

The WIC program also draws criticism because the few studies of its impact on children are not encouraging. Professor Douglas J. Besharov at the University of Maryland's School of Public Policy has studied the WIC program. His data suggest that, while WIC-provided prenatal care has led to improvements in the prenatal health of mothers, the program has had little impact on WIC children.[8]

Sometime between now and 2020 WIC benefits are expected to transfer from a voucher system to an electronic benefit transfer debit card system, which is cause for concern.[9] Many expect that WIC beneficiaries who are currently receiving nutritious food will no longer do so when their benefits come in the form of a cash card that allows them to purchase whatever they like; essentially the WIC cards will become an extension of SNAP.

Meanwhile there is already some fraud in the WIC system. Some retailers buy the vouchers at a discount, providing women with cash. A 2013 sting operation in New York involved nine grocery stores that were purchasing WIC vouchers at a 15–20% discount and then redeeming them through the WIC program for full face value. This operation uncovered $30 million in fraudulent redemptions.[10] In Augusta, Georgia, another sting operation in 2013 uncovered $8 million in WIC vouchers that were cashed in by thirteen phantom grocery stores whose "owners" didn't even bother to open storefronts to hide their fraud. They simply got the word out that they would buy WIC vouchers and SNAP benefit cards at a 30% discount, and then they cashed the cards for full face value.[11] The Web site Craigslist has recently agreed to cooperate with federal efforts to clamp down on food stamp trading carried on through its Web site, where buyers and sellers were openly advertising and purchasing federal benefits.[12]

Chapter 9

How We Disable the Disabled

This is painful for a liberal to admit, but conservatives have a point when they suggest that America's safety net can sometimes entangle people in a soul-crushing dependency—Nicholas Kristof

Poverty is where the money is—Malcolm X

We met Joe in Shoreline, Washington. He had been injured in a work-related truck accident and recently had been approved for disability payments. Being on disability, Joe says, is both a blessing and a curse. Joe is clearly not completely disabled (when we met him, he was carrying a backpack and rolling a suitcase full of books down a three-story staircase in the library) but he does have chronic pain from the accident. Although working in his former job as a construction manager is out of the question, he could work at least part time, and would like to do so. But part-time work is a problem. Joe can't earn more than $85 in any given month without worrying about whether he's earning enough to make it worth using up one of his nine permitted months of transitional work (see the section "The Nine-Month Rule" later in the chapter). He's pretty sure he could earn some money on his good days, but the risk of losing his benefits always seems too great.

For Joe and a great many other people, the disability programs often act as psychological and economic traps. Because benefits for the disabled are, understandably, quite generous, and because the rules about disability beneficiaries earning money in the private economy are frighteningly complex, very few people move out of these programs. What follows shows how and why many of the well-intended rules about disability benefits have backfired.

CASH ASSISTANCE PROGRAMS

Disabled Americans and their families have access to two different cash assistance programs, depending on their work history. Both Social Security Disability Insurance (SSDI) and Supplemental Security Income[1] (SSI) are administered through the Social Security Administration (SSA), and it is possible to receive payments from both, since the monthly SSDI payment may not be enough to bring recipients above the federal poverty guidelines.[2] As noted previously, SSDI is not a welfare program because it is not means-tested. Beneficiary payments are made from an insurance fund that payees have contributed to. We include it here because it falls under the Social Security Administration's disability umbrella, is often commingled with SSI (which *is* a means-tested program), and shares many characteristics with it.

The number of participants in these programs has grown rapidly, and continued growth appears certain. Nearly 19 million Americans are currently enrolled in one or the other or both. See Figure 9.1. The budget for SSDI grew from just under $80 billion in 2002 to $120 billion in 2012; SSI's budget increased from $34 billion to $51 billion in the same time frame.[3] Add medical care for those on disability and the bill comes to $260 billion a year, or almost $1,800 from every working American.

Disabled Americans and their families are also eligible for food stamps and public housing, and for either Medicaid or Medicare, depending on their age and income.[4]

The 2008 recession accelerated the growth in the number of beneficiaries of disability programs. Many workers who lost their jobs used up their unemployment benefits and then applied for disability coverage, essentially moving from a temporary safety net to a more permanent one. As the number of workers who were able to get unemployment benefits fell from six million in 2009 to less than three million in 2012, the number of SSI/SSDI beneficiaries increased by 1.5 million.[5] Since at least 1985, applications for disability have gone up and down with the unemployment rate. Relatedly, the definition of *disabled* has been continuously expanded, with many more people qualifying every year. "The percentage of workers who *actually* are physically or emotionally unable to work for reasons beyond their control has necessarily gone down [in recent decades]," notes Charles

Figure 9.1

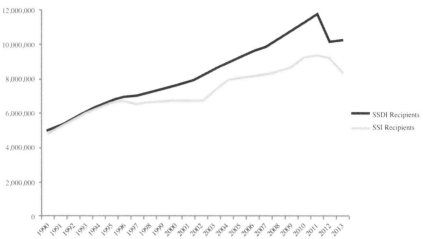

Source: U.S. Social Security Administration.

Murray. "Medical care now cures or alleviates many ailments . . . yet the percentage of people qualifying for federal disability benefits because they are unable to work rose from 0.7 percent of the size of the labor force in 1960 to 5.3 percent in 2010."[6] Meanwhile, Americans today also report that they are in better health than others have reported in previous decades.[7]

The expanding definition of disability is reflected in the types of medical conditions that currently qualify people for disability benefits. Today the predominant diagnoses for disability are musculoskeletal and connective tissue disorders and mental disorders, all of which are hard to assess and quantify.[8] See Figure 9.2.

If applicants complain of a chronic backache, or pains resulting from use of their arms, or of such mental disorders as depression, many doctors are prepared to certify them as disabled. Eligible conditions now also include autism and, in some cases, obesity.

SSDI

Social Security Disability Insurance, created in 1956, is part of the Old Age, Survivors, and Disability Insurance program of the Social Security Administration. All employed Americans pay in to SSDI through payroll

Figure 9.2

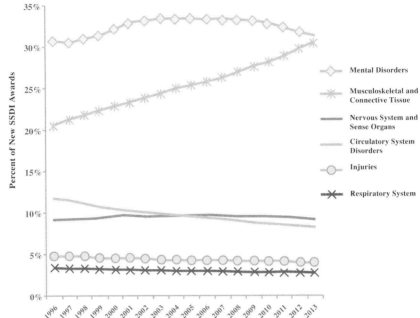

Diagnostic Causes of New SSDI Awards

Source: U.S. Social Security Administration.

deductions that are part of the Federal Insurance Contributions Act (FICA) deduction on all employee paystubs.[9] The overall FICA deduction includes 12.4% of the first $110,000 in income, which goes toward Social Security retirement and SSDI, with the employee paying 6.2% and the employer paying an equal amount. Also deducted from all paychecks is 1.45% for Medicare hospitalization insurance, which employers match. Self-employed workers pay the entire amount of both these taxes themselves.[10] Employees can tap into SSDI if they become disabled. Roughly 11 million Americans are on the program, which provides benefits to disabled workers who are under retirement age and who have paid into the disability insurance system for a sufficiently long time through payroll tax deductions at work. Their spouses, surviving spouses, and children are covered as well.[11]

SSDI is part of the overall Social Security system. The lion's share of the funds in the program goes to the retired elderly.

Benefits provided through SSDI are based on the insured's career earnings (see Appendix 3). For the 11 million disabled workers and their dependents currently receiving SSDI benefits, the average monthly benefit is $1,064 per disabled worker, $287 for his or her spouse, and $318 for each of their children.[12] Thus a family of three headed by a disabled worker might receive $1,669 per month or $20,000 per year. These payments are not taxed at either the state or federal level. Because this is an insurance program that participants have paid in to, there are no asset tests for participation—recipients may hold on to their homes, their cars, their bank accounts, and their retirement accounts.[13] If they choose to work once they are on SSDI, their earning limitations are less stringent than those for SSI beneficiaries, but there are limitations nonetheless; earnings normally must not exceed $750 a month. The nine-month rule also applies.

SSI

Supplemental Security Income, which covers almost eight million Americans, is a means-tested disability program that is not tied to previous work activity (see Appendix 4). Created in 1974 to benefit disabled Americans who are not covered by SSDI, it provides a flat cash benefit to the blind and disabled, including disabled children.[14] Currently, benefits are $733 per month per disabled single individual, $1,100 per eligible couple, and $367 per "essential person," usually a child. Thus a three-person household might receive $17,604 a year along with any other welfare benefits that members of the household qualify for.[15]

Since this program is means tested, theoretically applicants must have few assets and tightly limited income, usually no more than a meager $85 a month, to qualify.[16] Yet George Mason University professors David Armor and Sonia Sousa report in their examination of the American Recovery and Reinvestment Act of 2009 that "according to 2010 census data, 60% of SSI recipients have incomes above the poverty line, and 2.5 million of them (one third of the total) have incomes above 200% of poverty."[17] There are also "about a million recipients [who] are above the poverty line, are not [even officially] disabled, and are under age 65."[18]

Hank, a machinist who became disabled when he was exposed to toxic chemicals at the factory where he worked, finally qualified for SSI disability after several years of applying. We met him and his daughter Brittany in a cheap hotel in Atlanta, Georgia, where they live. Originally from California, Brittany and Hank have been moving around the country in search of work. Both are ambitious, having fallen from a middle-class background due to Hank's injury. Even though he is disabled, Hank would still like to earn a little money on his good days, but he worries about getting bumped from SSI, so his daughter trolls Craigslist and other temporary job sites and gets him odd jobs under the table. She scans the same sites, and others, looking for work for herself. When we spoke she was working off the books as a laborer for a local builder. Neither she nor her father can declare their income from working without the risk of losing his benefits, so they keep their earnings in cash in their room. Since the amount of money they would need to make to replace Hank's food stamps and disability payments is more than the two of them have been able to earn, they continue to do occasional day labor and hold their savings in cash.

Like Joe and Hank, Julie wants to work, but dares not risk the loss of disability income. A mother with two children who lives in Decatur, Georgia, Julie began receiving SSI when she was diagnosed with a terminal illness. Her doctor has estimated that she has two to three years to live and prescribed complete bed rest, but still she wants to work. Previously, Julie depended on TANF, the program of cash assistance for families with children. Now, she gets SSI, food stamps, housing assistance, and medical coverage. Since she doesn't know how much she will be able to work, Julie is afraid to start using up her nine months of benefits (see the section "The Nine-Month Rule" below). Instead, she plans to spend part of her disability income on small business training, and then scrimp and save as much as she can from disability payments and open her own business without reporting it. "Why not take that income, which I'm going to get anyway, and put it to work making money for myself and my family?" she asked. "I could double or triple that money if I put it to work in my business." Julie's business will be doing hair and nails and makeovers in her home. Since the tools of the beautician's trade are the same products any woman might reasonably have at home, she is confident that her small business will not be discovered even if a caseworker comes to visit. And she believes that the business will let her show her children that they had a mother who worked and made money, and wasn't "just another black lady on welfare."

If Julie's business is discovered, she could end up in prison. In 2013 Darlene Altvater of Mechanicsville, Maryland, was sentenced to five years behind bars for operating an exercise salon and spa at the same time she was collecting disability payments.[19] Her violation of the rules was clear, but the bizarre fact is that if she had sat at home doing nothing, she would not have been punished.

THE NINE-MONTH RULE

As repeatedly noted, one barrier that keeps Joe, Hank, Julie, and countless others from returning to work, or working for the first time, is the nine-month rule, a well-intentioned part of the disability welfare system that just doesn't seem to work. Both SSDI and SSI recipients can work for only nine months at or above certain income thresholds without losing their disability status (see Appendix 5). This policy and related complexities tend to undermine the Social Security Administration rules and programs that are meant to encourage work. Basically the rule allows SSDI and SSI beneficiaries to earn money without limitation for a total of nine months in any five-year period (a fuller description of the way it works appears in Appendix 5). The nine-month window with no earnings limitations is meant to give people who are genuinely interested in returning to the workforce the time they need to get established in the new job and possibly put aside some savings. But the rules here are complicated and require constant vigilance for those who take advantage of them. Beneficiaries must always be on guard against a "work" violation of the rules that will mean using up their nine-month allowance.

By way of illustration, suppose George is a 58-year-old man disabled by a back injury. He lives in Freeport, Maine, with his wife and he has qualified for SSDI, but his SSDI benefits do not bring him above the poverty line so he also receives additional payments under SSI. The combined benefits total $1,350 per month, or $16,200 per year with no taxes withheld. George is offered a peak-season position at L.L. Bean taking orders on the telephone from October through January. It's a sit-down job and he can move around from time to time so his back doesn't stiffen up. The pay is $2,000 per month ($1,750 after withholding) and George enjoys the work. He has been a Bean customer all his life and he knows their products. The other order takers sometimes consult him on camping gear—tent pegs for rocky areas, and the like. He enjoys talking with customers and his up-sell record is good. If someone buys boots, he sells them socks, and maybe a second pair of boots.

For two years George works those four-month shifts; his household income goes from $16,200 to $23,320 per year and he is happy. He's contributing. He's paying taxes, taking part in the community. He makes friends at work and joins the Elks Club. Life looks better. As the third October approaches, however, George realizes that he can work at L.L. Bean for only one more month without losing his benefits. He has used eight of the nine months when he is allowed to earn more than $750, and if he earns $2,000 in the tenth month, the benefits end. Even though pay for the Bean job averages only $667 a month over the full year, he is still disqualified by the nine-month rule because the limit is imposed each month. (Note that George's benefits could possibly continue for three more months beyond his violation of the $750 rule, but this is not guaranteed and it requires complicated requests for extension and advance planning.)

What if George reduced his hours and earned only $400 a month? The SSI part of his benefit would still be jeopardized since the SSI limit is just $85 a month, although SSDI permits monthly earnings up to $750. If George kept doing his job in November, he would be earning $7,000 after taxes at L.L. Bean and giving up perhaps $10,000 by losing his SSI benefit and part of his SSDI benefit as well. So, on Halloween, with great regret, George quits.

One way out of this dilemma might be for his wife to work, perhaps at the same job he's had to give up. But under SSI, his wife's income counts as if it were his income, although it doesn't count at all under SSDI. Since both their earnings affect the calculation of his benefits, George figured he would need a degree in advanced mathematics to calculate the optimum course. The couple's solution: his wife works as a part-time accountant for a local contractor who agrees to pay her in cash and not report the payments.

Table 9.1 is a page from the Social Security Administration's Red Book—a publication that provides information on SSA's programs—to show how the earned income exclusion is calculated, and it illustrates how complex these calculations can become.

Joe, Hank, Julie, and George want to be contributing members of society, to participate in the workforce to the extent they are able, and to be compensated. But the disability system makes calculating the risks of work extremely difficult, and the potential loss of income is substantial. The result is that fewer than 2% of SSDI/SSI recipients leave the system for work each year.

WHO ELSE GETS PAID

In an eye-opening report about the weeks she spent investigating the impact of disability welfare in Hale County, Alabama, in 2012, Chana Joffe-Walt of National Public Radio talks about what she has dubbed "The Disability-Industrial Complex," the many lawyers and companies that benefit from the disability welfare system and end up with a good deal of the program's money. One lawyers' group, headed by Charles Binder, specializes in filing motions with the government when an applicant is turned down for disability benefits. Appeals may be filed repeatedly, and when an appeal succeeds, the government calculates how much the applicant would have received between the date of the first application and the date that benefits actually begin. The lawyers get 25% of this sum, paid directly to them, with the balance going to the applicant. Binder's group took in $68 million on eligibility appeals this way in 2012, through 30,000 cases.[20]

Table 9.1   SSI Red Book Calculation of SSI Payment

Do we count all your earned income when we figure your SSI payment?

We do not count the first $65 of the earnings you receive in a month, plus one-half of the remaining earnings. This means that we count less than one-half of your earnings when we figure your SSI payment amount.

We apply this exclusion in addition to the $20 general income exclusion. We apply the $20 general income exclusion first to any unearned income that you may receive.

The following table shows two examples of how we apply the general income exclusion and the earned income exclusions.

Examples of the Earned Income Exclusion

Situation 1	Situation 2
Ed receives $361 SSDI each month, wages of $289 each month, and no other income.	Ed receives wages of $450 each month, no SSDI, and $13 of unearned income from another source.
$361 SSDI	$0 SSDI
−20 General income exclusion	$13 Other unearned income
$341 *Countable unearned income*	−20 General income exclusion
	$7 Remaining general income exclusion
$289 Earned income	
−65 Earned income exclusion	$450 Earned income
$224	−7 Remaining general income exclusion
−112 ½ remaining earnings	$443
$112 *Countable earned income*	−65 Earned income exclusion
	$378
$341 Countable unearned income	−189 ½ remaining earnings
+112 Countable earned income	$189 *Total countable income*
$453 *Total countable income*	
	$674 2011 Federal Benefit Rate
$674 2011 Federal Benefit Rate	−189 Total countable income
−453 Total countable income	$485 SSI payment
$221 SSI payment	
Available Income	**Available Income**
$361 SSDI	$450 Wages
+289 Wages	+13 Unearned income
+221 SSI Payment	+485 SSI Payment
$871 Total Monthly Income	**$948 Total Monthly Income**

Another set of professionals prospers by getting people off welfare programs such as TANF, which are largely funded by the states, and into disability programs entirely funded by the federal government. The biggest player in this business is the Public Consulting Group described below by Joffe-Walt:

PCG is a private company that states pay to comb their welfare rolls and move as many people as possible onto disability. "What we're offering is to work to identify those folks who have the highest likelihood of meeting disability criteria," Pat Coakley, who runs PCG's Social Security Advocacy Management team, told me.

The PCG agents help the potentially disabled fill out the Social Security disability application over the phone. And by help, I mean the agents actually do the filling out. When the potentially disabled don't have the right medical documentation to prove a disability, the agents at PCG help them.[21]

PCG gets paid on a per-case basis whenever they move someone off state-financed welfare and on to federally financed disability. A recent price was $2,300 per case.[22] States are glad to pay such fees because they save far more than that.

Vocational Rehabilitation Agencies (VRAs) and Employment Networks (ENs) also earn money from welfare programs (see Appendix 6). The VRAs are public agencies paid by the Social Security Administration to provide vocational training to the disabled. The ENs are public and private organizations paid by the SSA to provide job placement and employment.[23] VRAs and ENs can get as much as $23,000 for successful placement of a participant in a job that meets Substantial Gainful Activity (SGA) income-level requirements. And they get the maximum payment as soon as their clients reach the minimum income required to be removed from the disability rolls—about $13,000 a year. This means that the agencies paid to promote work for the disabled have no incentive to get them jobs that pay significantly more than the benefits that must be foregone. There is no incentive to train participants for higher paying jobs, or to place them in higher paying jobs. Faced with the choice between untaxed welfare benefits of $17,000 a year (for a family of three the typical benefit is $17,000–$20,000) or a job that yields less than that after taxes, staying on welfare is a rational choice. (For more information on payments to VRAs and ENs, see Appendix 6.)

It is worth remembering that most people on welfare live within hailing distance of subsistence. A drop in income of $100 or $200 a month can mean scrimping on food or needed clothes for a child. Thus it is easy to see why SSI and SSDI participants, however much they may prefer to be working, conclude that it is better to preserve the secure income from welfare programs than to give up welfare in exchange for a modestly paid job.

THE TESTS FOR DISABILITY

The Social Security Administration has more than 66,000 employees, about 6,000 of whom adjudicate the SSDI/SSI programs.[24] They screen applicants to ascertain if they have "a medically determinable physical or mental impairment" that makes it impossible for them to earn more than the Substantial Gainful Activity amount (usually about $1,080 a month). (See Appendix 7.) While the SSA claims that applicants can keep working during their application for disability as long as their income is under the SGA amount, it is widely acknowledged that working while applying for disability is a sure-fire way to be denied. Noted economist and disability expert David Autor of MIT puts it this way:

Rather than assisting workers with disabilities to stay employed . . . the SSDI program effectively bars them from participating in the workforce while seeking benefits. By law, the SSDI program can only award benefits to those who are "unable to engage in a substantial gainful activity." Hence, workers who participate in significant employment during the application period, even on a trial basis, are automatically denied benefits.[25]

This pushes most applicants to leave the workforce while applying. And since applications routinely take more than a year to process, people interested in working part-time once they're on disability have a very steep hill to climb; their skills, work connections, and employment habits have likely gone stale.

Children are treated slightly differently during the application process. To qualify, they must have "marked or severe functional limitation," and the medical listings for their disabilities differ slightly from those for adults, to adjust for age.[26]

People with nonpermanent disabilities are supposed to receive a medical review every three years, and 567,395 such medical reviews were conducted in 2009 (the most recent year with accessible records). However, the Social Security Administration estimates that less than 1% of the reviews resulted in termination of benefits. As Joffe-Walt notes, "Going on disability means you will not work, you will not get a raise, you will not get whatever meaning people get from work. Going on disability means, assuming you rely only on those disability payments, you will be poor for the rest of your life. That's the deal."[27]

The labyrinthine rule books on disability have other unintended consequences. When Joffe-Walt met with the doctor who makes most of the Hale County disability diagnoses, he told her: "We talk about the pain and what it's like." He added, "I always ask them 'What grade did you finish?'" As Joffe-Walt points out, this is not a medical question. "But the doctor feels he needs this information in disability cases because people who have only a high school education aren't going to be able to get a sit-down job."[28] Thus a back problem for a college grad might not be a qualifying disability, but for someone who finished only tenth grade the same back pain could be.

The fact that disability programs are growing so fast is worrisome enough, but an additional threat is that they will soon run out of money. In a 2013 *60 Minutes* interview, Senator Tom Coburn noted that our present disability programs are going broke. According to a 2012 Congressional Budget Office (CBO) report, the Disability Insurance Trust Fund will be exhausted by 2018:

> Under current law, the DI program is not financially sustainable. Its expenditures are drawn from the Disability Insurance Trust Fund, which is financed primarily through a payroll tax of 1.8 percent; the fund had a balance of $204 billion at the end of 2009. [We] project that by 2015, the number of people receiving DI benefits will increase to 11.4 million and total expenditures will climb to $147 billion. However, tax receipts credited to the DI trust fund will be about 20 percent less than those expenditures, and three years later, in 2018, the trust fund will be exhausted. . . . Without legislative action to reduce the DI program's outlays, increase its dedicated federal revenues, or transfer other federal funds to it, the Social Security Administration will not have the legal authority to pay full DI benefits beyond that point.[29]

In recommending changes, the CBO report dryly noted that "one approach to reducing expenditures on DI benefits would be to establish policies that would make work a more viable option for people with disabilities. However, little evidence is available on the effectiveness of such policies, and their costs might more than offset any savings from reductions in DI benefits."[30]

DOLLAR COSTS

Having so many people becoming dependent on our welfare system is obviously costly, and so is the impact of a dwindling labor force on the tax base required to support more and more beneficiaries. The number of disabled nonworkers is currently rising at an alarming rate, while the number of people engaged in the workforce and paying taxes is falling. See Figure 9.3.

The labor force participation rate depicted in Figure 9.3 is the percentage of working-age adults who are either working or seeking work. In the

Figure 9.3

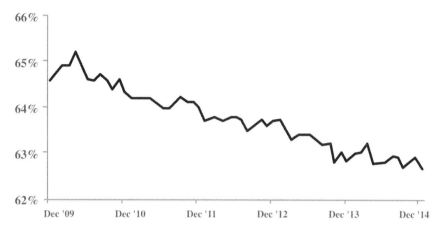

Source: U.S. Social Security, U.S. Bureau of Labor Statistics.

1960s the rate hovered around 60%, including more than 80% of men and 30% of women. After that, the rate rose steadily until 2007 when it reached 67%. But then it started to fall. In 2013, it reached 63%, roughly 70% of men and 60% of women. Over the years, more and more women have been working and fewer men have been. Overall, our labor force is dropping both in absolute terms and as a percentage of Americans.[31] In a 2013 *New York Times* column, David Brooks labeled this phenomenon "Men on the Threshold."[32] "In 1954," Brooks noted, "96 percent of American men between 25 and 54 years old worked. Today, 80 percent do. One-fifth of men in their prime working ages are out of the labor force." Brooks calls this a "catastrophe" and suggests that there is a mismatch between traditional male culture and the kinds of skills that are valued in today's economy. Thus many men may feel more disabled than they actually are. Economist Tyler Cowen adds that men's wages have done much worse than the averages suggest, noting that "wages for the typical or median male earner have fallen by about 28 percent" between 1969 and 2009.[33]

Note that the disabled are not included in our national unemployment statistics. Most are not looking for work and are therefore not technically unemployed, though they are of course out of the workforce.

Further exacerbating the labor force participation rate: more than two million Americans, most of them men of working age, are in jail, a substantial portion of them for nonviolent drug offenses.[34] Many of those men could be working. And, of course, those released from jail face multiple obstacles to employment.

These trends are troubling. As an ever smaller percentage of Americans—especially men—work or seek work, more and more are falling into a pattern of dependency. The United States has a population of 321 million, more than 204 million of them people of working age. Many working-age Americans now qualify for disability, and many more are on other government programs. Thousands of others have simply dropped out of the workforce. As a result we face two great dangers: losing our tradition of industriousness, and eroding the tax base that makes welfare and all other government programs possible.

Note that the increase in unemployed disabled is directly contrary to the Americans with Disabilities Act of 1990, which specifically calls for steps to help keep the disabled employed.[35]

EFFORTS TO ENCOURAGE WORK

In the face of these discouraging trends, the Social Security Administration has maintained and expanded several prowork initiatives. These include the Ticket to Work and Work Incentives Improvement Act,[36] a welfare-to-work program that has shown some successes. As an example, SSA's Red Book tells the story of Debra Gabriel, a talented and determined woman who suffered a terrible back injury in 2002. SSDI helped get her through the next four dark years, and she then took advantage of SSA's Ticket to Work program. The SSA explains:

The Trial Work Period (for SSDI recipients) allowed her to get trained and test her ability to work for at least 9 months while receiving cash benefits. . . .

The trial work period (TWP) and Expedited Reinstatement (ER) are just two of 20 Work Incentives that can help people who receive Social Security disability benefits return to work or work for the very first time.

Today, Debra is an independent contractor, working on projects for several clients. In spite of a slow economy, many organizations have benefited from Debra's skills since her return to the workforce in 2008.

"Employment has affected all of who I am in a positive way. I'm really thankful that Social Security was there when I needed it. I think the [Ticket] program is wonderful and wish more people would take advantage of it. When I look back I can see that I've achieved a lot!"[37]

To further encourage employment, the SSA has also changed health care benefits through Medicaid and Medicare so that disabled workers are now covered for up to eight years after they leave disability welfare for work; they don't have to worry about medical coverage while testing their ability to stay employed.[38] And reenrollment has been streamlined so that someone who tries employment and fails doesn't have to start from square one, but, for three years, can simply reenter the disability program after losing a job.[39]

Further, entering the workforce no longer triggers a medical review of a disabled person's case. Until changes were made in 1999, the fear of an immediate medical review in connection with an attempt at working prevented many people from considering employment.[40]

Despite these many well-intentioned efforts, there are precious few success stories like Debra Gabriel's. Less than 5% of SSDI or SSI recipients have ever participated in SSA's work programs.

Sadly, as Joffe-Walt notes, "Once people go onto disability they almost never go back to work."[41]

DIS-ABLING CHILDREN

"You want a child who can pull a check," disability recipients in Hale County, Alabama, told Joffe-Walt. A minor child officially classified as disabled can entitle a parent to a monthly payment, typically $700. In fact, 1.3 million children are now drawing such payments for their families. This number has more than quadrupled just since 1990.

As *New York Times* columnist Nicholas Kristof recently reported, parents in Appalachia have been removing their young children from a free literacy program provided in the local school. The kids' illiteracy qualified as a disability, so keeping their children illiterate meant continuing to get monthly disability checks. For many families, the income provided by illiterate offspring covers a substantial percentage of household expenses.

The problem, of course, as Kristof notes, is that these children "may never hold a job in their entire lives and are condemned to a life of poverty on the dole—and that's the outcome of a program intended to fight poverty."[42]

Along with illiteracy, autism is now included on the list of medical disabilities for SSDI and SSI, as noted above, and autism diagnoses are climbing nationwide.[43] While some of this increase is due to improved diagnostics, some is due to the fact that a diagnosis of autism allows children and their caregivers to get on the disability rolls. Given the low likelihood of autism cures, this disability can guarantee income for life.

Joffe-Walt provides an example of disability programs' downsides as she tells the story of Jahleel in Alabama:

Jahleel is a kid you can imagine doing very well for himself [in school]. He is delayed. But given the right circumstances and support it's easy to believe that over the course of his schooling Jahleel could catch up.

Let's imagine that happens. Jahleel starts doing better in school, overcomes some of his disabilities. He doesn't need the disability program anymore. That would seem to be great for everyone, except for one thing. It would threaten his family's livelihood. Jahleel's family survives off the monthly $700 check they get for his disability.

Jahleel's mom wants him to do well in school. That is absolutely clear. But her livelihood depends on Jahleel struggling in school. This tension only increases as kids get older. One mother told me her teenage son wanted to work, but she didn't want him to get a job because if he did, the family would lose its disability check.

[I think we'd all agree that] kids should be encouraged to go to school. Kids should want to do well in school. Parents should want their kids to do well in school. Kids should become more and more and more independent as they grow older and hopefully be able to support themselves at around age 18.

The disability program stands in opposition to every one of these aims.[44]

DISABILITY FOR VETERANS

All military veterans are eligible for a special disability program available only to them. Veterans coming home from combat and leaving the service learn they can get almost $3,000 in disability benefits a month if they qualify, along with medical care, and access to all other welfare programs. Or, they can try to find a job. For many, the enticement of a life on entitlements is hard to ignore.[45]

Lt. Col. Daniel Gade lost his leg in combat in 2005 and now teaches at West Point. He recently gave a talk to disabled veterans at Fort Carson, Colorado, in which he urged them to get in the workforce: "People who stay home because they are getting paid enough to get by on disability are worse off. They are more likely to abuse drugs and alcohol. They are more likely to live alone. . . . And the system is driving you to become one of them, if you are not careful."[46]

Former Navy SEAL Eric Greitens, the founder of The Mission Continues, a nonprofit that helps veterans become community volunteers, observes, "When vets come home from war they are going through a tremendous change in identity. Then the V.A., and others, encourage them to view themselves as disabled. We meet a number of veterans who see themselves as charity cases and are not sure anymore what they have to contribute."[47]

Disability for veterans now consumes $59 billion of the $151 billion Veteran Affairs budget.[48] Enrollment in veterans' disability programs rose from 2.3 million in 2001 to 3.9 million in 2014, with a doubling of the percentage of veterans receiving benefits, from 8.9% in 2001 to 18% in 2014.[49] In the 1980s and 1990s veteran males were more likely to be in the labor force than nonveterans, but since 2000 that has changed dramatically. Now there is a 4% gap between veteran and nonveteran participation, with veterans continuing their flight from the workplace.

One key driver of the growth of enrollment in the veterans' disability programs is the expansion of eligibility criteria. Stanford University economics professor Mark Duggan notes that in 2000 Type II diabetes was added because there was evidence of a link between exposure to Agent Orange and development of the disease. Disability claims among Vietnam era veterans grew substantially after that. Further, veterans who have served since the 1990s are much more likely to be on disability than their older counterparts; one in four younger veterans is on disability, versus one in seven from the wars prior to the 1991 Gulf War.[50] See Figure 9.4.

Most veterans on disability still have their prime working years ahead of them when they are discharged, and removing these young men and women from the workforce by putting them on disability and discouraging them from work is a profound disservice to them and their families. Notes Daniel Gade: "Veterans should be viewed as resources, not as damaged goods. . . . Efforts to help veterans should begin by recognizing their abilities, rather than focusing exclusively on their disabilities, and should serve

Figure 9.4

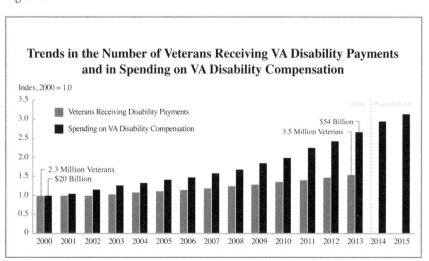

Source: Congressional Budget Office.

the ultimate aim of moving wounded soldiers . . . to real self-sufficiency." Sadly, he notes, the financial temptations of generous benefits lure many onto welfare. "From an economic standpoint, you would be crazy to get a job. It's a trap."[51]

Appendix 3: SSDI Eligibility

Eligibility for Social Security Disability Insurance is determined by counting the number of quarters per year the applicant worked, and how many of the quarters were in the past five years. An applicant must have worked at least 40 quarters in the years prior to the onset of the disability, and if the 40 quarters weren't contiguous, the applicant must have worked for at least one quarter in each year after 1950 or for at least one quarter each year since turning 21.[52]

The applicant must also have worked half the quarters in the past five years. Therefore, many part-time workers and workers who take significant time off, perhaps to raise children, cannot qualify for SSDI.

Once applicants qualify, there is a five-month waiting period before benefit payments begin, and there is a twelve-month waiting period before Medicaid or Medicare kick in.[53]

Appendix 4: SSI Eligibility

Supplemental Security Income recipients receive $710 in benefits per month and are also covered under Medicaid. Unlike SSDI beneficiaries, whose nine-month clock ticks only when they earn more than $750 a month, the SSI beneficiaries' clock starts ticking as soon as they earn anything over an almost absurdly meager $85 a month. Any earnings over $85 lead to a 50-cent reduction of their benefit for every dollar earned above the limit. Earn $105, get $700 instead of $710; earn a modest $500 and your benefit drops by $208, and so on until earnings reach $1,505 a month, at which point the benefits drop to zero.

For SSI beneficiaries the time barrier and income rules are so stringent that few take the risks of working for a living wage. Like the SSDI beneficiaries, they see using up their nine-month limit for just a few dollars in temporarily increased income as far too risky.

Although the SSA's Ticket to Work program is designed to provide a work opportunity for SSI recipients, it simply doesn't function well as a work incentive with the nine-month limit always hovering over recipients' shoulders.

Appendix 5: The Nine-Month Rule

As noted, both SSDI and SSI recipients can work for only nine months above certain income thresholds without losing their disability status. The nine-month work period is calculated over a maximum of five years, so it involves a rolling limit, with the oldest year falling out of the calculation at the end of each succeeding year.

For example, if Walter worked for three months a year for three years (say, 2009–2011), reaching his nine-month maximum at a salary that exceeds what he's allowed, and then he didn't work at that level for the next two years (2012–2013), he could then work another three months in the sixth year (2014) at any income level, because the oldest year of work (2009) would drop out of the calculation.

Also as noted, the nine-month window with no earnings limitations is meant to give people who are interested in returning to the workforce the time they need to get established in a new job. They are covered for medical care even after they leave SSDI, and if they lose the job or quit within 36 months, they can go right back on disability. But these provisions, while generous and reasonable, don't seem to offset all the uncertainties about earnings limitations.

Because they have paid in to the system, SSDI beneficiaries can earn up to $750 a month without being subject to the nine-month rule. But the rule kicks in again after any month in which they earn over $750. If they are still employed at more than $750 a month after the nine months, they become ineligible for SSDI until their income again drops below the substantial gainful activity threshold. However, they remain eligible to return to the disability program at any time within the following three years if they lose or quit a job.

Once any month is used—that is, once a recipient has earned more than the allowed limit in any given month—the recipient has one less month to take advantage of the "transition to work" program. Only people who are reasonably confident that their employment will eventually result in a living wage are willing to take that risk.

If these rules sound confusing, imagine what it must be like for a disabled recipient considering returning to the workforce. Only one thing may be clear: miscalculation can lead to a damaging loss of benefits.

Appendix 6: VRAs and ENs

SSDI and SSI recipients approach both vocational rehabilitation agencies and employment networks for help, and they engage their services by signing over a Ticket to Work provided by the SSA. This allows a VRA or EN to provide the requested services and bill the Social Security Administration for them.[54]

The incentives for the VRAs and ENs are substantial, with "milestones" ensuring additional payments to them. As you can see in Table 9.2, VRAs and ENs are paid $1,288 every time a participant reaches a Phase I milestone.

Milestone 1 means the participant has been employed for a month and earned $720; milestone 2 means the participant has been employed for three of the last six months and has earned $720 per month for each month of employment; and so on. If a participant manages to work for 9 out of 18 months and earns $720 each month, the EN or VRA earns $5,152. The incentive thresholds for the VRAs and ENS are nearly upside-down images of the earnings limit rules that apply to participants; for the participants, of course, approaching these limits means risking the loss of benefits rather than getting bonuses.

When an EN or VRA has a disabled client who progresses to earning $1,010 per month or a blind client who progresses to earning $1,690 per month, the agency is paid $222 per month for up to 18 months per SSI participant (for a total of $3,996) and $387 per month for up to 11 months per SSDI participant for a total of $4,257 each. The income level goals established for participants are important because they are the income levels that the Social Security Administration considers "Substantial Gainful Activity" (SGA) for purposes of qualifying for SSDI or SSI. In other words, the goal for the VRAs and ENs is to procure enough employment for each client so that the client will no longer need (and no longer be eligible for) the disability payment.

After that, ENs and VRAs can earn an additional $222 per month for each SSI participant and an additional $387 per month for each SSDI participant for each additional month, up to 60 months, in which a client continues to earn above the SGA. The total amount an EN or VRA can receive per client is $22,468 for an SSI participant and $23,341 for an SSDI participant.

Table 9.2 Milestone Outcome Payment Method

Payment Type	Beneficiary Earnings	SSI Payment Amount	SSDI Payment Amount
Phase 1 Milestones**			
Milestone 1	$720/mo. × 1 mo.	$1,288	$1,288
Milestone 2	$720/mo. × 3 mos. w/in 6 mos.	$1,288	$1,288
Milestone 3	$720/mo. × 6 mos. w/in 12 mos.	$1,288	$1,288
Milestone 4	$720/mo. × 9 mos. w/in 18 mos.	$1,288	$1,288
Total Potential Phase 1 Milestones		**$5,152**	**$5,152**
Phase 2 Milestones	Gross Earnings > SGA ($1,010/$1,690)***	$222/mo. for up to 18 mos. = **$3,996**	$387/mo. for up to 11 mos. = **$4,257**
Total Potential Phase 1+2 Milestones		**$9,148**	**$9,409**
Outcome	Earnings > SGA ($1,010/$1,690)*** and federal cash benefit = $0	$222/mo. for up to 60 mos. = **$13,320**	$387/mo. for up to 36 mos. = **$13,932**
Total Potential Milestones and Outcome Payments		$22,468	$23,341

* The payment rate in effect at the time the milestone or outcome is attained is the rate that will be paid for that particular month, regardless of when the payment request is submitted.

** Please call Account Manager for explanation [of] exceptions.

*** The 2012 monthly SGA amounts are $1,010 for nonblind and $1,690 for blind individuals.

Source: Social Security Administration, "Overview: The NEW Ticket to Work Program," SSA Publication no. 63-024 (2009).

Appendix 7: Medical Qualifications for Disability Benefits

There is a five-step process to determine eligibility for disability benefits. The first test is the work test. Theoretically, applicants can work during their application process, as long as they earn less than $1,040 per month (commonly known as "Substantial Gainful Employment," SGA), but as noted earlier any paid employment is likely to result in denial of the application.

Applicants who pass the work test move on to the severity test, where each applicant's condition is first evaluated to see if it is "severe enough to limit basic life activities for at least one year," and then they move on to the qualifying medical condition test. The SSA keeps a list of eligible medical conditions, and an applicant with a disability on that list progresses to the work tests. If it is determined that the applicant cannot do work previously done, and then it is determined that the applicant is not mentally or physically capable of doing any work in the national economy, that applicant may qualify for benefits. In theory, an applicant could earn up to the SGA amount and still qualify under this final test, but, as Autor, et al. note,[55] earners face intense scrutiny.

Chapter 10

Medicaid and the Affordable Care Act

We tried to provide more for the poor and produced more poor instead. We tried to remove the barriers to escape from poverty, and inadvertently built a trap—Charles Murray

A revolutionary change in health services for the poor unfolded in 2014 as the Affordable Care Act (ACA) expanded eligibility and mandated that most Americans get medical insurance, either through the private marketplace or through federal and state exchanges. Fifteen million additional Americans gained access to medical coverage and many of them got it for the first time. About ten million of those newly covered have qualified for Medicaid. The rest have obtained coverage under the new exchanges.[1]

Before the advent of the ACA—often known as Obamacare—Medicaid already covered nearly 50 million American citizens—16% of the population, including low-income parents and children, the elderly, and the disabled. It usually did not cover young people who were childless. Eligibility was tied to income; states could establish their own thresholds for coverage, and there was an asset test, with a $2,000 limit on savings. (Medicaid should not be confused with Medicare, the social insurance program available only to those over age 65 who have paid in to the Medicare system through their payroll taxes for 10 years or more. Forty-seven million Americans are currently enrolled in Medicare; it is not means-tested.[2])

Today, everyone whose income is below 138% of the poverty line is covered under the Medicaid program in the twenty-six states (and Washington, DC) that have opted in to the ACA's Medicaid expansion. To meet the income requirement in 2014, a single person had to earn less than $16,105. All applicants in all states have to produce proof of citizenship or legal status. States that opted out of expanding their Medicaid rolls continue to have more stringent Medicaid eligibility rules. Note that the number of opt-in and opt-out states is expected to fluctuate. The numbers cited here and in Appendix 8 are for 2014. See Figure 10.1.

In the states that opted out (details in Appendix 8), low-income pregnant women, disabled and elderly people, and people with children in the home are generally allowed to enroll. Single and married childless adults normally do not qualify. Because childless people are generally not eligible and because of stringent poverty guidelines for eligibility (and the fact that there will be less federal money granted to those states), Medicaid rolls are expected to increase much more slowly in opt-out states than in states that opted in.

Figure 10.1

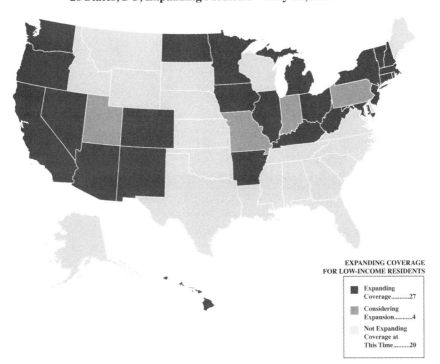

Where the States Stand on Medicaid Expansion
26 States, DC, Expanding Medicaid—May 22, 2014

EXPANDING COVERAGE
FOR LOW-INCOME RESIDENTS

Expanding
Coverage...........27

Considering
Expansion...........4

Not Expanding
Coverage at
This Time...........20

Nine of the twenty-five opt-out states do provide some form of state medical care to the childless. In fifteen opt-out states with no coverage for childless people, having a baby will continue to provide a ticket into the system for mothers poor enough to qualify.

The young mothers we met around the country counted their Medicaid benefit as one of the best things about having children, because the advent of a child meant Medicaid coverage for the mother as well as the infant.[3] "At least now that I have my son I have medical care that I don't have to worry about paying for," said Brittany. "If I had to pay for it myself, I'd have to go out and get a job, but this way we are doing okay."

Figure 10.2 shows the income limits required to qualify for Medicaid in each state. As you can see, many income ceilings are far below the federal poverty line.

Residents who earn between 138% of the federal poverty line ($16,105) and $46,700 in states that opted out can apply to get coverage through a federally run insurance exchange and receive subsidies to offset their costs. But this option is not available to people earning less than 138% of the poverty rate since they are supposedly eligible for Medicaid instead. As a result, residents in opt-out states who have incomes above the state limit but below the federal limit are out of luck. A single person earning $10,000 in Pennsylvania, for example, will not be eligible for either Medicaid or subsidized coverage under the ACA. Instead, that person will have to buy insurance or pay the penalty for staying uninsured.

Figure 10.2

Maximum Annual Income to Retain Medicaid Eligibility

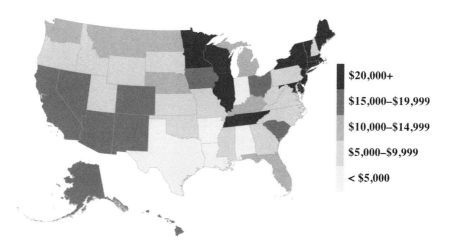

$20,000+

$15,000–$19,999

$10,000–$14,999

$5,000–$9,999

< $5,000

MEDICAID AND WORK

In announcing the implementation of the Affordable Health Care Act, the White House noted that people would no longer have to stick with employers they didn't like just to keep their health insurance.[4] However, that change is likely to mean that fewer people will work. A 2014 Congressional Budget Office report estimated that about 2.5 million Americans will quit their jobs, cut their hours, or stop looking for work in the next decade because of new benefits available under the health care law—far more than previously estimated.[5] Since the insurance subsidies paid to enrollees under the law grow less generous as income rises, workers are expected to be less motivated to do more work, or to work at all, once they do the math and figure out that the raise or promotion they were considering isn't worth the loss of the health insurance subsidy. Another study on medical coverage and employment, this one done in Tennessee, also suggests that the expanded medical coverage provided by the ACA "may cause large reductions in the labor supply of low income adults."[6] If that turns out to be the case, a possible and ironic result may be that those states that opted out of Medicaid expansion will have higher labor participation rates (and hence less poverty) than their subsidized counterparts.

Our interviews revealed that many Medicaid beneficiaries are especially concerned about exceeding their income and/or asset limits and risking their Medicaid coverage. Although opt-in states don't have asset limits, all states have income limits, and they are strictly enforced. Disabled and elderly* people will continue to get Medicaid even if they get jobs that pay above the poverty thresholds, at least for a year or two, depending on the state, but earning money can threaten medical coverage for the rest of Medicaid recipients.[7] Medicaid enrollees must report any changes in their financial status and update their case files regularly by showing bank statements, leases, and other proof of income and assets, and they must declare any changes that might affect their benefit level or ability to participate. In some states, if a participant has filed a universal application, any report to one program is reported to all, and any slip in one can lead to cancellation of all the others. This prospect makes the "welfare cliff" particularly ominous.

People we talked with were well versed in what to reveal and what not to reveal to their social workers, and how to declare or not declare income in

---

*The elderly who qualify for Medicaid are those who do not qualify for Medicare (not having adequately paid in) and who also meet the poverty guidelines.

order to maintain their status on the Medicaid rolls. Many worked part-time at off-the-books jobs that paid in cash. As Annie, a mother of two in Oregon, explained,

I'm not going to find a job that pays enough to make up for the value of my Medicaid coverage for me and my kids. It may pay enough to make up for losing my food stamps, or for losing my TANF benefits, but not both, and it certainly won't pay enough for me to be able to buy health insurance and get the coverage I get on Medicaid. With two kids needing regular checkups, immunizations, to say nothing of treating all the gunk they bring home from school and playgrounds . . . no way I could make it without Medicaid coverage. So I just do babysitting out of my house, for cash, for neighbors, and I rent out my garage to a guy who works on motorcycles on the side. That is all cash I don't declare, so I have some income, but I don't have to report it and lose my benefits.

While Annie displays a solid entrepreneurial spirit, she also exposes a recurring theme among beneficiaries of welfare benefits. They clearly are eager to work and would like to make some money, but they are also fully aware that doing so can result in an immediate loss of their Medicaid benefits, and Medicaid is especially important for many. Few have the skills needed to land jobs that will pay enough to cover all they will lose.

RISING COSTS

Medicaid costs have traditionally been covered jointly by state and federal funds and managed by the states.[8] For enrollees who were participating in Medicaid before the ACA was implemented, the states are reimbursed between 57% and 82% of costs, according to a formula recalculated every three years at the federal level. The costs of new enrollees under the ACA expansion will be covered 100% by the federal government for the first three years. After that, the states will be expected to pay 10%. The Center on Budget and Policy Priorities estimates that the federal government will bear about 93% of the costs of the Medicaid expansion over its first nine years (2014–2022).[9] Medicaid remains insurance based; doctors and hospitals provide services free of charge to patients, and then apply for reimbursement from the patients' insurance carriers. Some states contract with private health insurance companies to provide Medicaid coverage while others provide the insurance themselves.[10]

Even before the ACA, Medicaid enrollment was growing steadily, from 32.7 million in 2000 to more than 54.8 million in 2012.

Medicaid costs have gone up even more dramatically, from $2 billion in 1980 to $150 billion in 2000, to $432 billion in 2012, of which $251 billion was covered by the federal government and $181 billion was paid by the states. See Figure 10.4. The costs will balloon further to cover the ten million new Medicaid beneficiaries.

In a country with an aging population, with older baby boomers now starting to retire, and with rising numbers of people receiving disability benefits, elderly and disabled enrollees contribute disproportionally to Medicaid expenses. Five percent of Medicaid enrollees accounted for more than half of Medicaid expenditures in 2008,[11] for example, and those enrollees were heavily skewed toward the disabled and elderly.

It remains to be seen how health care costs will change under the ACA, but there is no question that overall costs for federal and state governments will continue to go up as Medicaid enrollment increases. Designers of the ACA envision that some of those costs will be offset by savings as a result of people with insurance getting treatment instead of needing the costly hospital stays that have been the norm for the uninsured until now.

In 2015 the *Washington Post* reported that half of the exchanges set up by the states and the District of Columbia were struggling financially. Growing costs for technology and customer call centers, combined with fewer enrollments than expected, were leading some states to consider closing their exchanges and to turn to the federal government to run their insurance programs.[12]

Figure 10.3

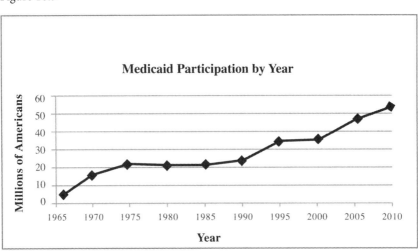

Source: Social Security Administration.

Figure 10.4

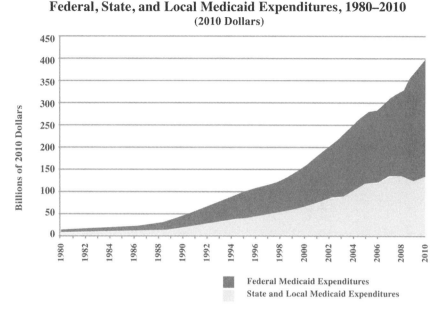

Federal, State, and Local Medicaid Expenditures, 1980–2010
(2010 Dollars)

Source: Centers for Medicare & Medicaid Services.

BENEFIT SHOPPING

States are now required to provide the mandatory benefits listed in Table 10.1 for Medicaid enrollees. Optional benefits are at the discretion of the states.

Because benefits differ from state to state (see Appendix 9), travel can be a great way to get medical care for poor people with serious health problems. In Maryland we met two women who had recently made the move. Bryanna, who is HIV positive, moved from Georgia when she discovered that her costly medications would be covered under Medicaid in Maryland. "I've never been to the Northeast, never been out of the South, and I left literally everything behind, including my girlfriend. It's pretty simple, really. I looked online and found the state where my health care would be covered the best; my meds are expensive and especially while I am looking for work, I need those costs covered."

Lauren, a disabled woman living in Seattle's Tent City #3, moved to Washington State from Wyoming. "I was living in a remote area, and there weren't any doctors who could take care of me," she told us. "But here in Washington State the Medicaid coverage is really good so I live here, even though all my family is in Wyoming. My fiancé is there too. Someday I

Table 10.1   Medicaid Benefits under the ACA

Ten Essential Health Benefits (EHBs)
1. Ambulatory patient services
2. Emergency services
3. Hospitalization
4. Maternity and newborn care
5. Mental health and substance abuse disorder services
6. Prescription drugs
7. Rehabilitative services and devices
8. Laboratory services
9. Preventative and wellness services/Chronic disease management
10. Pediatric services including oral and vision

hope he'll move here and we can get married, but for now I live here for the medical care."

This kind of benefit shopping is becoming more prevalent. It may mean that the most generous opt-in states will face unexpected costs.

PREVENTIVE MEASURES

While many private insurers take pains to encourage their clients to get physical exams, quit smoking, lose weight, and check and treat hypertension, Medicaid preventive care for beneficiaries remains much less thorough, especially in the opt-out states.[13] But it does include well child care visits and immunizations and is generally quite good for children.[14]

Medicaid has traditionally covered the cost of prescription contraceptives. The 2014 controversy over ACA coverage of several methods will result in some restrictions on birth control under the insurance provided by the ACA, but Medicaid beneficiaries will continue to be eligible for contraceptive coverage.[15] Still, the shortage of physicians who take Medicaid patients and the perceived lack of urgency in prescribing contraceptives can lead to unreliable birth control coverage. "Here in Georgia," said Terry, a mother of three in Mason, "it can be hard to stay on top of your pill prescriptions, because there are so few doctors willing to see us. You can only get an abortion through Medicaid in case of life endangerment, rape, or incest. Girls that want one have to lie and say they were raped or had sex with a relative, and now they even want the name of the father so they can file charges against him, so you really don't want to lie about that. You get pregnant, you have the kid, and then you sign them up for food stamps and stuff."

Under the ACA, states can earn additional funding for their Medicaid programs if they implement various preventive care services, but such care generally comes from primary care providers who are already in short supply.[16] The Health Resources and Services Administration reported in 2014 that there are more than 15,000 health professional–shortage areas in the United States and that we will need an additional 16,000 primary care physicians, 7,300 dentists, and 2,800 psychiatrists to alleviate these shortages.[17] Those figures do not include the additional providers who will be needed to cover new enrollees under the ACA. Clearly medical insurance will not guarantee access to medical care.

ABUSES AND FRAUD

Neither Medicaid nor SNAP food stamps cover over-the-counter treatments for routine symptoms like colds and headaches. As a result, a simple cold or headache that could be treated with NyQuil or Tylenol often leads to a costly 911 call by Medicaid patients. And because patients aren't responsible for the bill, they tend not to care about the cost.

John, a medic in Southern California, told us:

I went into medicine to help people, but five years in I'm ready to quit. I am so tired of getting called to houses in the projects, where the folks just call 911 whenever they want. They know we are required by law to respond. I can't tell you how many times we've shown up in our ambulance, knocked on a door, only to find some guy sitting on the couch, waiting for us to show up to give him Tylenol for his headache. Or they'll call us because they are having problems with their blood pressure meds and they don't want to sit at an emergency room all day, or wait the weeks it will take to be seen by a provider willing to take Medicaid reimbursement. Do you have any idea how much it costs to send an ambulance out on a call? For a Tylenol?

Over-the-counter medications are still unreimbursed under any program unless they're provided as part of hospital or home care treatment.[18]

Another expensive and wasteful practice is the use of emergency rooms by the uninsured. In 1986 Congress passed the Emergency Medical Treatment and Labor Act (EMTALA),[19] which requires hospitals to provide care to anyone needing emergency treatment regardless of citizenship, legal status, or ability to pay. Emergency rooms then became the go-to choice for those without health insurance, and hospitals do not get reimbursed for such expenses by any program.[20] They can only transfer patients needing emergency treatment or discharge them. Over time some provisions have aimed at limiting emergency room abuse by nonacute patients—including permitting hospitals to bill patients for their care and report them to credit agencies for failure to pay—but the American College of Emergency Room Physicians recently reported that 55% of ER costs were still not reimbursed, and those costs run to tens of billions of dollars.[21] Under the ACA, such inappropriate use of first responders and emergency rooms might be expected to decline because people who are insured can see their doctors before illnesses become acute. So far, however, the results are not promising; a preliminary study conducted in Oregon found that emergency room visits increased significantly as people used their new insurance to cover ER visits instead of going first to primary care physicians.[22]

Roughly $60 billion a year is lost to Medicaid fraud—more than $1 in $7 spent—according to an estimate from the U.S. Attorney General's Office. Since 2008 the federal government has spent $102 million on special audits to combat Medicaid fraud but was able to identify only $20 million in overpayments.[23] Abuses are likely to continue, and as the number of enrollees increases, the cost of losses due to fraud and abuse is likely to increase as well.

A wheelchair scam shows how easy it is to game the system. In 2003, scammers set up a number of electric wheelchair companies in several Western states and aggressively targeted retirees through print, radio, and TV advertising. Medicaid patients ordered $3,500 wheelchairs but received $1,500-value wheelchairs.[24] Before the scam was uncovered by ripped-off retirees, Medicaid had lost millions of dollars. Six years later, a wheelchair-bound Vietnam veteran received a $15 million whistleblower payment from Medicaid for his part in uncovering a massive scheme in 40 states involving home health care aide billings to Medicaid. His investigations started with a simple review of his own medical bills, which showed many hours of billing for nonexistent visits from home health care aides. Then follow-up investigations led to the discovery of more than $121 million in fraudulent claims[25] that Medicaid had failed to catch.

According to a recent joint report produced by the Center for Public Integrity and PBS's *Frontline*, many for-profit dental chains provide substandard dental care to Medicaid participants. The report, which focused on chains in 22 states that predominantly serve children on Medicaid, found that unnecessary and substandard care were quite prevalent. In one case, a four-year-old in Arizona received two stainless steel crowns, presumably on baby teeth.[26]

When we spoke with Reyna at a neighborhood park near her shelter in Brooklyn, she provided examples of other ways to cheat the system: "I worked for a company that did stress tests. The doctors would pay me for every person I'd bring to their office to get the tests. These were all people I knew how to find on the streets, in the shelters, and so on. They were all on Medicaid. They didn't have a diagnosis of anything that needed the test, but the doctors knew how to bill for it and get reimbursed. The doctors would give me $75 for each person. I'd give the person I brought in $25. The doctor would spend 20 minutes doing a stress test, and bill Medicaid hundreds of dollars."

Shared use of Medicaid cards is also common. "My aunt gives her Medicaid card to her friends who are the same age," Rita told us. "No one seems to be checking up, so you've got three or four people getting medical care off one card. They've been doing it for years."

Profit-oriented trade in Medicaid cards is brisk, much as it is with food stamp cards, since enrollees "rent" their cards for use by friends and family. The state of Georgia, having lost $26 million to Medicaid fraud in 2010, is trying to institute Medicaid "smart cards," which would include biometrics making them enrollee-specific.[27]

PROVIDERS' PROBLEMS

Many doctors and other health care providers do not accept Medicaid patients because of the low reimbursement provided for services. Accordingly, the ACA plans to increase reimbursements to doctors by significant amounts.[28] But low reimbursement is not the only reason many physicians try to avoid participating in Medicaid. Medicaid patients often have transportation challenges that lead to doctor visit no-shows, a further drag on the bottom line. And because their lives can be erratic, Medicaid patients are more likely to be sicker than patients with private insurance, who can usually take care of medical issues more promptly. Medicaid patients are also likely to have more trouble understanding and following their care regimens.[29]

Providers who do participate in the Medicaid system must accept what the federal and/or state governments will pay, even when it is much less than they get from private insurers.[30] As the ACA is implemented and the number of people on Medicaid expands substantially, especially in opt-in states, doctor shortages as well as increasing costs may result. California projected a severe shortage of primary care physicians after ACA implementation, according to a 2013 Robert Graham Center report.[31] The state's lawmakers are scrambling to address the issue, with bills to expand the use of physicians' assistants, nurse practitioners, optometrists, and pharmacists, but more physicians will also be needed. For all these reasons, doctors who do participate in Medicaid tend to be new physicians trying to build practices, physicians nearing retirement who have the time to deal with extra challenges, or physicians who otherwise have trouble landing patients.[32]

Under a separate program called the National Health Service Corps Loan Repayment program, funded through the Department of Health and Human Services,[33] newly minted physicians can receive extra compensation to pay off tens of thousands of dollars in student loans[34] by working for three or four years in "underserved" and minority areas, which typically include a lot of Medicaid patients. While these physicians are adequately trained, they are fresh out of their internships with very little experience, and they often get little support, especially in remote areas.

DIFFERING VIEWPOINTS

Federal guidelines issued in 1997 allow states to enroll state prison inmates in Medicaid.[35] States that do enroll them can get reimbursements of 57%–82% of prisoners' medical costs. Oddly, a *USA Today* article found in 2013 that only a dozen states participated. Some simply didn't want to deal with the hefty paperwork involved. But the main reason so few states participated has to do with the rules governing prisoner enrollment.[36] Until recently, prisoners had to consent to be enrolled in Medicaid, and most balked at doing so because they believed that the care provided through state programs was superior to the care Medicaid provides. Some states, California included, have now changed the enrollment process by empowering state prison officials to enroll prisoners in Medicaid without the prisoners' consent, and other states plan to do the same.[37] The prisoners' reluctance sends a clear signal about the reputation of medical services under the Medicaid program.

While Medicaid is riddled with flaws, including what seems to be endemic abuse, it is also highly valued by its beneficiaries. It remains a critical part of the safety net for the poor. And one of its greatest shortcomings—the exclusion of childless people in the opt-out states and the resulting incentive to bear a first child as a ticket into the system—will be ameliorated as the ACA takes hold in those states with expanded coverage.

Appendix 8: Opt-In and Opt-Out States and the District of Columbia, 2014

State	Number currently uninsured	Predicted number uninsured post-ACA
Opting in		
AR	534,965	262,117
AZ	1,198,325	599,767
CA	6,787,453	3,444,629
CO	704,533	360,757
CT	283,631	152,564
DC	49,735	25,487
DE	97,334	50,387
HI	104,845	51,460
IA	305,640	157,475
IL	1,731,845	878,954
KY	682,218	339,374
MA	272,126	145,020
MD	732,544	383,423
MI	1,059,696	547,897
MN	443,002	232,193
ND	79,739	42,223
NJ	1,223,216	640,020
NM	453,215	227,023
NV	642,493	329,945
NY	2,185,195	1,122,130
OH	1,401,784	1,148,496
OR	596,865	304,183
RI	127,703	66,831
VT	42,836	22,830
WA	932,584	481,870
WV	264,287	135,790
Opting out		
AK	133,848	107,010
AL	711,302	588,500
FL	4,116,399	3,365,447
GA	1,856,223	1,535,835
ID	252,948	209,156
IN	848,573	694,153
KS	358,399	298,923
LA	819,410	678,529

State	Number currently uninsured	Predicted number uninsured post-ACA
ME	126,202	101,234
MO	793,925	646,589
MS	443,685	370,177
MT	181,221	147,851
NC	1,658,330	1,350,588
NE	245,418	199,693
NH	157,199	125,790
OK	639,834	520,267
PA	1,520,611	1,229,171
SC	665,287	554,044
SD	118,760	98,143
TN	892,107	744,665
TX	6,425,592	5,268,845
UT	411,349	329,867
VA	977,655	808,966
WI	549,798	442,318
WY	88,797	70,998
Total	**47,950,687**	**32,202,633**

Appendix 9: The Cost of Serving Medicaid Enrollees by State

The Cost of Serving Medicaid Enrollees Varies Widely Across the State

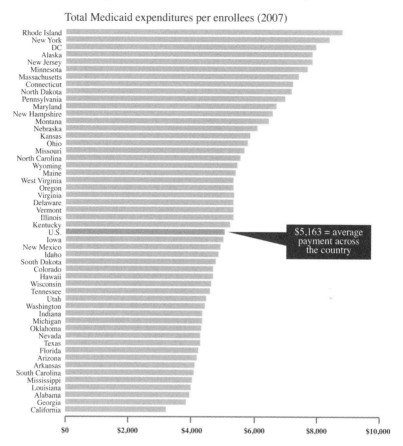

Total Medicaid expenditures per enrollees (2007)

Source: Kaiser Family Foundation.

Chapter 11

The Earned Income Tax Credit: Welfare Done (Almost) Right

For too long, we have measured compassion by how much we spend instead of how many people get out of poverty—Congressman Paul Ryan

Generally acknowledged to be the most successful of the U.S. means-tested antipoverty programs, the Earned Income Tax Credit (EITC) "has proven to be one of the most effective policy tools yet devised for encouraging work and eliminating poverty," in the words of a 2013 *Washington Post* editorial.[1] President Ronald Reagan called it "the best antipoverty, the best pro-family, the best job creation measure to come out of Congress."[2] The concept of fighting poverty by rewarding work generally appeals to people of all political persuasions, and the EITC is directly tied to work. To be eligible for benefits, a person must have reported earnings, normally provided on forms W-2 or 1099.

The original idea behind the earned income tax credit was to return any federal income tax that had been withheld from a low-income worker's salary. Today, however, the benefits of the EITC have little to do with withheld taxes. Accordingly, the EITC is now often called the EIC or Earned Income Credit. We will continue to use the term EITC here, though, because the program is still best known by that acronym.

Calculations of EITC benefits are now based on income level and number of children. At the bottom of the scale, for example, a worker who has one child and earns $2,000 in a given year automatically qualifies for an EITC credit of $689 even if no income tax has been withheld. The worker must file a return to get those funds, however. A Child Tax Credit (CTC) is linked to the EITC and adds additional funds for children. At annual earnings of $5,000 the automatic EITC is $1,709 for a worker with one child, and a Child Tax Credit of $300 is also allowed, for a total benefit of $2,009 and an increment on salary of 40%.[3]

At $10,000, the automatic benefit (with one child) is $3,250 plus the full CTC of $1,000, or a total benefit of $4,250, a 42% enhancement to earned income. At $20,000, the benefit starts phasing down and the increment to salary is 16% (EITC = $2,851; CTC = $387).[4]

All federal income taxes that have been withheld are also, of course, returned. But the payroll taxes known as FICA are not part of these calculations. All wage earners, including those eligible for EITC, must pay the FICA payroll taxes for Social Security (6.2% of gross earnings, matched with another 6.2% contributed by the employer) and Medicare (1.45% of gross earnings, also matched by the employer). This means that 7.65% is taken from every dollar that a low-income worker earns. Even at the rock-bottom $2,000 level, FICA taxes cost a worker $153, producing a net of $536 from the government. At $10,000, FICA is $765, so the worker's net benefit is $3,485.

Thanks in part to the EITC, tax rates for the poor have become negative, as the Congressional Budget Office (CBO) recently noted: "Between 2007 and 2009 [average tax rates] became increasingly negative for low income households (that is, on average, those households received money back from the federal government instead of owing income taxes)."[5] Thus, low-income workers, now about 40% of American wage earners, do not pay federal (or, usually, state) income tax. Instead, they get refunds of the income tax that had been deducted from their paychecks during the year, plus additional cash.

The Earned Income Tax Credit is the third most costly of all means-tested welfare programs. EITC expenditures increased from $23 billion in the mid-1990s to $60 billion by 2009 (see Figure 11.1).

The cost, however, is partially offset by the program's successes. The EITC's expansion during the 1990s, for example, might be the policy most responsible for the increase in employment and earnings among single mothers—"even more than the substantial changes to public assistance programs at the federal and state levels that occurred during that decade,"[6] according to the CBO study cited above. The CBO findings, in other words, suggest that the EITC may have made a greater difference than the TANF workfare and time-limit rules in getting women into the workforce and

Figure 11.1

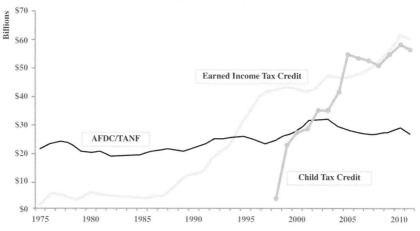

Real Federal Spending on EITC, CTC, and TANF 1975–2011
(2011 Dollars)

Sources: EITC/CTC: Internal Revenue Service, Statistics of Income
TANF: Health and Human Services, Office of Family Assistance.

earning money because EITC provided a tangible financial incentive to go to work at a regular paying job.

ELIGIBILITY

The vast majority of people who qualify for the EITC are low-income, working Americans. But the EITC has very few benefits for childless singles or couples, and that is the program's biggest flaw. In his second State of the Union address, President Obama noted that the EITC, while effective, "doesn't do enough for single workers who don't have kids."[7] While 40% of U.S. workers are eligible for the EITC (and owe no tax), only about half that number use the EITC system. Many others have no tax withheld and just don't bother to file tax returns, even though many of them would qualify for benefits.

About 20% of Americans who file tax returns do claim the EITC.[8] The percentage of filers who get the benefit varies widely by state. Mississippi leads the way, with almost 33% of filers receiving the credit, and Connecticut

Figure 11.2

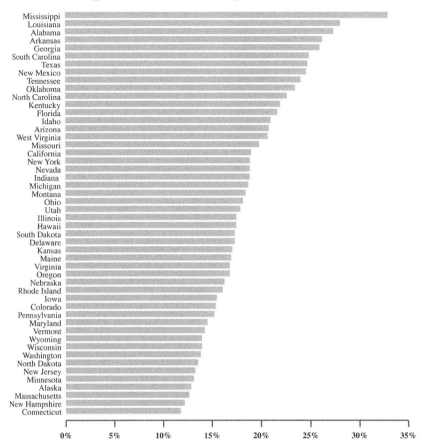

Percentage of Filers Receiving EITC, by State, 2010

Source: IRS Statistics of Income.

has the lowest rate with just over 12% of filers receiving it.[9] Figure 11.2 reflects poverty rates, with more residents of poorer states (Mississippi, Louisiana, Alabama, and Arkansas) and fewer residents of wealthier states (Alaska, Massachusetts, New Hampshire, Connecticut) receiving EITC benefits.

Half the states have instituted their own EITCs, and this trend is expected to continue.[10] Most follow the federal model, but three have a "nonrefundable EITC," which means filers can get back only as much state income tax as they paid in.[11]

Like virtually all other welfare programs, the EITC provides benefits that increase with each additional child.[12] Childless single people and married taxpayers without children can receive a maximum total benefit of only

$487 per year, and even that benefit starts to phase out on income above $8,000, dropping to zero on income over $19,000. In contrast, a single or married parent who has one child and earns $10,000 can receive more than $4,000; with earnings of $20,000 the benefit is $3,500. Additional children increase the benefit and the earnings limits. Single taxpayers with three children can qualify until earnings reach $42,000, and married taxpayers with three children can make up to $49,000 before the benefit phases out.[13] For more specifics, see Table 11.1, Appendix 10, and Appendix 11.

Nine million recipients of EITC benefits had incomes below the poverty line in 2010, while 17 million were above the poverty line, which means that 65% of recipients were nonpoor. The relatively high level of low-income, nonpoor participants is generally justified in this case because the EITC provides a way for the working poor to ease into higher levels of earned income without drastic reductions in EITC benefits. This is a sound principle, but for couples with children the $49,000 ceiling is too high; we believe the benefit could be phased out below $40,000.

Along with the EITC, the Child Tax Credit (CTC) of $1,000 per child is available to single heads of households earning up to $75,000 per year

Table 11.1   Earned Income Credit and Child Tax Credit Calculation, 2013

	Single Taxpayer			
		Childless	**One Child**	**Two Children**
Gross Income				
$10,000	EIC:	$330	$3,250	$4,010
	CTC:	$0	$0	$0
	ACC:	$0	$1,000	$1,050
	Federal Income Tax:	$0	$0	$0
	Total Credits:	$330	$4,250	$5,060
Total Annual Income Less FICA:		$9,565	$13,485	$14,295
$20,000	EIC:	$0	$2,851	$4,847
	CTC:	$0	$328	$0
	ACC:	$0	$672	$2,000
	Federal Income Tax:	$1,058	$328	$0
	Total Credits:	$0	$3,523	$6,847
Total Annual Income Less Federal Tax and FICA:		$17,412	$21,993	$25,317

and to married couples with incomes up to $110,000 per year. Childless workers cannot claim this credit. The CTC is supplemented with the Additional Child Credit (ACC) to help people who qualify for the CTC but pay no income tax. Table 11.1 provides an example showing that a single woman who earns $10,000 and has one child pays no income tax, and because of her low income, she qualifies for the Child Tax Credit. But the CTC of $1,000 can only refund federal income tax paid in, and since she didn't pay any income tax, she can't claim it. Instead she claims the Additional Child Credit, which is not tied to taxes. As a result, she gets the full $1,000 along with her EITC credit of $3,250—a 42% boost to her income (though she still pays $765 in FICA taxes). If her pay reaches $20,000 a year, following the same process, her IRS check will include her $2,851 EITC and $1,000 in child credits, less $328 in nonrefundable income taxes she owes (at $20,000 she must pay some income tax). She thus earns $20,000, pays FICA, and receives a $3,523 check from the IRS (which keeps $328 in income tax). Her net earnings for the year are $21,993. A single childless earner who makes $20,000 a year gets no EITC and ends up with $17,412. The child's "worth" in this scenario is $4,581. For further detail see Appendix 10.

Discrimination against low-income childless people is especially inappropriate for the EITC. The Center on Budget and Policy Priorities, which specializes in researching public policy that affects low-income families, notes that "childless workers are the sole group that the federal tax system taxes deeper into poverty. A childless worker making $12,566 will pay $1,016 in federal income and payroll taxes, yet be entitled to only $172 in EITC credits."[14] Reforming the EITC to include the childless would make it vastly more fair, provide a powerful incentive for the childless to find jobs, and make the incentive for childbearing much less powerful. Mary, a single, childless lab tech in suburban Maryland, shared her thoughts on the subject:

Most of the women who work here have kids; I'm the only one who doesn't. Every year around tax time I get so mad when they talk about what they are going to spend their tax checks on. They get a lot more than I do. My problem is not having any kids. I know kids are a lot more expensive than that check, but it did make me think a minute about whether it was worth it to have a kid. It isn't for me, but it may be for some.

In a recent study, the Brookings Institution found that a marriage penalty can also be associated with the EITC since certain married filers get lower refunds than single filers. "Taxpayers who might qualify for the EITC can suffer particularly large marriage penalties if the income of one spouse disqualifies the other from getting the credit,"[15] the study states, and it provides the following example:

A husband and wife with two children earn $20,000 each and claim the standard deduction of $10,900. Filing jointly, their taxable income is $15,100, on which their 2008 income tax liability is $1,510. They qualify for an EITC of $347 and a child credit of $2,000, yielding a net refund of $837. If they filed separately, the wife as a head of household with two children and the husband as single, the wife would have a tax bill of $150 minus an EITC of $3,927 and a child credit of $1,343, for a net refund of $5,119. The husband would owe $1,256 with no offsetting credits. Their separate tax bills would thus yield a combined net refund of $3,863, and so they incur a marriage penalty of $3,026, or 7.6 percent of their pretax income.[16]

When low-income parents do the calculations to figure out how to pay the bills and get through the day, every penny counts, and the system should not be sending the message that another child will increase your tax refund while getting married may reduce it. Holly, a middle-aged mother with two children in Oregon, got that message loud and clear.

When I got pregnant my husband and I got married. Six years later we realized that our benefits were going to run out unless we had another child, and our tax refunds would increase if we had another child as well. I'm not saying we had an- other kid to get continued benefits, but I can say that all those financial consider- ations influenced our decision to have our second daughter. I'm in my 40s now and I'm not going to have another child, but let's just say there was a reason we had that second child six years after the first one. And we have thought about getting divorced to increase our benefits, but that would be hard to explain to our family and friends. I admit, I have friends who chose not to marry because they knew they'd lose money in the process.

One of the surest ways to stay out of poverty is to get married before having children, notes Michael Tanner of the Cato Institute.[17] Our welfare system too often works against this.

EITC'S IMPACT

In 2014 the Center on Budget and Policy Priorities (CBPP) published a set of research findings about how the EITC affected children's success in school and promoted work habits among adults.[18] Several recent studies the CBPP reviewed found that "[t]he EITC and other income-enhancing measures improve the educational outcomes of young children in low-income families."[19] For example, Harvard and Columbia researchers looked at ten antipoverty and welfare-to-work experiments and found "a consis- tent pattern of better school results for low-income children in programs that provided more income [through credit programs such as the EITC and CTC]."[20] The CBPP also found that children from families that claimed the EITC did better, on average, on standardized tests than children in comparable poor families that did not claim the credit.[21] Similarly, a report in the *American Economic Review* found that additional income from the EITC correlated significantly with improved math and reading test scores of students.[22] The literature review also found that claiming the credit led to later success among children. One study, published by the CBPP, reported: "For children in low-income families, a $3,000 increase in family income . . . between a child's prenatal year and fifth birthday is associated with an average 17 percent increase in annual earnings and an additional 135 hours of work when the children become adults, compared to similar children whose families do not receive the added income."[23]

This study also found that the EITC increased the likelihood that adults would go to work. "EITC expansions between 1984 and 1996 accounted for more than half of the large increase in employment among single mothers," the authors note. "The most significant gain in employment attributable to the EITC accrued among mothers with young children and mothers with low education . . . [and] the EITC is particularly effective at encouraging work among single mothers working for low wages." Moreover, the authors said, "EITC expansions likely contributed about as much to the fall in the numbers of female-headed households receiving cash welfare assistance from 1993–1999 as the time limits on cash assistance and other changes under welfare reform."[24]

A recent working paper co-authored by Molly Dahl with the Congressional Budget Office found that the EITC not only helped increase the number of women entering the workforce, it helped them get jobs that increased their earnings over time.[25] The paper concludes that the women receiving the EITC "exhibit larger increases in [nonwelfare] earnings growth than other similar women," good news for women considering the leap from welfare to work.

EITC PROBLEMS

As noted, the EITC does practically nothing for childless workers. Low-income workers "*not* raising minor children receive little or nothing from the EITC," the Center on Budget and Policy Priorities found: "for example, a childless adult working full time at the minimum wage is ineligible, because his minimum wage earnings exceed the income limit for the very limited $487 maximum credit."[26]

There are other problems with the EITC, too. Getting the credit requires filing an income tax return, and many people who earn very little do not file tax returns, even if doing so would entitle them to a credit.[27] Also, because of the complexity of the current tax code, many who do file turn to professional tax preparers, who charge an average of more than $100 to prepare even the simplest return,[28] depleting the EITC advantage.

The cumbersome refund process is another problem. After an EITC-eligible return is filed with the IRS, there is usually a wait of four to six weeks for the check, but the wait is seven or eight months for those income taxes that are withheld over the course of the year. So, for example, if Mary has a job that pays $20,000 a year, and every month her employer deducts $250 in income tax (which she knows she will get back), she is, in effect, lending that money to the federal treasury, and meanwhile she has had no access to it. Many low-income taxpayers wonder about this. Sandy, a Washington mother of two, put it this way: "I qualify for the full refund, but I have to wait for it, so all year I'm putting things on layaway, or buying stuff on credit, because I know I'll get this big fat check after I file my return. But as a result I'm paying interest and I'm robbing Peter to pay Paul."

The lump sum refund can cause other problems. "It kinda feels like Christmas," says Paula, a Colorado mother of three. "I end up splurging on the kids, buying big-ticket items, because I'm just so excited to have such a big chunk of cash. It's stupid, I know, but when you scrimp all year and then this big check shows up it's hard not to just want to blow it on something. I wish I could just get it over the course of the year. Then I wouldn't blow it like that."

Those familiar with the EITC are not all fans. One woman we talked with comes from the African nation of Eritrea and works as a tax preparer in North Carolina. She prepares hundreds of EITC-eligible returns each year, often for people who will receive $6,000 or $8,000 in benefits when they file. And she is upset—even angry.

Why are we even giving them this money? I know it is supposed to be a helping hand. But we're creating poverty. The new generation, they are eighteen, coming in with babies in hand so they can get welfare. I try and get them to plan. But they want the check. This money is changing their lives. It is not making their life better. It is not a stepping-stone. They are stuck. And then off they go to Walmart to spend it on $100 tennis shoes for their toddlers, flat screen televisions. Walmart stocks up for tax season checks. And then when it is gone they come back into my office asking for loans. Americans need to see a light, somehow. When you hand out money and food to people, they will never work. You have to force them to work, somehow.

One year, I was volunteering at a Christmas event, handing out toys to poor children, and I took my eight-year-old son with me. He saw a helicopter and he really wanted that toy. I said, "No, that is for the poor children." On the way home in the car he said to me, "I wish you were poor, mommy, so I could have that toy."

Later, when he was thirteen, I made him come to the office with me and work, sorting papers, filing. He said to me, "I am the only teenager in America who has to work for food!" But he will not be lazy. He will work. He is my son and I am his mother and I show him work is important every day when I go to work.

FRAUD

Between 2006 and 2009, EITC beneficiaries were required to repay $2.3 billion in EITC overpayments,[29] according to a 2012 report from the U.S. Treasury Inspector General for Tax Administration. While some of these excess claims were the result of honest errors, most were not. The 2012 report noted weaknesses in auditing and estimated that between $13.7 and $16.7 billion had been lost through improper EITC payments in 2011 alone.[30] Overall, the estimate is that between 21% and 26% of EITC payments are improper.

Fraudulent claims typically involve filing a false tax return that lists nonexistent children, presents the worker's earnings as less (or sometimes more) than they were, or claims that withholding was more than it was.[31] Figures can normally be verified or refuted using accompanying forms from employers, but the system can clearly be gamed, sometimes with the help of fly-by-night tax preparers, also called "return mills," which often bill clients a percentage of the refund they generate. Many of these tax preparers manage to stay below law enforcement's radar.[32] One honest tax preparer in Southern California who hosts educational seminars in local neighborhoods had this to say about the temptations to cheat: "A lot of these folks, they get bad information from their neighbors and friends, and they see people getting these big checks and they think, 'Why shouldn't I do it too, no one is going to actually look at my return, are they?' And then they end up in a lot of trouble because they claimed more kids than they have, or lied about their income. But that is only if they get caught, and a lot of them don't get caught, so it's kind of a roll of the dice for them."

The result can be a double-whammy for taxpayers. When caught, a taxpayer must repay the fraudulent refund plus interest, frequently collected by deducting the amount from a subsequent year's EITC credits, and that taxpayer will be flagged by the IRS as having filed a fraudulent return, which increases the likelihood of future audits and possible severe punishment. Meanwhile the "professional" preparer has likely disappeared.

The government has been taking increasingly aggressive steps to counter this problem, including filing lawsuits against large tax preparation services found to be unreliable and imposing new monetary penalties for tax preparers found to have filed inflated claims.

Appendix 10: EITC and CTC Calculations: Single Taxpayers

		Childless	One Child	Two Children	Three Children	Four Children
Gross Income						
$2,000	EIC:	$155	$689	$810	$810	$810
	CTC:	$0	$0	$0	$0	$0
	ACC:	$0	$0	$0	$0	$0
	Income Tax:	$0	$0	$0	$0	$0
	Total:	$155	$689	$810	$810	$810
% of gross income:		8%	34%	41%	41%	41%
Total annual income less FICA:		$2,002	$2,536	$2,657	$2,657	$2,657
$5,000	EIC:	$384	$1,709	$2,010	$2,010	$2,010
	CTC:	$0	$0	$0	$0	$0
	ACC:	$0	$300	$300	$300	$300
	Income Tax:	$0	$0	$0	$0	$0
	Total:	$384	$2,009	$2,310	$2,310	$2,310
% of gross income:		8%	40%	46%	46%	46%
Total annual income less FICA:		$5,002	$6,627	$6,928	$6,928	$6,928
$10,000	EIC:	$330	$3,250	$4,010	$4,010	$4,010
	CTC:	$0	$0	$0	$0	$0
	ACC:	$0	$1,000	$1,050	$1,050	$1,050

(*Continued*)

Appendix 10: (Continued)

		Childless	One Child	Two Children	Three Children	Four Children
	Income Tax:	$0	$0	$0	$0	$0
	Total:	$330	$4,250	$5,060	$5,060	$5,060
% of gross income:		3%	43%	51%	51%	51%
Total annual income less FICA:		$9,565	$13,485	$14,295	$14,295	$14,295
$15,000	EIC:	$0	$3,250	$5,372	$5,372	$5,372
	CTC:	$0	$0	$0	$0	$0
	ACC:	$0	$1,000	$1,800	$1,800	$1,800
	Income Tax:	$503	$0	$0	$0	$0
	Total:	$503	$4,250	$7,172	$7,172	$7,172
% of gross income:		3%	28%	48%	48%	48%
Total annual income less FICA:		$13,350	$18,107	$21,025	$21,025	$21,025
$20,000	EIC:	$0	$2,851	$4,847	$4,847	$4,847
	CTC:	$0	$328	$0	$0	$0
	ACC:	$0	$672	$2,000	$2,000	$2,000
	Income Tax:	$1,058	$328	$0	$0	$0
	Total:	$1,058	$3,523	$6,847	$6,847	$6,847
% of gross income:		5%	18%	34%	34%	34%
Total annual income less FICA:		$17,412	$21,993	$25,317	$25,317	$25,317

$25,000		Childless	One Child	Two Children	Three Children	Four Children
	EIC:	$0	$2,052	$3,794	$3,794	$3,794
	CTC:	$0	$828	$438	$46	$0
	ACC:	$0	$172	$1,562	$2,954	$3,300
	Income Tax:	$1,808	$828	$438	$46	$0
	Total:	$1,808	$2,224	$5,356	$6,748	$7,094
% of gross income:		7%	9%	21%	27%	28%
Total annual income less FICA:		$21,279.50	$25,311.50	$28,443.50	$29,860.50	$30,181.50
$30,000						
	EIC:	$0	$1,253	$2,741	$2,741	$2,741
	CTC:	$0	$1,000	$938	$548	$156
	ACC:	$0	$0	$1,062	$2,452	$3,844
	Income Tax:	$2,558	$1,354	$938	$548	$156
	Total:	$2,558	$899	$3,803	$5,193	$6,585
% of gross income:		9%	3%	13%	17%	22%
Total annual income less FICA:		$25,147	$29,604	$31,508	$32,898	$34,290

Appendix 11: EITC and CTC Calculations: Married Taxpayers

		Childless	One Child	Two Children	Three Children	Four Children
Gross Income						
$2,000	EIC:	$155	$689	$810	$810	$810
	CTC:	$0	$0	$0	$0	$0
	ACC:	$0	$0	$0	$0	$0
	Income Tax:	$0	$0	$0	$0	$0
	Total:	$155	$689	$810	$810	$810
% of gross income:		8%	34%	41%	41%	41%
Total annual income less FICA:		$2,002	$2,536	$2,657	$2,657	$2,657
$5,000	EIC:	$384	$1,709	$2,010	$2,010	$2,010
	CTC:	$0	$0	$0	$0	$0
	ACC:	$0	$300	$300	$300	$300
	Income Tax:	$0	$0	$0	$0	$0
	Total:	$384	$2,009	$2,310	$2,310	$2,310
% of gross income:		8%	40%	46%	46%	46%
Total annual income less FICA:		$5,002	$6,627	$6,928	$6,928	$6,928
$10,000	EIC:	$487	$3,250	$4,010	$4,010	$4,010
	CTC:	$0	$0	$0	$0	$0
	ACC:	$0	$1,000	$1,050	$1,050	$1,050

Appendix 11: (Continued)

	Childless	One Child	Two Children	Three Children	Four Children
Income Tax:	$0	$0	$0	$0	$0
Total:	$487	$4,250	$5,060	$5,060	$5,060
% of gross income:	5%	43%	51%	51%	51%
Total annual income less FICA:	$9,722	$13,485	$14,295	$14,295	$14,295
$15,000					
EIC:	$356	$3,250	$5,372	$5,372	$5,372
CTC:	$0	$0	$0	$0	$0
ACC:	$0	$1,000	$1,800	$1,800	$1,800
Income Tax:	$0	$0	$0	$0	$0
Total:	$356	$4,250	$7,172	$7,172	$7,172
% of gross income:	2%	28%	48%	48%	48%
Total annual income less FICA:	$14,209	$18,103	$21,025	$21,025	$21,025
$20,000					
EIC:	$0	$3,250	$5,372	$5,372	$5,372
CTC:	$0	$0	$0	$0	$0
ACC:	$0	$1,000	$2,000	$2,550	$2,550
Income Tax:	$0	$0	$0	$0	$0
Total:	$0	$4,250	$7,372	$7,922	$7,922
% of gross income:	0%	21%	37%	40%	40%
Total annual income less FICA:	$18,470	$22,720	$25,842	$26,392	$26,392

(Continued)

Appendix 11: (Continued)

		Childless	One Child	Two Children	Three Children	Four Children
$25,000	EIC:	$0	$2,906	$4,918	$4,918	$4,918
	CTC:	$0	$111	$0	$0	$0
	ACC:	$0	$889	$2,000	$3,000	$3,300
	Income Tax:	$503	$111	$0	$0	$0
	Total:	$503	$3,795	$6,918	$7,918	$8,218
% of gross income:		2%	15%	28%	32%	33%
Total annual income less FICA:		$22,585	$26,883	$30,006	$31,006	$31,306
$30,000	EIC:	$0	$2,107	$3,865	$3,865	$3,865
	CTC:	$0	$613	$221	$0	$0
	ACC:	$0	$387	$1,779	$3,000	$4,000
	Income Tax:	$1,003	$613	$221	$0	$0
	Total:	$1,003	$2,494	$5,644	$6,865	$7,865
% of gross income:		3%	8%	19%	23%	26%
Total annual income less FICA:		$26,702	$30,199	$33,349	$34,570	$35,570

PART IV

Building Blocks for a Better Welfare System

Chapter 12

Patterns of Dependence and Independence: American Indians on Reservations, Barterers, and Immigrants

Government dependence, through current federal Indian policy, is killing people—Roland Morris Sr., Minnesota Chippewa tribal elder

I came here to work. I take no handouts. I work to take care of myself and my family, and this makes me a man—Chicago cab driver from Ethiopia

What drives long-term dependence on welfare? What encourages independence? Some clues have emerged from our examinations of welfare programs, and others come from examination of certain societal subsets. One group of citizens—those living on American Indian reservations—appears to be especially vulnerable to long-term dependency. Members of other groups, notably immigrants and barterers, seem especially determined to avoid dependence on government money.

AMERICAN INDIANS AND DEPENDENCE—THE FALLOUT FROM UNEARNED MONEY

On our travels around the country, our days on reservations were by far the most heartbreaking. If happiness comes from hard work, then low-income American Indians on reservations are destined to misery; the poor among them are trapped in a system that undermines all incentives for work, and the resulting misery is manifest.

Of course most Indians are not poor, and most do not live on reservations. More than 70% of Native Americans now live in cities and are integrated within mainstream American culture. Most are employed and doing well. Roughly 28% of Indians are poor, however, substantially more than the overall U.S. average of 15%, and their poverty seems to be endemic.[1]

According to the 2010 U.S. Census, 2.9 million Americans (almost 1% of the U.S. population) self-identified as American Indian or Alaskan Native and another 2.3 million identified as at least part Native American.[2] They are members of the 566 tribes registered with the Bureau of Indian Affairs (BIA) and the 72 tribes that have state, but not federal, recognition. Most refer to themselves and fellow tribal members as American Indians; in our travels we found the term *Native American* seldom used.

A close look at the roughly one million American Indians who live on reservations is instructive because a very substantial portion of them are poor and those who are impoverished are entitled to welfare and other payments that exceed, on average, twice the amounts available to other poor Americans. In many cases payments rise above $20,000 per person per year, enough to raise participants above the poverty line even with no other income. If more generous welfare payments can solve or substantially ameliorate America's poverty conundrum, there should be clues about that, and about the results of other sizable payments, on Indian reservations. What we found suggests that larger payments do not solve the poverty problem—at least not by themselves—and that so far they appear to have made things worse.

As Americans, American Indians qualify for all the federal welfare programs we have already described, including Temporary Assistance for Needy Families (TANF), Supplemental Nutrition Assistance Program (SNAP), Women, Infants and Children (WIC), Supplemental Security Income (SSI), Social Security Disability Insurance (SSDI), and Section 8 housing, and because of their tribal membership they are entitled to benefits from tribal welfare programs as well. In addition, many tribal members receive payouts from tribal investments in such businesses as casinos along with revenue from natural resource royalties. Tribal members also receive millions of dollars in annual payments from the federal government as the result of a settlement reached with the BIA after decades of court battles over mismanaged tribal funds.[3] Preparations for a similar settlement affecting additional tribes began in 2014.

Despite these multiple sources of income, American Indians die earlier and at much higher rates than other Americans from everything from tuberculosis to alcoholism, diabetes, vehicle crashes, and suicide.[4] According to scholar John Barnhill, writing in *The Encyclopedia of American Indian Issues Today*: "Native Americans . . . are five times as likely as other Americans to become addicted. . . . Drug abuse, specifically abuse of alcohol, is now the number one problem of Alaska Natives, who have a suicide rate four times the national average, and an astounding 80 percent of all deaths are related to alcoholism or alcohol abuse. Native Americans between the ages of 15 and 24 have a fatal accident rate three times the national average. Suicide is the second leading cause of death."[5] Average American Indian life expectancy is 73.7 compared to the overall U.S. average of 78.2.[6]

Although there is no "Indian gene" for alcoholism (an urban myth that persists to this day), alcohol remains a particularly serious problem for this population. A Navajo teen we met in a gas station parking lot on a reservation put it this way: "A lot of the kids here, they know they aren't going anywhere. Some might try and leave for a while, but they always come back. And here we are, with nothing to do. There's a big meth problem and a big drinking problem. We're bored. Nothing is happening, nothing is going to happen, our chances of ever leaving are low, our chances of finding work are even lower. So, why not get high, get drunk, and forget about it?"

A young Sioux in South Dakota concurred: "We don't work. Our parents don't work. Our grandparents don't work. We live on white man's guilt, which shows up as cash every month in the mailbox. We've got nothing to look forward to, nothing to plan for, except the next check, when we can go out and buy some weed, or meth, or some liquor and escape for awhile. And that is never going to change. It is what it is." These young men are trapped in a culture that tells them to live on the welfare the white man *owes* them, turning a blind eye to the fact that that very system is the cause of their ongoing misery.

Some reservations are "dry," which means that no alcohol can be sold or consumed there.[7] This has the perverse effect of increasing drunk driving, as tribal members drive off-reservation to purchase and consume alcohol. Pine Ridge (South Dakota) tribal members, for example, have traditionally made the two-mile journey south across the Nebraska border to the town of White Clay, where entrepreneurial liquor store owners on each corner of the only four-way stop in town are more than happy to ply their wares. The population of White Clay is 14,[8] yet 13,000 cans of beer are sold there daily.[9]

We decided to see for ourselves what happened to those 13,000 cans of beer. On our drive from Pine Ridge to White Clay we saw men, women, kids, and dogs walking the well-worn path that skirts the two-lane highway. Men and women were passed out on the side of the road and leaning against the few buildings in White Clay, clearly drunk. Men were urinating openly and staggering about, and two people were throwing up against the side of a truck, presumably a truck they had driven to get there from the reservation and would drive to get back. Partly in response to this public health disaster, the Pine Ridge tribe voted in 2013 to permit on-reservation alcohol sales with the profits to be used for alcohol treatment.

Native American women have an especially tough time. One in three has been the victim of rape or attempted rape, twice the national average.[10] Forty-six percent report being raped, beaten, or stalked by intimate partners.[11] A survey by the Alaska Federation of Natives estimated the rate of sexual assault in rural Alaska villages to be twelve times the national average.[12] One shy young woman we spoke with at the Taos Pueblo in New Mexico described a common life story. "I went off to college, but I got homesick and dropped out. I had never left home before and it was all the way down in Albuquerque. In Indian country we call it the 'reservation mentality'—the idea that no matter what, we end up back on the rez, with our family, no matter how bad it is. There aren't many jobs here, and now I have a couple of kids, so yeah, we basically live on welfare. I couldn't leave my husband now. I have no job skills, just a high school diploma, and no money to get far enough away."

Talking about her experiences with abusive clients, a longtime social worker on the Pine Ridge reservation told us, "By giving women the welfare check you took away what was traditionally the responsibility of the man of the family, providing for his family, and gave it to the woman. This made the man feel weak and useless, which in turn led to drink, and then to spousal abuse."

For all its faults, "the rez" has a powerful pull on its members. A friendly young college graduate living on the Yankton Sioux reservation in South Dakota looked somewhat abashed when asked why she had returned after going to college in Omaha. "I know. It doesn't make any sense. I won't find work here. I won't ever 'amount to anything' and will probably waste my degree. But my great-grandma, my grandma, my mom . . . they all live here, and we're really close. Even they say I should leave. 'What are you staying here for? We'll be here forever. You can always come visit. We aren't going anywhere, but you should.' You've heard of the 'rez mentality,' right? Well, it is a real thing, and it's like glue. Or a rubber band. You can walk away, but it pulls you back."

Shame and Secrecy

It is hard for outsiders to get information about reservation life. "We don't want [white] people looking around here," said one tribal member in Colorado. "We are ashamed, and we are angry, and we are upset, but we fear what happens if we draw attention to ourselves, because then everyone points their finger and says 'Those damned Indians, we give them so much and they're still so poor. What's their problem?'"

Our visit to the Ute Mountain Ute reservation in southern Colorado bore this out. When we went to the tribal offices in search of tribal workers to talk to, three different employees shuffled us along to colleagues until one finally told us point blank: "No one here will talk to you. We would have to get clearance from the Bureau [of Indian Affairs] and from our supervisor—who is on permanent leave—and that isn't going to happen. We don't talk to outsiders." Later in the week we were informed that payday was coming and we were encouraged to hit the road, as the reservation would be awash in alcohol; apparently there is a violent reservation subculture fueled by "payday" alcohol consumption that makes the streets unsafe at night, payday being the day tribal members receive their monthly welfare checks.

We fared no better in South Dakota on the Pine Ridge reservation. People left the aisles in the supermarket as we entered them, and tribal policemen in patrol cars followed us everywhere we went. Attempts to approach tribal members at the local grocery store were met with stares and stony silence.

Despite such obstacles we were able to interview a number of American Indians, including elders on the Taos, Yankton Sioux, Southern Ute, and Onandaga reservations, with most success coming through chance encounters in laundromats, parking lots, and gas stations, away from the prying eyes of fellow tribal members. Some were eager to share their grim views about how their tribes have fared under the reservation system and the supervision of the BIA. Many waxed nostalgic for the days when hunting, fishing, and farming were the norm, and tribal members were self-sufficient. Said one, "I don't understand my grandsons and great-grandsons—they don't know how to do anything anymore. If the government disappeared tomorrow I think they would all starve pretty quick. This reservation has taken away any gumption they were born with."

Payment Streams

In the last twenty years the number of tribes seeking federal recognition and the number of Americans claiming Native ancestry rose almost 20%.[13]

Tribes have petitioned for recognition in suburbs and cities around the country, not because they want to return to reservation life but because of the lure of increased financial support, including possible income from casinos and other profit-making ventures.[14]

"Each member is worth about $5,000 to [my] tribe in federal aid," said Choctaw attorney S. Kayla Morrison. "And this begins when children are born in the Indian Health Service hospital and lasts until the time they die in the same hospital. With more members, we get more money, so we have a vested interest in swelling our membership."[15]

California State Polytechnic University professor Debra Bucholtz explains another reason tribes continue to apply for federal recognition: "Federal recognition and the quasi-sovereign status it entails also enable tribes to enter into gaming compacts with the state where they are located and open bingo parlors and casinos. . . . Critics of the federal recognition system, as well as some tribal leaders, argue that entities without legitimate claims are now seeking federal recognition so that they can open and profit from their own casinos."[16]

The Southern Ute tribe—whose reservation sits in the southwest corner of Colorado and straddles thousands of acres of farmland and hunting grounds—gained control of the natural gas resources beneath the land in 1980, and natural gas fracking there has now become big business.[17] The tribe has built gleaming new office buildings and expanded tribal services. They have a successful casino and a new museum in rural southern Colorado, and natural gas continues to flow. Early on, this tribe made the decision to put its earnings into trust for the tribal membership.[18] "We thought we were doing the right thing," former chief Matthew Box said. "With the Bureau of Indian Affairs you never know what might happen, and we really wanted to leave a legacy for our kids. So we decided to start a trust fund, and pay out earnings to each tribal member. Today, that payout is about $70,000 annually per tribal member, including kids." He paused before continuing. "Sadly, it isn't turning out how we had hoped."

With evident sorrow, the former chief explained that the children on the reservation have no interest in going to school or pursuing a career. Teachers are at their wit's end trying to inspire the children to get an education. The children say, in essence, "Why bother, when I know I have a middle-class income promised to me for life?" Although the tribe has instituted a college scholarship program that not only pays for tuition, books, and housing, but also pays incentive bonuses for each quarter or semester completed,[19] the number of tribal youth taking advantage of the opportunity is very low.

A tribal member described her son's experience. "He got that money from a young age. He had a car, cash in his pocket, and people started taking advantage of him. The non-Indians in town know about these tribal dividends, so the Indian kids become targets for all kinds of moochers. Other kids ask them for loans (that never get paid back); they hassle them for gifts and rides and expect them to pay for everything if they go out, because they have money. We gave our children this gift, but they have no sense how to make use of it responsibly. My son wrecked his car and started driving mine, wrecked mine—no big deal, there will be another check soon. Now he is in trouble with the law for drunk driving. This is a kid with all the financial advantages you could have, and he's just blowing through it."

These children are not poor. Indeed, poverty has been eliminated on this reservation, fulfilling what for many people elsewhere is a near-impossible dream. But giving American Indians on reservations ample amounts of money seems to create or exacerbate more problems than it solves.

Were things better before the natural gas windfall? One elder thinks so. "We didn't know we were poor then. We were happy. We worked hard, building our homes from wood off this land, putting up food for winter. Now we are all rich. The children don't listen to us. . . . We made it too easy for them. I know we had the right idea and did it with a pure intention—we wanted to protect them from the white man and make it so they would never have to be dependent the way we had to be dependent for handouts and welfare and commodities—but now they are even more dependent because they have no skills at all. They don't even take their education seriously so they face a lifetime of unemployment. If these checks go away some day, these kids are lost."

At the Ute Mountain Ute reservation, tribe members demanded their checks from the BIA settlement even before the funds were available, which meant that the tribe had to borrow money. This is how one tribal member described what happened next: "There were fights in the line at the tribal office where they handed out the checks. People were mad that the checks didn't get handed out quick enough. It wasn't big money, I think we each got about $2,000, but that is big money around here. People went and spent it on trips to Vegas, or another car, or booze . . . within a week, that money was gone. And for what? Did anyone save it? Not many people did. Most just spent it on stuff. So what good did it do?"

Indian Gaming

One of the most visible American Indian enterprises nationwide is gambling, known as Indian gaming. Since Indian gaming was approved by the federal government in 1988, more than 460 American Indian casinos have opened, and their aggregate annual income in 2011 was more than $36 billion.[20] The Shakopee tribe of Minnesota—by far the wealthiest tribe in the nation—generated $1.4 billion in 2013 casino revenues at their Mystic Lake casino and entertainment complex outside Minneapolis–St. Paul. Like the Southern Utes, this tribe pays out monthly dividends to each tribal member—a staggering $84,000 apiece to 600 people.[21] Unemployment is 99%. Why should anyone work when they don't have to, the tribal elders say.

Tribal elder Keith Anderson elaborated in an interview for London's *Daily Mail*: "Why dig a hole when you don't need to dig it—when you can pay someone to dig a hole? Instead of budgeting a dinner and a movie, you can go to dinner and a movie and then go to dinner again and see another movie, but you can't see enough movies and dinners to spend all your money."[22]

Not surprisingly, the Shakopee tribe struggles to motivate its young people. While 83% of Americans over 25 in Minnesota hold high school diplomas, the Shakopee tribe's graduation rate is just 55%.[23] Shakopee Mdewakanton Community chairman Charlie Vig agreed in a recent interview with the *Minnesota Post* that inspiring the tribe's youth is becoming more difficult. "One of our challenges in this community is, because of our success, I think we have to work a little harder at getting our children to understand the importance of being good citizens, doing what they need to do for our community. And part of that is graduating from high school and going on to further their education."[24]

While there have been movements among tribal leadership to invest gaming money and other windfall income in job creation, public works, or other projects, the leaders who vote for cash payments remain in the most important decision-making positions because cash payments remain universally popular.

Bright Spots

The picture is more hopeful for some tribes, including the Yakama Nation of eastern Washington. Arguably the most economically diversified tribe in the United States, it does have tribal casino operations, but its leaders decided early on to diversify holdings and invest in many long-term projects. The tribe's 1.3 million acres boast five tribal enterprises including the Yakama Land Enterprise, which manages fruit orchards, timberlands, a timber mill, and an RV park. The tribe also has a wildlife range, a vegetation and resource management program, a tribal museum and cultural center, and a tribal casino called Legends. And it maintains fishing, hunting, and food gathering rights on 12 million acres of ceded land. Its most impressive project is Yakama Power, which provides electricity on tribal land and the Yakama Network wireless Internet service.[25]

Although the tribal unemployment rate remains extremely high with heavy welfare dependency, members we spoke with are optimistic. More good jobs are available on Yakama land than on most reservations, and young people appear to be getting the training and education they need to fill them.

Positive developments are also evident among the Eastern Band of Cherokee Indians in North Carolina. This tribe does not have the wealth of the Shakopees and Southern Utes and pays only modest stipends from casino revenue. Located in the Blue Ridge Mountains, their casino is not a powerhouse entertainment venue, but by 2001 the 8,000 tribal members were each receiving $6,000 a year in profit sharing; by 2006 the number was $9,000 yearly, enough to take the edge off poverty.[26] Jane Costello, an epidemiologist with Duke University Medical School, studied the effect of the cash flow on the Cherokee children's psychological health. In 2006, four years after the payments started, Dr. Costello noted "marked improvements in those who moved out of poverty [as a result of the payments]. The frequency of behavioral problems declined by 40 percent," she found, "nearly reaching the risk level of children who had never been poor."[27] Moreover, the earlier the children started receiving the supplemental income, the better their mental health in adulthood. And the poorer the child was when a family started receiving the payments, the greater the improvement in the child's psychological health.

Today the tribe has a 58% labor force participation rate, not far below the average of 62.7% for all of North Carolina. The tribe's high school graduation rate is 78%, higher than the state average.[28]

The Future of Tribes

Despite these relatively bright spots, American Indians living on reservations generally find themselves, by all measures, much worse off than other Americans. Access to many more welfare benefits than ordinary Americans receive plus unearned windfall payments from Indian gaming and natural resource exploitation continue to have perverse effects, with human misery continuing to increase on the reservations. Suicides, accidents, spousal abuse, diseases, and alcohol and drug abuse all testify to this. While these tribal communities have some distinguishing characteristics—the "reservation mentality," the strong sense of being owed reparations from the white man—the basic problem appears to be the same as the basic problem with welfare dependency in the rest of America. Without the challenge that comes from the necessity to make a living, without the sense of pride and self-respect that comes from providing for oneself and others, the system, in Charles Murray's words, takes the life out of life,[29] and the results are dismal.

Native American leaders are becoming increasingly concerned about problems associated with dependency on welfare and other unearned money, and that is good news. Dave Anderson, a wealthy American Indian entrepreneur, investor, and member of the Lac Courte Oreilles Lake Superior Band of Ojibwa of northwest Wisconsin, said in a 2012 interview with *Native Sun News*:

> I believe that the real reason why our elders and our forefathers were respected, it wasn't because they knew how to harvest wild rice or they knew how to take down a deer and turn that hide into moccasins . . . what they were doing was surviving successfully in their environment.
>
> [Our] elders or forefathers might be horrified that we are trying to teach our young people how to make moccasins if we can't first sit our child down in front of a computer and teach that child how to [use it].[30]

Native entrepreneur and attorney Calvin Helin is more blunt. The author of *The Economic Dependency Trap,* Helin says: "Look what Native Americans have traded for their welfare crumbs: they have lost complete control over their lives, and their self-worth and self-determination has been replaced with a crippling economic dependency, a loss of community cooperation, and a diminishing sense of personal, tribal, and community responsibility."[31] The path to success is available to those willing to take responsibility for themselves and their families by getting off the welfare rolls and into the mainstream workforce, Helin insists, and his book has gained enormous popularity among tribal Indians as a guide to avoiding welfare dependence and gaining (or regaining) one's self-respect.

We met many tribal elders who privately agreed that the tribal system is bad for Indians and should be abolished, but they nearly always toe the line when in the presence of other tribal members for fear of repercussions. It is blasphemy to suggest that the tribes have outlived their purpose and that American Indians should be assimilated, but that is what many elders we met secretly wished for. "We have won many battles," said one Taos Pueblo elder. "We have won land from the federal government. Our pueblo is a United Nations World Heritage Site. People come from all over the world to visit us. But what do they see? A people still living in mud huts, like some archaeological curiosity left over from centuries past. They peek in our windows like we are zoo animals, snapping photos. And where does that leave our youth? They go to school; they get on the Internet; they live in the modern world. They could find work if they left and joined the rest of the world, but they will stay dependent if they stay here. Yet, because we want to be a tribe we hold them back, telling them to hold on to traditions. It is hard for me to admit, but the best way forward for our children would be to leave tribal life behind and move on."

UNEARNED MONEY IN OTHER CONTEXTS

Interestingly, studies of lottery winners support findings about reservation Indians and unearned money. Forty-three states have state lotteries in this country. Together they sold $78 billion in lottery tickets in 2012.[32] The largest payout ever made occurred the same year, when the multistate Mega Millions lottery paid out $656 million to three ticket holders.[33] Every day millions of Americans buy lottery tickets, mostly winning little or nothing, but sometimes winning big.

When researchers at the University of California at Santa Barbara set out to see what happened to the happiness and well-being of big winners, they found that winning the lottery had negative effects on happiness, for two reasons. Winners tended to view the experience as very positive, of course, but they used it as a new set-point for comparing other life events. As a result, they found themselves less able to appreciate mundane life experiences that previously would have brought them joy. Winners also eventually became accustomed to their well-endowed circumstances, at which point buying more things simply stopped making them any happier.[34]

In his book *The Battle,* Arthur Brooks of the American Enterprise Institute described a study with similar findings:

In 1978, researchers at the University of Michigan tracked down and interviewed a group of major lottery winners. They found that although the newly rich experienced an immediate boost to their cheeriness, their mood darkened within months to levels around where they were to begin with.[35]

But there's worse news. The initial high that came from winning actually reduced the impact of simple pleasures—things like talking with a friend, getting a compliment, or buying clothes.

"If not money, then what do people really crave?" Brooks asks in his most recent book, *The Road to Freedom.* "The answer is *earned success,* the ability to create value with your life or in the lives of others. It does not come from a lottery check or an inheritance. . . . To earn your success is to define and pursue your happiness as you see fit."[36]

INDEPENDENCE (AND AVERSION TO HANDOUTS)

Achieving independence from welfare seems to be more a matter of individual decision than of public policy. But low-income individuals seeking to earn their own way do cluster in several categories. One consists of that very significant number of Americans who so dislike the idea of being dependent that they hurry to get out of welfare programs. Another—easily identifiable—comprises immigrants. A third, which we are labeling *barterers*, consists of people who achieve independence mostly through cashless transactions.

In 2004, nine years into the 1996 welfare reform changes, Jason DeParle's book *American Dream—Three Women, Ten Kids, and a Nation's Drive to End Welfare*[37] chronicled the seven years he spent observing the experiences of three women and their ten children as they moved from welfare to work. DeParle, a reporter for the *New York Times*, found that none of the women wanted to return to the welfare rolls. One of them, Angie Jobe, expressed a particular determination to continue working—and not go back on welfare—despite some leading questions from a member of Congress during a radio interview:

> **Angie Jobe:** No, I don't want to stop working.
>
> **Rep. Gwen Moore:** Not even if it meant you could take a semester off and get your GED?
>
> **Angie:** I enjoy working. That's what I get up for. You know, it just makes me feel good . . . to know I can get out and do something to help my kids.[38]

Several people we met expressed similar attitudes. Connie, a mother of two in Decatur, Georgia, who recently lost her job and ended up on TANF, couldn't wait to get off. "I just have to keep telling myself it's temporary. It's here for a reason, and I will take advantage of all the training and job placement assistance I can get, but I want to get off as soon as possible. It should definitely be temporary—no one should look to welfare like 'I'm gonna live on it for life.' That isn't any way to live or raise children."

Tanisha, who was working as a bartender on the waterfront in Washington, DC, told us: "I was on welfare for a while when I first had my son. I hated it but I didn't have a choice. During the recession my boyfriend and I both lost our jobs. Those were tough days, but we both knew pretty quick welfare wasn't for us. We're too independent to be happy relying on handouts. As soon as we could find jobs, even before we got our first paychecks I think, we went down and told the social worker to take us off, we didn't want it. We could have stayed on for a while, but it just didn't feel right to us. We're young, able-bodied, and taking welfare seems like giving up."

Jeanine, a mother of four grown children living in rural Washington State, echoed the sentiment. "I went on welfare when I left my husband. I was a battered wife, I had been a stay-at-home mom for years, and when I left he emptied our accounts. I was grateful for the welfare support, even though it was grueling meeting all their rules and standards, but pretty soon I started to feel guilty—I mean, I had two teenage sons, two middle school daughters, there was no reason we couldn't come up with jobs. So I went back to college and got a teaching certificate, and my sons got jobs in construction, and one day we all decided we were done with dealing with those offices, we wanted to be free of that yoke. We've never looked back."

"Early on I saw my choices as a single teen mom with two kids," Shari, a California realtor, told us. "I could go on the dole, or get to work. I went to work, and did what I needed to do to take care of my kids. I raised three kids, never took a dime from the government. That's the American way, right?"

What is the difference between these women and people who feel trapped on reservations? The reasons are almost infinitely complex, but those people who resist welfare dependency, who are simply uncomfortable in that condition, surely sense that a good life means earned accomplishment. They know, somehow, that there is no happiness without effort and that fending for oneself is a key to life's satisfactions. We found that people on welfare, with few exceptions, also sense these things; their dependency is enervating: it undermines their dignity and self-respect. It often makes them angry. Most welfare recipients want to work, and many work at part-time jobs and often off the books for reasons detailed earlier, which means that they are not counted as working. But of course knowing that it's important to get off or stay off welfare is not the same as accomplishing that.

There is a phenomenon at work here that Professor Charles Hynam at the University of Alberta calls the dysfunctionality of unrequited giving. "An outright gift without any question of repayment is a . . . violation of the norm of reciprocity," he asserts. "Giving in a situation where the receiver cannot repay creates reciprocal imbalance. . . . [Thus], unwittingly, a form of exploitation can result from giving with the purest of motives."[39] Although Hynam was focusing on individuals who give and get charitable contributions, his point about the harmful imbalance between giver and receiver holds true within the welfare system for welfare recipients, who can never expect to repay what they receive. The ablest welfare recipients do what they can to right this imbalance, to make themselves something more than passive recipients. Some do this by getting off welfare, some by working at something, anything. In an interview with National Public Radio in 2013 an employee at Walmart showed her determination to be an equal even though she depended on welfare. "I *earn* my food stamps!" she asserted.[40]

Others just get angry, or depressed. It feels good to be needed; it feels bad to be dependent. The best private charities recognize this and demand program participation—usually work—from those being helped. See, for example, the description of the Doe Fund in chapter 13. Or imagine a soup kitchen where the beneficiaries are asked to bus their own dishes or clean up, acts of participation that might make them feel a bit more equal.

Former Florida representative Steve Southerland has long focused on this sort of welfare issue. In 2013, the *Washington Post* reported on a conversation between him and a welfare recipient that shows him searching for reciprocal acts to help balance the scales between giver and receiver. Noting that she had raised three children on food stamps, an older mother in the audience told Southerland: "I've been through dark times. I needed help, and I got it. Is that wrong?" "I believe if you're going to eat you should bring something to the table," Southerland replied. "That can be volunteering, that can be delivering meals on wheels. But somehow you've got to contribute."[41]

IMMIGRANTS

A 2012 National Bureau of Economic Research paper compared sources of income in 2009 in households with children below the poverty line for immigrants and for nonimmigrant Americans. Marianne Bitler and Hilary Hoynes, the paper's authors, found that more than 70% of income came from earnings in low-income immigrants' households. For equally low-income nonimmigrant citizens, only 45% of household income was from earnings, with the balance coming from welfare payments, particularly food stamps.[42]

One of the most remarkable things we noticed in our travels was the number of immigrants hard at work. While the economy struggled to shake off the worst of the recession, these immigrants (especially undocumented immigrants), who usually can't qualify for welfare programs, were busy scraping together all manner of paid employment—driving taxis, doing lawn work, harvesting plastic bottles from trash cans, cleaning houses. In Chicago, we met a cab driver from Ethiopia who had been in the United States for seven years. "When I got here there were some ladies who came and talked to us at our church and said they could give us some assistance, and then they got out a big stack of papers and started asking all manner of personal questions," he told us. "This is not right. I will not give them my freedom. I came here to work, not to have to answer to someone else. I take no handouts, I work to take care of myself and my family, and this makes me a man. Those people living on welfare, that is not living, that is not a life."

Taking an early morning walk through a park in Harlem, we met a Latino man pushing a stroller with two children in tow. In the stroller was an enormous plastic bag bulging with plastic bottles; the man was checking the trash cans lining the park, removing all the recyclable plastic bottles that could be exchanged for cash. His children were along for the walk, playing in the park, pointing out places to look, and as the bag filled to bursting, helping by filling smaller plastic bags with more bottles. "I am the father of these children," he said. "I show them there are many ways to make money here, if you just try. This is what I want them to learn. Some day they will be American citizens, and they will get good jobs, but until then, they know we can find ways to eat and live from our own hands."

Visiting Mt. Rushmore in the Black Hills of South Dakota, we hit upon a concession stand in the walkway leading to the monument, selling drinks and hot dogs in the 100 degree heat. The young men behind the counter told us they were cousins who had found their way to South Dakota from Russia. They had somehow managed to get a permit for their stand and could barely keep up with demand. "We had one uncle who ended up here in South Dakota, and he managed to get us all here, and now we all work and live together," one said. "It's hard work, we stay open as many hours as we can. We pool our earnings to pay rent for our apartment and for the car we share. We are making very good money. It is not glamorous, but it is a start. Someday we will be sitting behind the desks at our big chain of restaurants, but for now, we work."

In Oxnard, California, we met the owner of a honey bee business who maintains hives all over the country. "I tried and tried to hire Americans," he said. "I pay good money. It is a hard job, but it's a good job, tending the hives. Too hard for Americans, I guess. Sometimes I wouldn't get a single response to my ads. I finally gave up and started sponsoring workers from Nicaragua. Now my entire crew comes up from there. They enter on work visas, work the season, and then head back home. Sure, I'd rather hire Americans, but I can't find any."

It is often argued that immigrants do the work Americans are no longer willing to do (and perhaps, shouldn't "have" to do). But until very recently, those were the same jobs that most Americans expected their teenage children to spend summers doing.

"Any job is better than no job," notes Michael Tanner at the Cato Institute. "And a key indicator of future success is the willingness to take any job and stick with it. Immigrants appear to have inherited the work ethic that many Americans are giving up on."[43]

BARTERERS

Every year there are dozens of festivals and gatherings that attract hundreds of thousands of participants who are drawn to the idea of radical individual liberty, independent communities, and self-sufficiency through barter. These range from the Barter Festival in Washington State to the Country Fair in Eugene, Oregon. The most well known is Burning Man, a week-long event in the Nevada desert that hosts 50,000 "burners." They represent a particular sort of self-sufficiency.

"I don't have much money, but I have a network of people that I can absolutely trust to help me out if I need help," said Annie in Sedro-Wooley, Washington. "I always have a place to stay, and I always find a way to barter and trade for what I need. I work as a DJ, and I knit, and I have a sewing machine, and those skills can be traded for lots of other things."

Like the women who talked about getting off welfare quickly, people who join these support networks feel better when they are self-reliant and are contributing to their community. They don't want to be independent from their friends, neighbors, and trading partners; rather they choose to take part in reciprocal arrangements where they can contribute their fair share.

Bartering is also common in poor neighborhoods of inner cities, where many people manage to stay afloat without welfare support in the hidden, underground economy. Estimates are hard to come by, but judging by the experiences Sudhir Alladi Venkatesh reports in *Off the Books: The Underground Economy of the Urban Poor*, the underground economy is both substantial and intricate. Venkatesh spent two decades studying a small neighborhood in inner-city Chicago, and the stories he tells of residents' creative ways of paying the bills reveal a vast, interwoven web of economic exchange, the "product of perpetual negotiations, of collusion and compromise, of the constant struggle to survive, to find purpose for your life, to fulfill your desires, to feed your family."[44]

Off the Books describes a fascinating variety of work, barter, and trade arrangements, some legal, some not: tenants who pay the rent by baby-sitting for the landlord; pastors who place maids with wealthy church members in exchange for a 10% cut of the earnings (or, sometimes, for sexual favors in lieu of cash); landlords who rent their houses out to gangs to process drugs; mothers who trade driving for babysitting, or home-cooked meals for oil changes; and mechanics who trade their automotive skills for the right to park and work on cars in parking spots in front of houses. The ways these residents cover their expenses and manage to support themselves are endless.[45]

One of the women Venkatesh interviewed had lived on welfare for years but hated it. Today, she trades and sells home-cooked meals, an underground, cash-only business she runs out of her kitchen. It has become so successful that she now pays her children's public school teachers $20 a day to let her kids ditch school at midday so they can help deliver lunches, an interesting example of how this underground economy interacts with the above-ground one, with sometimes dubious results.

There are other downsides to the underground economy, of course. As Venkatesh concludes, "the underground enables poor communities to survive but can lead to their alienation from the wider world. For groups and organizations, as well as individuals, surviving in the ghetto via shady means can result in their overall removal from the [economic life of the] city."[46] Still, these residents, in difficult circumstances, come up with ways to make the rent, feed the kids, and participate in the life of their community. In the most fundamental sense they are earning their way.

PATTERNS IN THE BROADER POPULATION

How far should public policy go when it comes to encouraging work? There is little doubt that people seek work more urgently when faced with a cutoff of government benefits. In 2014, the North Carolina unemployment rate dropped noticeably when the legislature ended unemployment benefits (though the drop was partly due to dropouts from the workforce).[47] Similarly, the employment rate in Tennessee ticked upward after the state in 2005 took 170,000 adults off Medicaid.[48] A National Bureau of Economic Research (NBER) paper in 2015 analyzed the nationwide impact on jobs and work when the recession-induced extensions in unemployment benefits were abruptly cut off by Congress at the end of 2013. The authors found that a drop in the duration of unemployment benefits led to a significant increase of employment: "1.8 million additional jobs were created in 2014 due to the benefit cut. Almost 1 million of these jobs were filled by workers from out of the labor force who would not have participated in the labor market had benefit extensions been reauthorized."[49]

"Some people need a real push," noted Patty Smith, a social welfare official we interviewed in Champagne County, Illinois. Sometimes that push may require that we make welfare less comfortable, or that we limit its duration.

"Not having to work is a problem," notes Barbara Blovin, who studies inherited wealth, which, like other unearned income, "can fatally undermine any sense of purpose, any reason for doing anything at all."[50]

If people are forced to work in order to survive, do they end up happier? Less poor? Is society better off? These are vital questions for welfare policy makers in America. If it weren't for most Americans' antipathy to being on welfare, the present system would be pushing us dangerously close to an untenable welfare state.

"There is nothing to suggest that people on welfare are lazy," notes Cato's Michael Tanner. "But there is also nothing to suggest that they are stupid. If you pay someone as much for not working as you do for working, it should come as no surprise that many take advantage of the offer."[51]

Chapter 13

What Should Be Done: From Incentives to Special Savings Accounts, Solutions Abound to Get Americans Back to Work

Welfare doesn't end poverty; work does—Yair Lapid, Israeli finance minister

We cannot solve our problems using the same thinking we used when we created them—Albert Einstein

In our trips around the country to meet welfare recipients, we also talked with the social workers and service providers who work on the inside, implementing these programs on the ground. Toward the end of our conversations, whether with recipients or administrators, we discussed solutions. Everyone was eager to talk about possible fixes to the programs they knew, and everyone wanted to know what our conclusions and recommendations would be. "How are you going to fix these problems?" said Caroline, a veteran social worker who spent her career working all over the Midwest. "My clients didn't want welfare, most of them, and they'd be happy to work if they could, but the system is full of barriers to employment. It always seemed like such a waste to me, all these wasted lives that could have had meaning and purpose."

What follows includes a variety of recommendations—some simple, some complex, some easy, some hard—that respond to today's welfare problems. Taken together, they offer an alternative vision with a focus on work, which we believe is the key to a better system for America's poor. The most promising recommendations from scholars, thinkers, authors, and others are included along with many ideas and recommendations arising from our own work.

The recommendations are arranged in three categories:

Section 1. Strategies and programs related to work and to making work pay off.
Section 2. Strategies that promote work and reduce welfare indirectly.
Section 3. Strategies to alleviate poverty and thus reduce welfare.

SECTION 1. STRATEGIES AND PROGRAMS RELATED TO WORK AND TO MAKING WORK PAY OFF

Our main proposal for welfare reform is to make work more profitable for those on the lower levels of the wage scale. This can be accomplished by supplementing the wages of low-income workers and/or by reducing or eliminating the taxes they must pay. Specific steps include fixing the Earned Income Tax Credit (EITC), reducing or eliminating FICA taxes on all low-income earners, and instituting an across-the-board program to subsidize wages on a sliding scale for low-income workers.

Fix the EITC

The EITC, which already acts as a significant work incentive, has produced generally positive results and is favored by parties across the political spectrum. But the program has flaws, and we recommend three steps that would improve it.

First, the EITC should be available to the childless at about the same rate as it is now available to those with one child. This simple step would improve many lives by drawing more childless people into work and removing welfare-related incentives to have children. It would also reduce welfare fraud, since claiming bogus children would have much less payoff. Two scholars at the Brookings Institution recommend "a tripling of the childless EITC to $1,625, while requiring recipients to work more hours to qualify."[1] President Obama promoted this change in his second State of the Union speech, praising the EITC but noting that it does far too little for those who don't have children. Second, the EITC should focus more on the poor by setting the maximum income level for EITC benefits a little below $40,000 (in 2015 dollars) and phasing out benefits for people with earnings above that figure. Present limits go as high as $49,000. Third, we see no reason to withhold income taxes from low-income taxpayers. The EITC should be structured so that earned money stays in their pockets, providing more immediate rewards for working and counteracting the tendency to splurge with refund checks.

It would be quite simple to set a standard, perhaps $1,000 a month, below which no federal income taxes would be withheld. In a few cases, low-wage employees might end the year owing taxes, in which case they would be required to pay them. It would also help a great deal if more employers paid better wages at the lower end of the scale. In early 2015, the CEO of Aetna, the insurance giant, announced that the company's lowest-paid workers would get a substantial wage increase—from $12 to $16 an hour in some cases.[2] Many employers have found that more generous wages have paid for themselves through reduced turnover and better employee morale. As James Surowiecki observed in *The New Yorker*, "A substantial body of research suggests that it can make sense to pay above-market wages—economists call them 'efficiency wages.' If you pay people better they are more likely to stay, which saves money. . . . Better-paid employees tend to work harder, too."[3] While there may be some wishful thinking here, it does work for some.

Eliminate or Reduce FICA Taxes

FICA taxes are job killers. Penalizing employers for hiring and employees for working, they deduct 6.2% of an employee's earnings for Social Security and another 1.45% for Medicare, even when the employee is a poverty-level worker.[4] The elimination of the FICA tax has a good deal of support. Then–House Ways and Means Committee chairman Dave Camp put forward a proposal in 2014 that included a rebate of employees' FICA tax payments as a partial replacement for the EITC.[5] Earlier, former Treasury secretary Lawrence Summers proposed a reduction in that tax to 3%.[6] And in 2014, *New York Times* columnist Ross Douthat observed:

> Payroll taxes are a relic of New Deal Machiavellianism: by taking a bit of every worker's paycheck and promising postretirement returns, Franklin Roosevelt effectively disguised Social Security as a pay-as-you-go system, even though the program actually redistributes from rich to poor and young to old. . . . But the costs of this disguise have grown too great to bear. . . . It makes no sense to finance our retirement system with a tax that falls directly on wages and hiring and imposes particular burdens on small business and the working class.[7]

It would also make sense to eliminate FICA taxes paid by employers on poverty-level workers. Most Americans, nearly all economists, and voices from the entire political spectrum consistently call for more jobs as the fundamental cure for our economic (and other) ills; in this context it seems nonsensical to slap a tax on employers for hiring people. Most economists also believe that if employers did not have to pay their half of the FICA tax (also 6.2% + 1.45%), they would pay their low-wage employees more.[8]

In any event, eliminating the FICA tax on low-income workers would have several salutary consequences. Currently, the counterproductive results of the tax include transferring wealth from today's younger workers to the retired elderly, many of whom are wealthier than the workers. Households headed by people over 75 have the highest net worth of any American age group.[9] "Yes, they say it's for when I get old," said Twan, a checker at a Virginia Safeway. "But they keep bumping the retirement age up so it's like a carrot you can never actually reach. And I hear the money is going to run out in 15 years or something, so basically I'm paying so old people now get a retirement but there isn't going to be anything in there for me when I retire."

The FICA payroll tax system also penalizes high school graduates and dropouts who start work at a younger age than their college-bound peers. Because they begin paying into the system sooner than higher-income earners, and because they die earlier on average,[10] they reap fewer benefits at the end of life. Today's Social Security system could never be enacted by a contemporary Congress, Milton Friedman observed a few years ago.[11] It is much too regressive.

Of course the poor should not be eliminated from the Social Security system as long as it continues to function. Funds lost through FICA tax elimination would therefore have to be made up from other sources. But this is not as radical a step as it sounds. First, for most of its beneficiaries, the present EITC system refunds or rebates more than enough to offset FICA anyway, so a simple adjustment to the EITC payment could cover the tax shortfall, easing the FICA burden on employers. Second, the United States had a 2% partial FICA elimination on all taxpayers during 2011 and 2012. Employees paid only a 4.2% payroll tax in those years instead of 6.2%.[12] The change was instituted as part of the postrecession recovery plan and, while this step increased the budget deficit, neither Democrats nor Republicans raised serious objections. Eliminating all of the tax for the poor would promote jobs and work, with more taxpayers chipping in as a result.

Subsidize Wages on a Sliding Scale for Low-Income Workers

We would take the amended EITC one step further and provide a straightforward across-the-board wage subsidization program. A formula could be set so that people who work for, say, $8 an hour would have that amount increased by 30%–90% depending on hours worked during the year. This would make entry-level work dramatically more attractive, turning a full-time minimum-wage equivalent (roughly $17,000 in 2015) into an annual income of $22,000 (see Table 13.1). People making $20,000 a year in unsubsidized wages would be entitled to a 17% increment for a total of $23,400. The formula would be set so that additional work would always result in more income even as the subsidy diminishes. We suggest that the subsidies be paid monthly to bring the payments close to the work effort, but subsidy payments could also be tied to the filing of an annual income tax return as they are currently with the EITC.

Table 13.1   Suggested Scale for Supplementing the Wages of Low-Income Workers

Proposed additions to annual earnings (in 2014 dollars)		
Earnings	**Program Adds**	**Resulting Pay**
$5,000	$5,000	$10,000
6,000	6,000	12,000
7,000	6,000	13,000
8,000	6,000	14,000
9,000	6,000	15,000
10,000	6,000	16,000
11,000	6,000	17,000
12,000	6,000	18,000
13,000	6,000	19,000
14,000	5,800	19,800
15,000	5,600	20,600
16,000	5,300	21,300
17,000	4,900	21,900
18,000	4,400	22,400
19,000	3,900	22,900
20,000	3,400	23,400
21,000	2,900	23,900
22,000	2,400	24,400
23,000	1,800	24,800
24,000	1,100	25,100
25,000	400	25,400
26,000	0	26,000

The program could be administered by employers, who would be getting a very good deal by having more and higher level employees than they would otherwise be able to afford.

While we believe these plans for supplementary earned wages constitute the best pro-work, antipoverty public policies, they inevitably have some antiwork impact during phase-out. In Table 13.1, for example, a worker whose earned wages go from $16,000 to $17,000 loses $400 in subsidies in the process. Thus, while the worker's total income goes up from $21,300 to $21,900, there is no avoiding the fact that she or he is performing work valued at an additional $1,000, while the net result for that effort is $600. This is sometimes referred to as a high marginal tax rate: losing $400 in benefits as $1,000 is added to income is equivalent to a tax of 40%, and this can act as a disincentive to climbing the income ladder. The same problem applies to the phase-out of the FICA tax. Care must be taken to see that the phasing out of the subsidies as earned income increases is never too steep. If the phase-out is gradual and at sufficiently high income levels, it seems likely that most workers will find that they are on a path to a real living wage and keep going.

Another approach to enhancing wages, and one that avoids the phase-out problem, is to pay wage subsidies to employers rather than to workers. That approach is spelled out by Edmund S. Phelps, a Nobel Prize–winning economist, in his 2007 book *Rewarding Work*. Phelps proposes that eligible firms be paid for as many workers as they employ, and he maintains that wage subsidies paid to employers—in amounts similar to those in Table 13.1—would greatly increase hiring, which would, in turn, reduce the available labor supply and thus lead to rising wages. Such a program could work well, but with less immediate impact than one giving payments directly to workers. As both approaches are fairly radical, experimentation would be needed to compare the impact of employer vs. employee payments. A combination of the two might also be considered. In any case we agree with Phelps that "low wage employment subsidies, their imperfections notwithstanding, are the most effective instrument we have available to re-create lost opportunities for work and self-support, to restore inclusion and cohesion, and to reclaim responsibility for oneself and others."[13]

A possible caveat: It can be argued that too many of our citizens are not fully invested in our country or its politics. If 40% of American workers pay no income taxes (as is now the case),[14] a very substantial part of our population is literally not invested in the workings of government. This may be a problem but there appears to be no way to ameliorate it; if we wish to provide supplementary income to our lowest-income citizens, there is no logical way to impose income taxes on them.

Other Improvements

Another category of pro-work welfare improvements entails changes to the rules that govern today's programs. Such changes, discussed below, would include requiring work for benefits, especially food stamps; adjusting overgenerous benefits so they don't exceed minimum-wage pay; letting people earn more before cutting off their benefits; eliminating welfare recruiting; changing rules so as to help the disabled start (or keep) working; offering more apprenticeships; and exploring Opportunity Grants.

Require Work for Benefits

The law authorizing food stamps requires beneficiaries to work—or to be looking for work—but this requirement is practically never enforced. It should be. All other welfare benefits, except those for the truly disabled and some that cover medical costs, should also require work and/or preparation for work. If loopholes that have softened TANF work requirements were closed, if work was (really) required for SNAP, and if the disabled got the help they need to hold jobs, the entire welfare system would be greatly improved. People receiving welfare would be literally working for it; they would, in a very real sense, be earning it, and getting a major boost to their self-respect and their happiness, like the Walmart employee who asserted, "I *earn* my food stamps!"[15] Earned welfare is less of a dole of the kind Roosevelt called a narcotic.[16] And of course enforcing and instituting work requirements would bring welfare costs down markedly as the working option takes hold.

"I *want* to work. My dad *wants* to work," Rebecca told us in the hotel for the homeless in Georgia where she and her father live. "He worked his whole life to raise me, then he got injured, and now he has medical problems. The system just holds you down and makes it so you're better off not working, on the edge of poverty but at least with some security."

Make Welfare Pay Less Than Work

Welfare benefits should be more in line with pay for low-wage work. In at least eight states the dollar value of a typical welfare package in 2013 exceeded that of full-time work at minimum wage, even allowing for EITC.[17] But if nonworking welfare beneficiaries in Hawaii, Massachusetts, and other especially generous states got the lower benefits paid in Pennsylvania or Wisconsin, far fewer potential workers would have to fear taking a cut in after-tax income by getting a job.

Let People Earn

The other side of this coin entails raising the earnings caps for all welfare programs. Welfare beneficiaries should be able to reach a reasonable level of earned income before losing benefits. The SSI (Supplemental Security Income) limit of $85 a month is absurd. Most other programs begin phasing out benefits when beneficiaries reach an earnings level between $750 and $1,100 a month. If welfare programs continue to be structured as they are, we believe that benefits should be phased out more gradually so that fewer welfare beneficiaries would avoid work in fear of the welfare cliff cutoff. This may require some compromise with a more nearly exclusive focus on the truly poor, but only those people who are working and earning would be entitled to benefits when their income is above the poverty line.

Stop Recruiting

As noted in chapter 7, the government pays recruiters to find people who are eligible for welfare and sign them up for benefits. This should stop. Many of the people who are recruited may not need benefits, whether or not they are entitled to them according to published criteria.

"Yeah, my parents give me money for food," said Karl, a University of Washington student in Seattle. "And they pay for my dorm room. And pay my tuition. But some lady set up a table at the farmer's market in the U. District and it's right next to campus. I went over there and she signed me up for food stamps. It's cool, and it's a little extra cash for me, so I spend it at the farmer's market buying organic."

Help the Disabled Keep Working if They Can

David Autor, professor of economics at Massachusetts Institute of Technology, and his colleagues have rigorously analyzed the U.S. disability programs, especially SSDI (Social Security Disability Insurance), and their impact. Their conclusion: The present system pushes the disabled away from work. "[T]he program provides strong incentives to applicants and beneficiaries to remain permanently out of the labor force," they report, "and it provides no incentives to employers to implement cost-effective accommodations that enable employees with work limitations to remain on the job."[18] Autor notes that such policies are at odds with the Americans with Disabilities Act of 1990, which stresses the rights of the disabled to engage fully in society, including in employment, and requires employers to take reasonable steps to accommodate disabled workers.

As noted in chapter 9, the present system makes it very difficult for people disabled on the job to successfully apply for SSDI or SSI benefits if they continue working. And if they don't work during the normal period when their cases are under review—typically a year or more—they will probably lose work contacts, work skills, and work habits, making the slide into permanent dependency more likely.

During our travels we met people living on disability benefits, and in most cases their story was the same. The wait to get on disability is so long, they said, that by the time they got approved their old jobs were gone and they had been out of the workforce too long to be attractive candidates for employers. To turn these incentives around, Autor and Duggan recommend adding a "front end" to the SSDI system with "workplace accommodations, rehabilitation services, partial income support, and other services to workers who suffer work limitations, with the goal of enabling them to remain in employment," and they also recommend providing financial incentives to encourage employers to accommodate workers who become disabled and minimize the chances that those workers will move from their payrolls onto the SSDI system. The authors propose doing this with the addition of an inexpensive private disability insurance system, which could be added to the present SSDI structure. Private disability coverage is already common in the workplace and in this context would pay for itself many times over by helping millions of workers to stay in or regain employment.

Provide More Apprenticeships

Many European countries—including both Germany and England—invest in apprenticeships to train young people and put them on a pathway to permanent work. Authors Stuart Eizenstat and Robert Lerman suggest that the United States could quadruple current apprenticeship slots to great benefit.[19] Apprentice pathways to employment are appropriate for people who work in manufacturing, chefs and bakers, computer network administrators, commercial sales representatives, health technicians, and others, they say. "[Apprentices] have a chance to gain and demonstrate skills such as reliability, teamwork, and problem solving—all while earning money instead of borrowing it."[20] Apprenticeships also provide an effective way of getting young people connected with employers, who are the ones who know what skills are needed for the current economy.

Explore Opportunity Grants

Congressman Paul Ryan's Opportunity Grant is a relatively new entrant among proposed welfare reforms. Then–chairman of the House Budget

Committee, Ryan outlined his plan in remarks at the American Enterprise Institute in July 2014. The plan has much to recommend it. The experimental approach he advocates would send the states funds representing the cost of 11 federal programs to use for experimental, personalized poverty relief programs. The test programs would have to adhere to the following principles:

- The funds must be spent on the poor.
- Every person who can work should work.
- Whether through state agencies, nonprofits, or for-profits, there must be options offered to the beneficiaries.
- Results must be measured.[21]

Because Ryan puts a good deal of emphasis on personalized services in contrast to the one-size-fits-all nature of federal programs, his approach would be costly and it would probably require even more caseworkers (or their equivalents in the private sector) than welfare programs have now. This is not ideal. Critics of the plan are particularly concerned about sweeping SNAP into what looks like a block grant, fearing that SNAP beneficiaries could suffer. Still, many features of the plan represent improvements over the present system and, with its emphasis on experimentation and measurement, it should result in a lot of successful initiatives that could be widely adopted.

SECTION 2. STRATEGIES THAT PROMOTE WORK AND REDUCE WELFARE INDIRECTLY

Another set of strategies would promote work less directly but in important ways. The first among these are policies that make it easier for employers to hire people and for entrepreneurs to start new businesses. These include better control of onerous regulations, backing off on dysfunctional licensing requirements, ameliorating mandates on employers, reducing or eliminating the corporate income tax, and helping workers find work by moving. In addition, there are powerful arguments for delivering more of our welfare through private institutions.

Help Employers Create Jobs

America recently fell to seventeenth place as a good country to do business in, according to the Fraser Institute's Index of Economic Freedom, having fallen from third place at the beginning of this century.[22] Although the United States is becoming increasingly unfriendly to business, and especially to small businesses whose owners have no friends in high places, more than 550,000 new businesses are started every year and they employ millions of Americans, including many who are working for the first time. Unfortunately regulations and other legal requirements are making this process harder and harder.

Back Off on Onerous Regulations

Statistics vary, depending on definitions, but the costs of regulation on U.S. employers—especially on small businesses—are huge. According to one report, "In 2013 Washington imposed an additional $112 billion in regulatory costs and 157.9 million paperwork burden hours on Americans."[23] That year "80,224 pages of regulations were added to the *Federal Register,* a 3.8 percent increase over 2012,"[24] while the number of economically significant regulations increased by 25% and the number of rules imposing unfunded mandates on states or private entities grew by 38%.

A major source of new regulations, the Dodd-Frank law, enacted in 2010, has become a paperwork nightmare for financial institutions. Companies struggling to conform to this law, and the hundreds of regulations that go with it, are never quite sure what it requires. Four years after its passage, its regulations were still being promulgated.

The Occupational Safety and Health Administration is also famous for its regulations and requirements. Some years back, a brick factory was cited for having certain railings 40 inches high, instead of the regulation 42 inches. In the same factory, managers were required to put up POISON signs in a shed storing bags of ordinary sand. (Under entirely different conditions, the silica in sand was considered problematic.[25]) OSHA seems more concerned with regulation compliance than with common sense. Accordingly, the most common OSHA violation is failure to keep paperwork correctly.

The case of Marty the Magician illustrates nonsensical regulations run amok. Marty Hahne has a magic act for young children that features a rabbit named Casey. Under the Animal Welfare Act, the rabbit requires a license and the regulations don't stop there. The inspectors who initially imposed licensing requirements on Marty have now visited his home *ten times*, unannounced, to force him to comply with all relevant regulations, including the 30-page disaster plan for Casey in the event of a blizzard, tornado, or fire.[26]

On a broad scale, overregulation is making a big dent in the number of well-paid manufacturing jobs, especially for men. A recent National Association of Manufacturers study noted that the average U.S. manufacturer spends $19,564 per employee each year to comply with regulations,[27] nearly twice the cost incurred by nonmanufacturing companies. Small manufacturers have an even tougher time; those with fewer than 50 employees pay an estimated $34,671 per worker.[28] "If you're a small business you're getting a double whammy from the cost of regulation," said economist W. Mark Crain, one of the study's authors.[29] What's needed is far more rigorous review of the costs, benefits, and reasonableness of both new and old regulations.

Eliminate Dysfunctional Licensing Requirements

Similarly, licensing requirements and a number of other government mandates should be reviewed and reformed. Imposed mainly by state and local governments, licensing requirements make it especially difficult for entrepreneurial workers to make a living. Back in the 1950s, only one out of every 20 workers needed a license to work. Today, that number has jumped to one in three, according to the Institute for Justice, a nonpartisan, public interest law firm.[30] Even the most harmless activities can be subjected to stringent licensing requirements. Until IJ won a lawsuit in 2012, hair braiders in Utah were required to take 2,000 hours of cosmetology training, which cost $16,000 and didn't even include hair braiding.

Eliminating unnecessary licensing requirements would create new jobs and lower prices for consumers, all at no cost to the taxpayer. Morris Kleiner, the AFL-CIO chair and professor at the University of Minnesota, estimated that "licensing results in 2.85 million fewer jobs with an annual cost to consumers of $203 billion." Scaling back occupational licensing "could translate into significantly higher employment, better job matches, and improved customer satisfaction."[31]

Ease Up on Employer Mandates

Government mandates usually mean fewer jobs, too. The more government demands that businesses provide to their employees, the more expensive it is for employers to hire people. Consider, for instance, the Affordable Care Act. In the past, many employers provided health care voluntarily, but the Affordable Care Act made that mandatory, increasing the cost of employment for almost all employers.[32] In 2015 a health insurance premium for a family of four averaged over $15,000, more than a lot of workers are worth, noted economist Tyler Cowen.[33]

Or consider wage mandates. A higher minimum wage will help some workers (although most of them will not be from poor households), but employers will have to take those wages into account when hiring. Higher mandated wages and benefits not only mean fewer jobs at the very bottom of the scale, they also push employers to automation and offshoring.

Eliminate or Reduce the Corporate Income Tax

Doing away with the corporate income tax sounds like a benefit for the wealthy, but it could save and create a significant number of jobs. This tax is a major reason for the loss of many American jobs to workers overseas and the vulnerability of those exportable jobs depresses wages here at home. Professor Laurence Kotlikoff of Boston University has made a powerful case for abolishing the tax:

Fully eliminating the corporate income tax and replacing any loss in revenue with somewhat higher personal income tax rates leads to a huge short-run inflow of capital, raising the United States' capital stock (machines and buildings) by 23 percent, output by 8 percent and the real wages of unskilled and skilled workers by 12 percent. Lowering the corporate rate tax to 9 percent while also closing loopholes is roughly revenue neutral and also produces very rapid increases in capital (by 17 percent), output (by 6 percent) and real wages (by 8 percent).[34]

Help Workers Find Work by Moving

In our travels around the country we often asked the people we met whether they had considered moving to places with better employment prospects, and we were surprised to find that very few had. "It's just too hard," said Devon, an unemployed demolition worker in the Bronx. "Once you get signed up for all the benefits and get yourself all situated and go through all that paperwork, you kinda feel like you don't want to move because it is going to cause so much trouble with all the different offices. Even moving apartments, having to do change of address, can lead to a suspension of benefits." Here again, welfare inertia acts as a barrier to paid employment.

As Arthur Brooks of the American Enterprise Institute has pointed out, though:

[The] government could help cover costs for chronically unemployed Americans to move to areas with more plentiful opportunities. Obviously, not everyone will pick up and move, however generous the voucher. But at a time when economic conditions vary widely between regions, the opportunity is a powerful one. Thousands of low-income families would probably prefer to pursue hope and prosperity in booming states such as North Dakota (where unemployment sits at 2.6 percent [in 2013]) than continue cashing government checks and despairing in say, Michigan (8.7 percent) or Rhode Island (9.0 percent). Relocation might well offer the spark they need to begin rebuilding their resumes—and their lives.[35]

Privatize Welfare

There are many advocates of privatization of the welfare system, and many arguments that support them. Much welfare assistance, of course, already comes from the private sector. Of America's 1.8 million charitable organizations, a substantial fraction are active in efforts to assist America's poor, and many more easily could be. Approximately $80 billion in donations is spent on these private efforts each year, plus an unspecified portion of the $96 billion donated to religious institutions. Total charitable giving in the U.S. exceeds $300 billion annually.[36] We believe that our welfare system would be improved if a larger share of welfare money came from non-government sources. Here are some of the reasons:

First, locally focused assistance for the poor is much more personalized than a one-size-fits-all policy originating from Washington or a state capital. Government welfare must treat all people equally, regardless of their circumstances. In a hospital setting, commentators John C. Goodman and Michael D. Stroup suggest, "no one in his right mind would recommend that the chronically ill be given the same medical treatment as the short-stay patient, or that all short-stay patients . . . be treated in the same way, regardless of medical condition. Yet that is precisely the way the federal government runs the welfare state."[37]

Michael Tanner provides a simple example: "[A] poor person . . . has a job offer. But she can't get to the job because her car battery is dead. A government welfare program can do nothing but tell her to wait two weeks until her welfare [check] arrives. Of course, by that time the job will be gone. A private charity can simply go out and buy a car battery (or even jump-start the dead battery)."[38]

In addition to being more personalized and focused, private charity is more efficient. "[W]hen spending decisions are made through the political process, it is inevitable that powerfully organized special interests have considerable influence over how the dollars are spent," Goodman and Stroup point out. "Thus, it is no accident that [much] federal welfare spending ultimately ends up in the pockets of people who are distinctly not poor."[39] Administrative costs paid to caseworkers, recruiters, food retailers, lawyers, and health care administrators eat up a good deal of the government's welfare budget, and these groups are effective at lobbying. Private charities are less susceptible to political pressures and far more likely to spend most of their resources on the needy beneficiaries of their programs, with a minimum of red tape.

A further advantage to private welfare support is that it is often easier to get but harder to keep getting. "Most government programs, by contrast, have the opposite characteristic: It's hard to get on welfare, but once on it, it's easy to stay there,"[40] in the words of Goodman and Stroup.

A quick thought experiment underlines the fundamental point: Contemplating a personal donation to help the poor, how many of us would voluntarily make a charitable contribution to SNAP or TANF? We all know, in our heart of hearts, that private charities do a better job.

An important, intangible value of private charity stems from the fact that it is voluntary. When we contribute our hard-earned dollars to a private charity we are being personally generous. Often we are taking part in our own local communities, sharing our spirit with our fellow Americans. Tax dollars, however, are coerced from us. Even if we submit cheerfully to taxation, paying taxes is not an act of personal generosity. Instead of displacing local initiatives, as government-funded welfare tends to do, privatizing welfare enhances them. In a remarkable passage from the papal encyclical *Centesimus Annus*, Pope John Paul II eloquently summed up this principle:

> By intervening directly and depriving society of its responsibility, the welfare state leads to a loss of human energies and an inordinate increase in public agencies, which are dominated more by bureaucratic ways of thinking than by concern for serving their clients, and which are accompanied by an enormous increase in spending. In fact, it would appear that needs are best understood and satisfied by people who are closest to them and who act as neighbors to those in need.[41]

A fairly simple formula for privatization, suggested by Goodman and Stroup, Tanner, and others, would permit taxpayers to designate part of their taxes—perhaps part of the portion normally used by government for welfare programs—directly to qualified private charities and to deduct that amount from their tax bills. For every contribution dollar so designated, one dollar would be deducted from federal welfare budgets.

This would immediately increase the funds flowing to private charitable organizations. Those organizations would have to compete, as they do now, for contributions, and they would be accountable to their donors for helping our neediest citizens in a dignified and efficient manner.

Some Sample Programs in the Private Sector

Literally thousands of private charities and programs across the country currently help the poor, especially the very poor. These programs, free of government control and oversight, are generally focused on bringing people out of poverty. A few examples:

- *The Center for Neighborhood Enterprise* is headed by Bob Woodson, a man who is skeptical about most poverty programs. "Around 70 cents of every dollar designated to relieve poverty goes not to poor people but to people who serve the poor," he notes. CNE's approach relies heavily on faith-based remedies, especially for drug addicts and former prisoners. The organization has trained 2,500 grassroots leaders in thirty-nine states and has an excellent record of rehabilitating some of the most difficult-to-reach populations.[42]

- *Year Up*, a training program for low-income people who are "determined" to move up, is funded by the same corporations that hire many of the program's graduates. Participants undergo intensive technical training and training in social skills. Eighty-five percent of the trainees who complete the program go on to college and most have a job waiting when they get out.[43]

- The *Doe Fund* in New York City runs a successful program for homeless men. Program participants must work—"You get up every day and stay drug-free [and do your job] and we will pay you and house you and feed you," says the couple in charge. Rules are strict and the jobs—cleaning and maintaining commercial strips all over the city—are real. More than half the men who complete the six-month program get continuing jobs at $10+/hour.[44]

Such initiatives should be encouraged.

It is tempting to suggest that more government welfare spending should go through private charities. However, charitable organizations that receive large parts of their revenue from the government begin to lose their private nature so that many of the strengths of privatization can be undermined. With more government involvement, politicians, lobbyists, and local government employees move in. Charities heavily dependent on government funds fear losing those funds and adopt practices they believe the government (and government stakeholders) favor. While we are chary of regulations generally, we favor restricting tax-favored contributions to charities that get no more than one-third of their revenue from governments.

A more radical move to privatization would simply phase out government-funded welfare, all $680 billion of it (counting only federal expenditures), and rely on private charities and private initiatives to fill the gap. This could work better than most people think. It would not take nearly as much money to do the same job without that army of almost two million bureaucrats, inspectors, and caseworkers. Further, communities and organizations (and volunteers) of all kinds would step up to the plate. "When government says it will take some of the trouble out of doing things that families and communities evolved to do," notes Charles Murray, "it inevitably takes some of the action away from families and communities."[45]

SECTION 3. STRATEGIES TO ALLEVIATE POVERTY AND THUS REDUCE WELFARE

Alleviating poverty has been a millennia-long quest. Countless ideas have been put forward over the centuries, and many are relevant today. One approach is to provide people with money directly with no strings attached. Others include focusing our welfare resources more firmly on the poor, ending our current policies for mass incarceration of nonviolent offenders, putting greater emphasis on birth control, and addressing the many issues surrounding the deterioration of the two-parent family.

Provide Money

Many of those who address issues of poverty have concluded, not un-reasonably, that poverty problems can be solved by giving people money. If the poverty income line is $11,700 (as it was in 2014), then providing sufficient funds so that everyone receives something close to this amount would eliminate poverty virtually by definition.

The idea behind such plans has been discussed for centuries. It was first mentioned in Sir Thomas More's *Utopia*,[46] when the traveler Raphael Nonsenso suggests in a conversation with the Archbishop of Canterbury that a basic income for the poor would be a much better solution to thievery than the common practice at the time of hanging thieves.[47] Interest in it revived in the 1960s when Nobel laureate Milton Friedman suggested a negative income tax, and economists James Tobin and John Kenneth Galbraith published a series of articles in support of a minimum basic income. In the spring of 1968 more than 1,000 economists signed a petition to Congress urging the passage of a series of reforms including a basic income. This is the closest the United States has ever come to a minimum income, although the Alaska Permanent Fund is credited as the first American attempt at a "national income," since it regularly distributes Alaskan oil revenue to each Alaskan.[48]

The guaranteed minimum income, or negative income tax, entails government covering any shortfall between the amount a person makes and a certain minimum level. This model has been tested extensively over the years, most notably in the United States during the 1970s in Iowa, New Jersey, Indiana, Pennsylvania, and Washington State.[49] The approach appears to be a work-killer, and it is easy to see why. For the poor, the system leaves little incentive to earn money. If the minimum income level is $12,000, someone who earns $9,000 a year will get $3,000 from the government and have absolutely no reason to work harder to bring his or her earned income up to, say, $11,000.

A far better approach entails simply giving every adult citizen a fixed sum of money and letting people keep anything they earn above that amount. Reporter Rutger Bregman provides an example from the United Kingdom:

In May 2009, a small experiment involving 13 homeless men took off in London. Some of them had slept in the cold for more than 40 years. The presence of these street veterans was far from cheap. Police, legal services, health care: Each cost taxpayers thousands of pounds every year.

That spring, a local charity decided to make the street veterans—sometimes called rough sleepers—the beneficiaries of an innovative social experiment. No more food stamps, food-kitchen dinners or sporadic shelter stays. The 13 would get a drastic bailout financed by taxpayers. Each would receive 3,000 pounds (about $4,500) in cash, with no strings attached. The men were free to decide what to spend it on.

The only question they had to answer: What do you think is good for you? "I didn't have enormous expectations," an aid worker recalled a year later. Yet the homeless men's desires turned out to be quite modest. A phone, a passport, a dictionary—each participant had ideas about what would be best for him. None of these men wasted his money on alcohol, drugs or gambling. A year later 11 of the 13 had roofs over their heads. (Some went to hostels; others to shelters.) After decades of authorities' fruitless pushing, pulling, fines and persecution, 11 vagrants moved off the street.

The cost? About 50,000 pounds, including the wages of the aid workers. In addition to giving 11 individuals another shot at life, the project has saved money by a factor of multiples. Even the *Economist* concluded: "The most efficient way to spend money on the homeless might be to give it to them."[50]

This approach has been given some recent support from work done by Professor Sendhil Mullainathan at Harvard, whose research suggests that poverty itself may interfere with the sort of sound decision making that could help impoverished people better themselves. When he began his work he believed he and his colleagues could demonstrate experimentally that "poverty imposed a kind of 'bandwidth tax' that impaired people's ability to perform. 'To put it crudely,' he explains, 'poverty—no matter who you are—can make you dumber.'"[51] In one experiment a group of Indian farmers were given IQ tests at harvest time when they had plenty of cash, and before the next harvest when they were strapped for money. Their IQs were significantly lower when they were cash-strapped. Daniel Kahneman, a psychologist who works in this field, notes that this work "inverts the long-held thinking that the poor are poor because they make bad decisions." Instead, he says, "people make bad decisions *because* they are poor."[52]

Providing money to people with very low incomes means that, at least temporarily, they are relieved of some of the stress of scarcity and should be thinking more clearly as a result.

The *In Our Hands* Approach

A much more detailed plan for a guaranteed basic income is proposed by Charles Murray in his 2006 book *In Our Hands.* His approach got renewed attention in 2013 when a group of Swiss citizens dumped a huge heap of gold coins in front of the Parliament building in Bern to publicize a referendum on awarding each citizen $34,000 per year.[53] While this is an unrealistic amount, Swiss backers collected 126,000 signatures to put it on the ballot.

Murray's plan calls for a deposit of $10,000 to be made into every American's bank account every year, in monthly installments, starting when a person reaches the age of 21. That's it. No other welfare or Social Security, no medical benefits, no disability, no TANF, no food stamps. Murray assumes that $2,000 of the $10,000 will go to health insurance, and in one variation of the plan that purchase is mandatory. Combined with even very modest earnings, such payments could provide enough to live on at a subsistence level and they contain no penalties for work. Family members (or others) living together could do fairly well with each adult getting the $10,000 a year until reaching an earned income level of $25,000 (in 2006 dollars), at which point a surtax would kick in and the benefit would be gradually reduced.[54]

The advantages to Murray's plan are substantial. Except for a fraud suppression team and some workers to help all Americans open bank accounts, the entire welfare bureaucracy could be dismantled and the government would no longer poke its nose into poor people's lives. Dignity and self-respect would be enhanced. Nearly everyone would have enough to survive, but a comfortable life would require work. No financial incentive to have babies. No financial disincentives to marry. Some people might find a way to live well without working. But, Murray argues, there would almost surely be an increase in work performed because work itself would carry no penalties, only benefits.

This approach also eliminates all aspects of coercion of the poor. Advocates for the poor have often lamented that the rules imposed on welfare recipients are just a way of controlling them,* and welfare beneficiaries uniformly despise the patronizing aspects of the system. Under Murray's plan, no one is coerced, regulated, or patronized. Still, the plan does not require or directly facilitate work, and that is a major shortcoming.

---

*See, for example, F. F. Piven and Richard Cloward's *Regulating the Poor.*

Murray's critics suggest that the major flaw in this plan is that Congress would never bring itself to enact it and, if enacted, the plan would soon unravel as Congress decided, for example, that the legally blind should get more, and then another group, and so on. However, getting jiggered back to a system as bad as the one we have now would take perhaps 20 years and for those 20 years, we'd all be better off, especially the poor.

Focus More Firmly on the Poor

As noted in chapter 3, more than half the spending for welfare programs now goes to Americans above the poverty line. Fulfilling the system's proper mission—serving the poor—requires reinstating more rigorous means testing and limiting assistance to low-income individuals and families. Targeting our welfare dollars to the truly poor could save nearly $170 billion a year even if earnings up to 200% of the poverty line were allowed for the disabled, according to calculations by authors Armor and Sousa.[55]

Stop Incarcerating People for Nonviolent "No-Complaint" Crimes

Long sentences for nonviolent drug crimes have many dreadful consequences. Men and women are separated from their families, tearing apart family and social structure. People who do time are often criminalized in jail and, in any case, find it very hard to get jobs upon release, although many of them have been and could be productive members of their communities. "From 1980 to 2000, the number of children with fathers in prison rose from 350,000 to 2.1 million," according to a 2014 article in the *New York Times*, which went on to observe: "Since race and poverty overlap so significantly, the weight of our criminal justice experiment continues to fall overwhelmingly on communities of color, particularly on young black men. . . . The research is in, and it is uncontestable. The American experiment in mass incarceration has been a moral, legal, social, and economic disaster. It cannot end soon enough."[56] Since that time, momentum for reform of prison sentencing and incarceration practices has been building among the public, in Congress, and in the law enforcement community.

A New Reason to Save: Lottery Savings Accounts

Noting that low-income Americans spend a disproportionate share of their income on lotteries, writer Tina Rosenberg suggests that we consider more savings plans that include a chance to win big. Banks can't do this, but several credit unions have shown promising results. In 2009 the Michigan

Credit Union League introduced "Save to Win," an imaginative lottery/ savings scheme for low-income members.

> For each deposit of $25, savers got interest, plus one entry to the annual grand prize of $100,000 and monthly smaller prizes of between $25 and $100. More deposits meant more chances to win. . . . [Michigan] now has 34 credit unions involved with 12,000 accounts in total, an average of $2,596 in each account . . . [more] than 9,000 prizes have been awarded.[57]

Credit unions in three other states—Washington, Nebraska, and North Carolina—have started similar programs.

Promote Birth Control

America's welfare programs are strongly pronatalist. Benefits under TANF, SNAP, SSI, SSDI, and Section 8 all go up substantially with each additional child. And in some states pregnancy is a woman's entry ticket to Medicaid. While evidence is scanty that these policies actually cause many women to decide to get pregnant, there is no doubt that having children while unmarried exacerbates and perpetuates poverty and reinforces intergenerational poverty cycles. Time after time, the women we interviewed, while they loved and appreciated their babies, revealed the negative effects of childbearing on their ability to work, make a living, or climb out of poverty.

"Birth control? Nah," said Sadie, a teenage California mother. "That wasn't on my list of things to think about. It was all about having a baby. And in my high school they even have day care for the kids of the students, and all this extra help, and you don't see the same from the clinics. The school clinics can't give out birth control, but they can take care of us and our babies."

At the very least, we should do what we can to make all childbearing intended. "[Seventy] percent of pregnancies among unmarried women under 30 are unplanned," Nicholas Kristof noted in 2014. "The Guttmacher Institute calculates that without family planning services, the rate of unintended teen pregnancies would be 73 percent higher."[58] Knowledge about birth control starts with science-based sex education. States should promote and the federal government should favor accurate sex education. "Abstinence-only" programs should be dropped. Such programs are not really sex education at all, but rather part of a cultural propaganda effort that ends up depriving young people of accurate information about sex and birth control that they need and are entitled to have.

A comprehensive study in the *Journal of Adolescent Health* in 2008 reported, "The impact of formal sex education programs on teen sexual health using nationally representative data found that abstinence-only programs had no significant effect in delaying the initiation of sexual activity or in reducing the risk of teen pregnancy or STDs. In contrast," the report continued, "comprehensive sex education was significantly associated with reduced teen pregnancy."[59]

Stress LARCs

There is growing evidence that long-acting reversible contraceptives (LARCs) can effectively prevent unwanted pregnancies among the poor. IUDs and hormonal implants last for several years unless removed, and they are 99% effective at preventing pregnancy. A 2014 privately funded Colorado study found that the birthrate among low-income women between the ages of 15 and 19 who were given free access to LARCs fell by 29%; those age 20 to 24 reduced their birthrate by 14%. Abortion rates also fell. Even allowing for preexisting trends (which were also positive), the changes were substantial. Most strikingly, enrollment in welfare programs for low-income mothers fell by 23% during the study period.[60]

Author Isabel Sawhill notes that LARCs, because they require no attention once in place and last for years, can change the birth control "default": A woman need not think about the LARC until she actually wants to become pregnant.[61]

Aggressive social marketing campaigns that inform Americans about birth control options, especially long-term reversible methods, should be undertaken, preferably by the private sector. The MTV reality-style show *16 and Pregnant* provides a promising example.[62] Widely watched by teenagers, the show was especially effective in getting them to talk with peers and even their parents about sex and pregnancy, "and how to avoid it," according to an evaluation by Melissa Kearney and Phillip B. Levine in their 2013 study for the National Bureau of Economic Research.[63] Such campaigns should also include well-researched messages designed to counteract the notion that men who father babies out of wedlock are manly.

Early-trimester abortions should be paid for by any program that reimburses the costs of low-income women's basic or reproductive health care.

Tackle Issues Surrounding Family Structure

There is a fair unanimity of opinion among experts on American poverty that the massive trend toward single parenthood must be addressed if we are to solve the poverty problem. The correlative data are powerful and even people who are most sympathetic to the poor are deeply concerned about this trend. "Though many single mothers are admirable parents, it remains true that, on average, children raised outside of marriage typically learn less in school, are more likely to have children while they are teens, are less likely to graduate from high school and enroll in college, and have more trouble finding jobs as adults," Edin and Kefalas reported in *Promises*.[64] We discussed this issue in chapter 4, and we recognize that changing the current cultural pattern of premarital childbearing is unquestionably daunting. Still, a number of steps may mitigate it.

Making long-acting birth control methods such as IUDs and implants easily and cheaply available could do a lot to reduce or postpone unintended pregnancies.

New messages for young women should be tried and evaluated. Several authors[65] note that addressing messages to young women about the importance of a stable married household *to their children's welfare* might have an impact. As Isabel Sawhill notes in *Generation Unbound*: "By appealing to the desire among low-income parents to give their children a chance for a better life, we might still turn the tide."[66]

"If they really care for the kids that they bring into this world," states W. Bradford Wilcox in *Poverty in America,* "they should do that in the context where those kids have two parents who are committed to one another . . . and are ready to become parents."[67]

SUMMING UP

Earned accomplishment is a key to human happiness, and work at a paid job is the commonest route to earned accomplishment. We especially recommend two plans for encouraging and enabling work among people in need:

- Greatly improving the EITC to make it more generous and consistent, with worker benefits available for childless people as well as for those with children.
- Subsidizing wages so that entry-level workers can see and have a realistic path to self-sufficiency.

Both initiatives aim to accomplish the same things, and they could be implemented in combination. Elimination or significant reduction in the FICA tax in conjunction with these changes or others will also benefit the poor and reward work, while reducing the tax burden imposed on employers when they hire people.

Along with the welfare recipients we talked with and many of the analysts and scholars we have quoted, we believe that substantially improving the rewards for work is the most promising public policy approach, because work is the key to a better life. Work brings immediate and substantial benefits, as reported throughout this book, and as it does, the enervating trends of poverty and welfare dependence can be reversed.

Accordingly, legislation to reform welfare that is based on helping people find work and keep working is essential not just to repair our broken and increasingly expensive welfare system but, as so many welfare recipients have testified, to improve the quality of individual lives. If America is to remain a nation of workers, of dreamers, of citizens who thrive rather than just exist, all our citizens deserve the chance to earn their own success.

Happiness stems from work, and in the United States the pursuit of happiness is an inalienable right.

Notes

INTRODUCTION: WELFARE REFORMS NEED REFORMING

1. "The Recovery Act," The American Recovery and Reinvestment Act, http://www.recovery.gov/arra/About/Pages/The_Act.aspx.

2. U.S. Department of the Treasury, "Recovery Act," http://www.treasury.gov/initiatives/recovery/Pages/recovery-act.aspx.

3. David J. Armor and Sonia Sousa, "Restoring a True Safety Net," *National Affairs* no. 13 (2012): 9–10, 19.

CHAPTER 1: WHAT DOES WORK HAVE TO DO WITH HAPPINESS?

1. Rachel Jones, "Welfare Reform Changes Women's Lives," *National Public Radio*, August 22, 2006, http://www.npr.org/templates/story/story.php?storyId=5688674.

2. John Ifcher, "The Happiness of Single Mothers after Welfare Reform," *B. E. Journal of Economic Analysis & Policy* 11, no. 1 (2011): 1–29.

3. Chris Herbst, "Welfare Reform and the Subjective Well-Being of Single Mothers," *Journal of Population Economics* 26, no. 1 (2013): 203–238.

4. Ibid., 238.

5. Ibid., 203.

6. Ifcher, "Happiness of Single Mothers," 1.

7. "G-SOEP—German Socio-Economic Panel (DIW Berlin)," European University Institute, http://www.eui.eu/Research/Library/ResearchGuides/Economics/Statistics/DataPortal/GSOEP.aspx.

8. Richard Layard, Andrew Clark, and Claudia Senik, "Chapter 3: The Causes of Happiness and Misery," *World Happiness Report 2013* (New York: Columbia Earth Institute, 2013), 67.

9. Studs Terkel, *Working: People Talk about What They Do All Day and How They Feel about What They Do* (New York: New Press, 2013), 295. Quoted in Charles Murray, *In Pursuit of Happiness and Good Government* (New York: Simon and Schuster, 1988), 145.

10. Arthur C. Brooks, *Gross National Happiness: Why Happiness Matters for America—and How We Can Get More of It* (New York: Basic Books, 2008), 162.

11. Aaron Reeves, Martin McKee, and David Stuckler, "Economic Suicides in the Great Recession in Europe and North America," *British Journal of Psychiatry* 205, no. 3 (2014).

CHAPTER 2: THE WAR BETWEEN WELFARE AND WORK

1. Charles Murray, *Losing Ground: American Social Policy, 1950–1980* (New York: Basic Books, 1984), 212.

2. "Resource Guide: Lifting Asset Limits in Public Benefit Programs," Corporation for Enterprise Development (2012), 1.

3. Ibid., 17.

4. "Supplemental Nutrition Assistance Program (SNAP): Eligibility," U.S. Department of Agriculture Food and Nutrition Service, http://www.fns.usda.gov /snap/eligibility.

5. Gary D. Alexander, "Welfare's Failure and the Solution," Pennsylvania Department of Public Welfare (2012).

6. Ibid.

7. "Shelter and Housing: Reduced Fare Bus Tickets," Seattle Human Services Department, http://www.seattle.gov/humanservices/emergencyservices/shelter/bus .htm.

8. "King County and Seattle Clothing Closets," *Need Help Paying Bills,* http:// www.needhelppayingbills.com/html/king_county_free_clothing_clos.html.

9. "Supplemental Nutrition Assistance Program (SNAP): Eligibility," U.S. Department of Agriculture Food and Nutrition Service, http://www.fns.usda.gov /snap/eligibility.

10. Liz Schott, "Policy Basics: An Introduction to TANF," Center on Budget and Policy Priorities (2012).

11. Ibid., 4.

12. Jane L. Collins and Victoria Mayer, *Both Hands Tied: Welfare Reform and the Race to the Bottom in the Low-Wage Labor Market* (Chicago: University of Chicago Press, 2010).

13. Ibid., 55.

14. *Wisconsin Works (W-2) Manual: 8.3.2 Education and Training Activities for Community Service Jobs and W-2 Transition Placements*, Wisconsin Department of Children and Families (2014).

15. Personal conversation with participant, August 2012.

CHAPTER 3: WHAT COUNTS AS POVERTY

1. "Poverty Overview," World Bank, http://www.worldbank.org/en/topic/poverty/overview.

2. "2014 Poverty Guidelines," U.S. Department of Health and Human Services, http://aspe.hhs.gov/poverty/14poverty.cfm.

3. William Voegeli, *Never Enough: America's Limitless Welfare State* (New York: Encounter Books, 2013), 52.

4. Kathleen Short, "The Research Supplemental Poverty Measure: 2011," U.S. Census Bureau, Current Population Reports P60-244 (2012): 3.

5. American Recovery and Reinvestment Act of 2009, U.S. Government Publishing Office, H.R. 1, 111th Congress (2009): 31, 65.

6. Ibid.

7. David J. Armor and Sonia Sousa, "Restoring a True Safety Net," *National Affairs* no. 13 (2012): 1.

8. Gene Falk, "The Temporary Assistance for Needy Families (TANF) Block Grant: Responses to Frequently Asked Questions," Congressional Research Service, RL32760 (2013): 11.

9. State of Hawaii, Department of Human Services, "Benefit, Employment and Support Services," http://humanservices.hawaii.gove/bessd/snap/.

10. Nicholas Eberstadt, *The Poverty of "The Poverty Rate": Measure and Mismeasure of Want in Modern America* (Washington, DC: AEI Press, 2008), 62.

11. Annie Lowrey, "Changed Life of the Poor: Better Off, but Far Behind," *New York Times*, April 30, 2014, http://www.nytimes.com/2014/05/01/business/economy/changed-life-of-the-poor-squeak-by-and-buy-a-lot.html?_r=0.

12. Ibid.

13. Nicholas Eberstadt, *Poverty of "The Poverty Rate,"* 62.

CHAPTER 4: MARRIAGE, CHILDBEARING, AND TEEN PREGNANCY

1. "2014 vs. 2013 Food Stamp (SNAP) Income Eligibility Levels, Deductions and Benefit Allotment Payments," *Saving to Invest*, http://www.savingtoinvest.com/2012-food-stamp-snap-income-eligibility-levels-deductions-and-benefit-allotment-payments/.

2. "About Teen Pregnancy," Centers for Disease Control and Prevention (2014), http://www.cdc.gov/teenpregnancy/aboutteenpreg.htm.

3. "Teenage Pregnancy Prevention: Statistics and Programs," Congressional Report Service, no. RS20301 (2011): 1–2.

4. Carmen DeNavas-Walt and Bernadette D. Proctor, "Income and Poverty in the United States: 2013," U.S. Census Bureau, *Current Population Reports* (2014): 16.

5. Joyce A. Martin, Brady E. Hamilton, Stephanie J. Ventura, Michelle J. K. Osterman, Elizabeth C. Wilson, and T. J. Mathews, "Births: Final Data for 2010," Centers for Disease Control and Prevention, *NVSS* 61, no. 10 (2012): 44.

6. "Moynihan Report," *International Encyclopedia of the Social Sciences* (2008), *Encyclopedia.com,* http://www.encyclopedia.com/doc/1G2-3045301638.html.

7. George Will, "What Patrick Moynihan Knew about the Importance of Two Parents," https://www.washingtonpost.com/opinions/what-patrick-moynihan-knew-about-the-importance-of-two-parents/2015/03/13/2cdf9bae-c9a4-11e4-aa1a-86135599fb0f_story.html.

8. Nicholas Kristof, "When Liberals Blew It," *New York Times*, http://www.nytimes.com/2015/03/12/opinion/when-liberals-blew-it.html?_r=0.

9. Robert A. Moffit, *The Effect of Welfare on Marriage and Fertility: What Do We Know and What Do We Need to Know?* Institute for Research on Poverty, Discussion Paper no. 1153–97, Johns Hopkins University, 1997.

10. Gene Falk, "Temporary Assistance for Needy Families (TANF): Eligibility and Benefit Amounts in State TANF Cash Assistance Programs," Congressional Research Service, R43634 (2014).

11. Melissa Schettini Kearney, "Teen Pregnancy Prevention," *Targeting Investments in Children: Fighting Poverty When Resources Are Limited* (Chicago: University of Chicago Press, 2010), 244.

12. Annie Lowery, "Can Marriage Cure Poverty?" *New York Times*, February 4, 2014, http://www.nytimes.com/2014/02/09/magazine/can-marriage-cure-poverty.html?_r=0.

13. Belinda Luscombe, "Teens Answer: Why I Had a Baby," *TIME*, February 3, 2011, http://healthland.time.com/2011/02/03/teens-answer-why-i-had-a-baby/.

14. Kathryn Edin and Maria Kefalas, *Promises I Can Keep: Why Poor Women Put Motherhood Before Marriage* (Berkeley: University of California Press, 2007), 205.

15. Ibid., 10.

16. Ibid., 204–205.

17. Sue Ricketts, Greta Klingler, and Renee Schwalberg, "Game Change in Colorado: Widespread Use of Long-Acting Reversible Contraceptives and Rapid Decline in Births Among Young, Low-Income Women," *Perspectives on Sexual and Reproductive Health* 46, no. 3 (2014): 125–132, http://dx.doi.org/10.1363/46e1714: 125.

18. Ibid., 129.

19. Kristina M. Tocce, Jeanelle L. Sheeder, and Stephanie B. Teal, "Rapid Repeat Pregnancy in Adolescents: Do Immediate Postpartum Contraceptive Implants Make a Difference?" *American Journal of Obstetrics and Gynecology* 206 (2012): 481, e1–7.

20. Heather D. Boonstra, "Leveling the Playing Field: The Promise of Long-Acting Reversible Contraceptives for Adolescents," *Guttmacher Policy Review* 16, no. 4 (Fall 2013).

21. Ricketts, Klingler, and Schwalberg, "Game Change," 132.

22. Alan J. Hawkins, Paul R. Amato, and Andrea Kinghorn, "Are Government-Supported Healthy Marriage Initiatives Affecting Family Demographics? A State-Level Analysis," *Family Relations* 62, no. 3 (2013): 502.

23. Susan L. Brown, "Marriage and Child Well-Being: Research and Policy Perspectives," *Journal of Marriage and the Family* 72, no. 5 (2010): 1039–1479.

24. Jane G. Mauldon, Rebecca A. London, David J. Fein, and Steven J. Bliss, "What Do They Think? Welfare Recipients' Attitudes Towards Marriage and Childbearing," Welfare Reform and Family Formation Project, Research Brief no. 2 (2002): 7.

25. Sanders Korenman, Ted Joyce, Robert Kaestner, and Jennifer Walper, "What Did the 'Illegitimacy Bonus' Reward?" National Bureau of Economic Research, Working Paper no. 10699 (2004): 32.

26. Hawkins, Amato, and Kinghorn, "Government-Supported Healthy Marriage Initiatives," 502.

27. Ibid.

28. Korenman, Joyce, Kaestner, and Walper, "What Did the 'Illegitimacy Bonus' Reward?" 6.

29. Ted Joyce, Robert Kaestner, Sanders Korenman, and Stanley Henshaw, "Family Cap Provisions and Changes in Births and Abortions," National Bureau of Economic Research, Working Paper no. 10214 (2004).

30. Korenman, Joyce, Kaestner, and Walper, "What Did the 'Illegitimacy Bonus' Reward?" 6.

31. Ibid.

32. Jason F. Fichtner and Jacob Feldman, "Taxing Marriage: Microeconomic Behavioral Responses to the Marriage Penalty and Reforms for the 21st Century," Mercatus Center, Working Paper no. 12–24 (2012).

33. Elizabeth Stuart, "How Anti-Poverty Programs Marginalize Fathers," *The Atlantic*, February 25, 2014, http://www.theatlantic.com/politics/archive/2014/02/how-anti-poverty-programs-marginalize-fathers/283984/.

34. Edin and Kefalas, *Promises I Can Keep*, 5.

35. Justin Wolfers, David Leonardt, and Kevin Quealy, "1.5 Million Missing Black Men," *New York Times*, http://www.nytimes.com/interactive/2015/04/20/upshot/missing-black-men.html?abt=0002&abg=1.

36. James Pethokoukis, "Can Anything Really Be Done about Family Breakdown and American Poverty? A Q&A with Brad Wilcox," American Enterprise Institute (2014).

37. Maureen A. Pirog and Kathleen M. Ziol-Guest, "Child Support Enforcement: Programs and Policies, Impacts and Questions," *Journal of Policy Analysis and Management* 25, no. 4 (2006).

38. National Conference of State Legislatures, *Criminal Non-Support and Child Support: 50 State Table,* http://www.ncsl.org/research/human-services/criminal-nonsupport-and-child-support.aspx#50%20State%20Table.

39. Daniel L. Hatcher, "Child Support Harming Children: Subordinating the Best Interests of Children to the Fiscal Interests of the State," *Wake Forest Law Review* 42, no. 4 (2007), http://ssrn.com/abstract=1113165.

40. Maureen Waller and Robert Plotnick, "Child Support and Low-Income Families: Perceptions, Practices, and Policy," Public Policy Institute of California (1999).

41. Ibid.

42. Robert Doar, Mordgridge Fellow in Poverty Studies, American Enterprise Institute, personal communication, August 13, 2015.

CHAPTER 5: TANF: THE CHANGING FACE OF CASH ASSISTANCE

1. Sheila Zedlewski, Thomas Callan, and Gregory Acs, "TANF at 16: What Do We Know?" Urban Institute (2012).

2. Liz Schott, LaDonna Pavetti, and Ife Finch, "How States Have Spent Federal and State Funds under the TANF Block Grant," Center on Budget and Policy Priorities (2012): 15.

3. Ibid., 5.

4. David J. Armor and Sonia Sousa, "Restoring a True Safety Net," *National Affairs* no. 13 (2012): 1.

5. "Spending for Federal Benefits and Services for People with Low Income, FY2008–FY2011," Congressional Research Service, no. R41625 (2012): 4–11.

6. Zedlewski, Callan, and Acs, "TANF at 16."

7. Ife Floyd and Liz Schott, "TANF Cash Benefits Continued to Lose Value in 2013," Center on Budget and Policy Priorities (2013).

8. "State Fact Sheets: How States Have Spent Federal and State Funds under the TANF Block Grant," Center on Budget and Policy Priorities, http://www.cbpp.org /cms/?fa=view&id=3809.

9. Ibid.

10. Zedlewski, Callan, and Acs, "TANF at 16."

11. Welfare Rules Database, http://anfdata.urban.org/wrd/Query/query.cfm.

12. Social worker at Washington State Department of Social and Health Services, Economic Services Administration, Clarkston office, personal communication, May 2013.

13. Ibid.

14. Ibid.

CHAPTER 6: A HOUSING SYSTEM LEAVES THE NEEDY OUT IN THE COLD

1. "Housing Choice Vouchers Fact Sheet," U.S. Department of Housing and Urban Development (2015).

2. "Resident Characteristics Report," U.S. Department of Housing and Urban Development (2015), http://portal.hud.gov/hudportal/HUD?src=/program_offices /public_indian_housing/systems/pic/50058/rcr.

3. Ibid.

4. "Chart Book: Federal Housing Spending Is Poorly Matched to Need," Center on Budget and Policy Priorities, http://www.cbpp.org/research/chart-book-federal -housing-spending-is-poorly-matched-to-need#Three.

5. Will Fischer, "Expanding Rental Assistance Demonstration Would Help Low-Income Families, Seniors, and People with Disabilities," Center on Budget and Policy Priorities (2014): 2.

6. "Fiscal Year 2014: Budget of the U.S. Government," Office of Management and Budget (2014): 115.

7. David J. Armor and Sonia Sousa, "Restoring a True Safety Net," *National Affairs*, no. 13 (2012): 22.

8. Ibid., 23.

9. Office of Inspector General, United States Department of Housing and Urban Development, Audit Report no. 2015-KC-0001, February 13, 2015, https://www.hudoig.gov/sites/default/files/documents/2015-KC-0001.pdf.

CHAPTER 7: WHO GETS FOOD STAMPS?

1. Robert Rector and Katherine Bradley, "Reforming the Food Stamp Program," Heritage Foundation, no. 2708 (2012): 4.

2. Ibid., 1.

3. "Building a Healthy America: A Profile of the Supplemental Nutrition Assistance Program," U.S. Department of Agriculture Food and Nutrition Service (2012): 1.

4. Rector and Bradley, "Reforming the Food Stamp Program."

5. "Maine Enforces Work Requirements for Able-Bodied Food Supplement Recipients," U.S. Department of Health and Human Services, Press Release (2014).

6. Eli Saslow, "In Florida, a Food-Stamp Recruiter Deals with Wrenching Choices," *Washington Post*, April 23, 2013, http://www.washingtonpost.com/national/in-florida-a-food-stamp-recruiter-deals-with-wrenching-choices/2013/04/23/b3d6b41c-a3a4-11e2-9c03-6952ff305f35_story.html.

7. Ibid.

8. Ibid.

9. United States Department of Agriculture, Office of Communications, Press Release 0254.07, http://www.usda.gov/wps/portal/usda/usdahome?printable=true&contentidonly=true&contentid=2007/09/0254.xml.

10. Paul Krugman, "From the Mouths of Babes," *New York Times*, May 30, 2013, http://www.nytimes.com/2013/05/31/opinion/from-the-mouths-of-babes.html.

11. Alisha Coleman-Jensen, Mark Nord, and Anita Singh, *Household Food Security in the United States in 2012*, ERR-155, U.S. Department of Agriculture, Economic Research Service, September 2013.

12. Sheryl Gay Stolberg, "On the Edge of Poverty, at the Center of a Debate on Food Stamps," *New York Times*, September 4, 2013, http://www.nytimes.com/2013/09/05/us/as-debate-reopens-food-stamp-recipients-continue-to-squeeze.html?pagewanted=all&_r=0.

13. Ibid.

14. Jeff Sessions, "Food Stamp Reforms Will Help Both the Recipient and the Treasury," United States Senate Budget Committee (October 18, 2012).

15. Editorial Board, "Congress Should Close a Food Stamp Loophole," *Washington Post*, December 30, 2013, http://www.washingtonpost.com/opinions /congress-should-close-a-food-stamp-loophole/2013/12/30/23736316-699c-11e3 -8b5b-a77187b716a3_story.html.

16. Ibid.

17. Randy Alison Aussenberg and Libby Perl, "The 2014 Farm Bill: Changing the Treatment of LIHEAP Receipt in the Calculation of SNAP Benefits," Congressional Research Service, no. R42591: 2.

18. "Supplemental Nutrition Assistance Program (SNAP): Eligible Food Items," U.S. Department of Agriculture Food and Nutrition Service (2014).

19. Luke Rosiak, "Top Secret: $80B a Year for Food Stamps, but Feds Won't Reveal What's Purchased," *Washington Times* (June 24, 2012), http://www.washingtontimes .com/news/2012/jun/24/top-secret-what-food-stamps-buy/?page=all.

20. Ibid.

21. Ibid.

22. Steve Young, "Court Rules for Argus Leader over USDA in Access to Food-Stamp Data," *Argus Leader*, http://archive.argusleader.com/article/20140129/NEWS /301290023/Court-rules-Argus-Leader-over-USDA-access-food-stamp-data.

23. "Supplemental Nutrition Assistance Program (SNAP): Eligible Food Items," U.S. Department of Agriculture Food and Nutrition Service (2014).

24. Randy Alison Aussenberg, "Supplemental Nutrition Assistance Program (SNAP): A Primer on Eligibility and Benefits," Congressional Research Service, no. R42505 (2014): 19.

25. James Malbi, Stephen Tordella, Laura Castner, Thomas Godfrey, and Priscilla Foran, "Dynamics of Supplemental Nutrition Assistance Program Participation in the Mid-2000s," U.S. Department of Agriculture Food and Nutrition Service (2011): 84–87.

26. Michael D. Tanner, "SNAP Failure: The Food Stamp Program Needs Reform," Cato Institute, Policy Analysis no. 738 (2013): 13.

27. Maya Rao, "Minnesota Targets Food Stamp Fraud," *Star Tribune*, June 1, 2012, http://www.startribune.com/local/minneapolis/156544515.html.

28. Matthew Hendley, "State Auditor: Prisoners, Dead People Got Food Stamps and Welfare Benefits," *Phoenix New Times*, April 30, 2014, http://blogs .phoenixnewtimes.com/valleyfever/2014/04/welfare_food_stamps_fraud_elgibility _arizona_inmates_dead.php.

29. Kevin Miller, "Rooting Out EBT Fraud More Complex Than It Seems," *Press Herald*, January 12, 2014, http://www.pressherald.com/2014/01/12/rooting_out_ebt _fraud_morecomplex_than_it_seems_/.

30. Karen Tumulty, "'Obama Phones' Subsidy Program Draws New Scrutiny on the Hill," *Washington Post*, April 9, 2013, http://www.washingtonpost.com /politics/obama-phones-subsidy-program-draws-new-scrutiny-on-the-hill/2013 /04/09/50699d04-a061-11e2-be47-b44febada3a8_story.html.

31. Ibid.

32. Rochelle Finzel, "Restrictions on the Use of Public Assistance Electronic Benefit Cards," National Conference of State Legislatures, http://www.ncsl.org /research/human-services/ebt-electronic-benefit-transfer-card-restrictions-for -public-assistance.aspx.

33. A. G. Sulzberger, "States Adding Drug Test as Hurdle for Welfare," *New York Times*, October 10, 2011, http://www.nytimes.com/2011/10/11/us/states-adding -drug-test-as-hurdle-for-welfare.html?pagewanted=all.

34. Ibid.

35. Ibid.

36. Elizabeth Condon, Susan Drilea, Keri Jowers, Carolyn Lichtenstein, James Mabli, Emily Madden, and Katherine Niland, "Diet Quality of Americans by SNAP Participation Status: Data from the National Health and Nutrition Examination Survey," 2007–2010 (2015).

CHAPTER 8: WIC: MISSTEPS WITH WOMEN AND CHILDREN

1. "Frequently Asked Questions about WIC," United States Department of Agriculture (2014).

2. Committee on Dietary Risk Assessment in the WIC Program, *Framework for Dietary Assessment in the WIC Program: An Interim Report from the Food and Nutrition Board* (Washington, DC: National Academies Press, 2000), 59.

3. Michael Martinez-Schiferl, "WIC Participants and Their Growing Need for Coverage," Urban Institute (2012): 2.

4. Ibid., 1.

5. Victor Oliviera, Elizabeth Frazao, and David Smallwood, "Rising Infant Formula Costs to the WIC Program: Recent Trends in Rebates and Wholesale Prices," U.S. Department of Agriculture, Economic Research Report no. 93 (2010).

6. "WIC Breastfeeding Data Local Agency Report," U.S. Department of Agriculture Food and Nutrition Service (2012): 4.

7. United States Department of Agriculture, Women, Infants and Children (WIC), "Final Rule, Revision in the WIC Food Packages," http://www.fns.usda.gov /wic/final-rule-revisions-wic-food-packages.

8. Douglas J. Besharov and Peter Germanis, "Evaluating WIC," *Evaluation Review* 24, no. 2 (2000): 58–59.

9. Martinez-Schiferl, "WIC Participants and Their Growing Need for Coverage," 7.

10. Daniel Prendergast, "Multi-Million Dollar Welfare Scam Busted," *New York Post*, November 20, 2013, http://nypost.com/2013/11/20/multi-million-dollar -welfare-fraud-scheme-busted-in-nyc-bodegas/.

11. Bianca Cain Johnson, "Food Stamp, WIC Fraud Leads to Conviction," *Augusta Chronicle*, November 8, 2013, http://chronicle.augusta.com/news/crime -courts/2013-11-08/food-stamp-wic-fraud-leads-conviction.

12. David Goldstein, "Investigation Uncovers People Selling Taxpayer-Funded Food Stamps," *CBS Los Angeles*, February 16, 2012, http://losangeles.cbslocal.com /2012/02/16/investigation-uncovers-people-selling-taxpayer-funded-food-stamps/.

CHAPTER 9: HOW WE DISABLE THE DISABLED

1. "2015 Red Book," Social Security Administration, SSA Publication no. 64-030 (2015): 1.

2. Ibid., 48.

3. David H. Autor, "The Unsustainable Rise of the Disability Rolls in the United States: Causes, Consequences, and Policy Options," National Bureau of Economic Research, Working Paper no. 17697 (2011): 118.

4. "2015 Red Book," Social Security Administration, 22.

5. "Annual Statistical Report on the Social Security Disability Insurance Program, 2013," Social Security Administration, http://www.ssa.gov/policy/docs /statcomps/di_asr/.

6. Charles Murray, *Coming Apart: The State of White America, 1960–2010* (New York: Crown Forum, 2012), 174–175.

7. David H. Autor and Mark G. Duggan, "The Growth in the Social Security Disability Rolls: A Fiscal Crisis Unfolding," *Journal of Economic Perspectives* 20, no. 3 (2006).

8. "2011 CDA Long-Term Disability Claims Review," Council for Disability Awareness (2011).

9. "2015 Red Book," Social Security Administration, 7.

10. "Social Security & Medicare Tax Rates," Social Security Administration, http://www.ssa.gov/oact/progdata/taxRates.html.

11. "2015 Red Book," Social Security Administration, 8.

12. "Social Security Disability Insurance: December 2010 Baseline," Congressional Budget Office (2011), http://cbo.gov/sites/default/files/3-di.pdf.

13. Umar Moulta-Ali, "Primer on Disability Insurance (SSDI) and Supplemental Security Income (SSI)," Congressional Research Service, no. RL32279 (2014).

14. Ibid.

15. "SSI Federal Payment Amounts for 2015," Social Security Administration, http://www.ssa.gov/oact/cola/SSI.html.

16. Ibid.

17. David J. Armor and Sonia Sousa, "Restoring a True Safety Net," *National Affairs*, no. 13 (2012): 21.

18. Ibid.

19. "Former Postal Service Employee Sentenced to Prison for Making False Statements to Obtain Federal Disability Benefits," Office of the United States Attorneys, Press Release (2013).

20. Channa Joffe-Walt, "Unfit for Work: The Startling Rise of Disability in America," *National Public Radio*, March 26, 2013, http://apps.npr.org/unfit-for-work.

21. Ibid.

22. Ibid.

23. "2015 Red Book," Social Security Administration, 24.

24. "Clearing the Disability Claims Backlogs: The Social Security Administration's Progress and New Challenges Arising from the Recession," House hearing, 111th Congress, http://www.gpo.gov/fdsys/pkg/CHRG-111hhrg63016/html/CHRG -111hhrg63016.htm.

25. David H. Autor and Mark Duggan, "Supporting Work: A Proposal for Modernizing the U.S. Disability Insurance Program," Center for American Progress and the Hamilton Project (2010): 10.

26. Paul O. Deaven and William H. Andrews, *Social Security: New Issues and Developments* (New York: Nova Science, 2008), 118.

27. Joffe-Walt, "Unfit for Work."

28. Ibid.

29. "Policy Options for the Social Security Disability Insurance Program," Congressional Budget Office (2012), https://www.cbo.gov/sites/default/files/112th -congress-2011–2012/reports/43421-DisabilityInsurance_print.pdf.

30. Ibid.

31. David Brooks, "Men on the Threshold," *New York Times*, July 15, 2013, http:// www.nytimes.com/2013/07/16/opinion/brooks-men-on-the-threshold.html?_r=0.

32. Ibid.

33. Tyler Cowen, *Average Is Over: Powering America beyond the Age of the Great Stagnation* (New York: Penguin Group, 2013).

34. Tyjen Tsai and Paola Scommegna, "U.S. Has World's Highest Incarceration Rate," Population Reference Bureau (2012), http://www.prb.org/Publications/Articles /2012/us-incarceration.aspx.

35. "Information and Technical Assistance on the Americans with Disabilities Act," United States Department of Justice, Civil Rights Division, http://www .ada.gov/.

36. "2015 Red Book," Social Security Administration, 28.

37. "Debra Gabriel's Success Story," Social Security Administration, Ticket to Work, http://www.chooseworkttw.net/library/debra-gabriels-success-story.

38. Ibid., 31.

39. Ibid., 29.

40. "Program Operations Manual System: DI 13010.012," Social Security Administration (2015), https://secure.ssa.gov/apps10/.

41. Joffe-Walt, "Unfit for Work."

42. Nicholas D. Kristof, "Profiting from a Child's Illiteracy," *New York Times*, December 7, 2012, http://www.nytimes.com/2012/12/09/opinion/sunday/kristof -profiting-from-a-childs-illiteracy.html?pagewanted=all.

43. "Prevalence of Autism Spectrum Disorder among Children Aged 8 Years," Centers for Disease Control and Prevention, *Morbidity and Mortality Weekly Report* 63 (SS02) (2014).

44. Joffe-Walt, "Unfit for Work."

45. Dave Phillips, "Iraq Veteran, Now a West Point Professor, Seeks to Rein in Disability Pay," *New York Times*, http://www.nytimes.com/2015/01/08/us/iraq-veteran-now-a-west-point-professor-seeks-to-rein-in-disability-pay.html.

46. Ibid.

47. Ibid.

48. Congress of the United States, Congressional Budget Office, "Veterans Disability Compensation; Trends and Policy Options," August 2014, https://www.cbo.gov/sites/default/files/45615-VADisability_2.pdf.

49. Ibid.

50. Mark Duggan, "The Labor Market Effects of the VA's Disability Compensation Program," Stanford University, Stanford Institute for Economic Policy Research, Policy Brief, November 2014, https://siepr.stanford.edu/?q=/system/files/shared/pubs/papers/briefs/Policy-Brief-Nov14-Duggan.pdf.

51. Ibid.

52. Code of Federal Regulations: § 404.130, Social Security Administration (2014), http://www.ssa.gov/OP_Home/cfr20/cfrdoc.htm.

53. Umar Moulta-Ali, "Social Security Disability Insurance (SSDI): The Five-Month Waiting Period for Benefits," Congressional Research Service, no. RS22220 (2013).

54. "2015 Red Book," Social Security Administration, SSA Publication no. 64-030 (2015): 24.

55. David H. Autor, Nicole Maestas, Kathleen J. Mullen, and Alexander Strand, "Does Delay Cause Decay? The Effect of Administrative Decision Time on the Labor Force Participation and Earnings of Disability Applicants," National Bureau of Economic Research, Working Paper no. 20840 (2015).

CHAPTER 10: MEDICAID AND THE AFFORDABLE CARE ACT

1. "Total Monthly Medicaid and CHIP Enrollment," Kaiser Family Foundation (2014), http://kff.org/health-reform/state-indicator/total-monthly-medicaid-and-chip-enrollment/.

2. "2014 CMS Statistics," U.S. Department of Health and Human Services, Centers for Medicaid and Medicare Services (2014), https://www.cms.gov/Research-Statistics-Data-and-Systems/Statistics-Trends-and-Reports/CMS-Statistics-Reference-Booklet/Downloads/CMS_Stats_2014_final.pdf.

3. "What the Medicaid Eligibility Expansion Means for Women," National Women's Law Center (2012): 4.

4. Jay Carney, "Statement by the Press Secretary on Today's CBO Report and the Affordable Care Act," White House Press Office (2014), https://www.whitehouse.gov/the-press-office/2014/02/04/statement-press-secretary-today-s-cbo-report-and-affordable-care-act.

5. "The Budget and Economic Outlook: 2014 to 2024," Congressional Budget Office, Publication no. 4869 (2014): 123.

6. Craig Garthwaite, Tal Gross, and Matthew J. Notowidigdo, "Public Health Insurance, Labor Supply, and Employment Lock," National Bureau of Economic Research, Working Paper no. 19220 (2013).

7. Michelle Andrews, "Quick Income Changes Can Threaten Coverage for Those on Medicaid," *Washington Post*, April 7, 2015.

8. Christopher J. Truffer, John D. Klemm, Christian J. Wolfe, Kathryn E. Rennie, and Jessica F. Shuff, "2013 Actuarial Report on the Financial Outlook for Medicaid," U.S. Department of Health and Human Services (2013).

9. January Angeles, "How Health Reform's Medicaid Expansion Will Impact State Budgets," Center on Budget and Policy Priorities (2012).

10. "Medicaid Third Party Liability & Coordination of Benefits," Centers for Medicare and Medicaid Services, http://medicaid.gov/medicaid-chip-program-information/by-topics/eligibility/tpl-cob-page.html.

11. Robert Gettings, Charles Moseley, and Nancy Thaler, "Medicaid Managed Care for People with Disabilities: Policy and Implementation Considerations for State and Federal Policymakers," National Council on Disability (2013): 52.

12. Lena H. Sun and Niraj Chokshi, "Almost Half of Obamacare Exchanges Face Financial Struggles in the Future," *Washington Post* (May 1, 2015), https://www.washingtonpost.com/national/health-science/almost-half-of-obamacare-exchanges-are-struggling-over-their-future/2015/05/01/f32eeea2-ea03–11e4-aae1-d642717d8afa_story.html.

13. "Preventive Services without Cost Sharing. New Private Health Plans Must Pay for Screenings and Other Preventive Services. Will the Benefits Outweigh the Costs?" Robert Woods Johnson Foundation Health Policy Brief (December 28, 2010), http://healthaffairs.org/healthpolicybriefs/brief_pdfs/healthpolicybrief_37.pdf.

14. "Core Set of Children's Health Care Quality Measures for Medicaid and CHIP (Child Core Set): Technical Specifications and Resource Manual for Federal Fiscal Year 2014 Reporting," Centers for Medicare & Medicaid Services (2014).

15. "Contraception in Medicaid: Improving Maternal and Infant Health Questions and Answers," Department of Health and Human Services, Centers for Medicaid and Medicare Services (June 19, 2015), http://www.medicaid.gov/medicaid-chip-program-information/by-topics/quality-of-care/downloads/contraception-q-and-a.pdf.

16. Cindy Mann, "RE: Affordable Care Act Section 4106 (Preventive Services)," Centers for Medicare and Medicaid Services (2013).

17. "Shortage Areas," United States Department of Health and Human Services, Health Resources and Services Administration, http://datawarehouse.hrsa.gov/topics/shortageAreas.aspx.

18. "Supplemental Nutrition Assistance Program (SNAP)—Using SNAP Benefits," United States Department of Agriculture, Food and Nutrition Service, http://www.fns.usda.gov/snap/using-snap-benefits.

19. "Emergency Medical Treatment & Labor Act," Centers for Medicare and Medicaid Services (2012), https://www.cms.gov/Regulations-and-Guidance/Legislation/EMTALA/index.html?redirect=/emtala/.

20. "The Impact of Unreimbursed Care on the Emergency Physician," American College of Emergency Physicians, http://www.acep.org/Clinical—Practice-Management/The-Impact-of-Unreimbursed-Care-on-the-Emergency-Physician/.

21. Ibid.

22. Sarah L. Taubman, Heidi L. Allen, Bill J. Wright, Katherine Baicker, and Amy N. Finkelstein, "Medicaid Increases Emergency-Department Use: Evidence from Oregon's Health Insurance Experiment," *Science* 343, no. 6168 (2014): 263–268.

23. "National Medicaid Audit Program: CMS Should Improve Reporting and Focus on Audit Collaboration with States," U.S. Government Accountability Office, GAO-12-627 (2012): 26.

24. Erin McCormick, "Elderly Immigrants Used in Medicare Scam: Unneeded Tests, Supplies May Have Cost Taxpayers Millions; FBI Raids 2 Clinics, but So Far No Arrests, No Charges," *SF Gate*, April 17, 2005, http://www.sfgate.com/health/article/Elderly-immigrants-used-in-Medicare-scam-2686630.php.

25. "Wheelchair-Bound Vietnam Vet Uncovers Multimillion Dollar Medicaid Fraud," *Fox News*, September 14, 2011, http://www.foxnews.com/us/2011/09/14/wheelchair-bound-vietnam-vet-uncovers-multimillion-dollar-medical-aid-fraud/.

26. David Heath, "Dollars and Dentists: Dental Chain May Be Booted from Medicaid Program," Center for Public Integrity and PBS (May 19, 2014), http://www.publicintegrity.org/2014/03/11/14395/dental-chain-may-be-booted-medicaid-program.

27. Andy Miller, "Smart Cards Pushed to Reduce Medicaid Fraud," *Georgia Health News*, March 9, 2011, http://www.georgiahealthnews.com/2011/03/smart-cards-reduce-medicaid-fraud.

28. Laura Snyder, Julia Paradise, and Robin Rudowitz, "The ACA Primary Care Increase: State Plans for SFY 2015," Henry J. Kaiser Family Foundation (October 28, 2014), http://kff.org/medicaid/perspective/the-aca-primary-care-increase-state-plans-for-sfy-2015/.

29. "America's Health Literacy: Why We Need Accessible Health Information," U.S. Department of Health and Human Services, Office of Disease Prevention and Health Promotion, Health Communication Activities, http://health.gov/communication/literacy/issuebrief/#adults.

30. Chapin White, "A Comparison of Two Approaches to Increasing Access to Care: Expanding Coverage versus Increasing Physician Fees," *Health Services Research* 47, no. 3. pt1 (2012): 963–983.

31. Stephen M. Petterson, Angela Cai, Miranda Moore, and Andrew Bazemore, "State-Level Projections of Primary Care Workforce, 2010–2030," Robert Graham Center (2013).

32. Sandra L. Decker, "In 2011 Nearly One-Third of Physicians Said They Would Not Accept New Medicaid Patients, But Rising Fees May Help," *Health Affairs* 31, no. 8 (2012).

33. "National Health Service Corps Loan Repayment Program: Fiscal Year 2015 Continuation Contract Application & Program Guidance," U.S. Department of Health and Human Services (2014).

34. Ibid.

35. Christine Vestal, "Medicaid for Prisoners: States Missing Out on Millions," *USA Today*, June 25, 2013, http://www.usatoday.com/story/news/nation/2013/06 /25/stateline-medicaid-prisoners/2455201/.

36. Ibid.

37. Ibid.

CHAPTER 11: THE EARNED INCOME TAX CREDIT

1. Editorial Board, "Slowing the Decline in the Size of the Labor Force," *Washington Post*, September 7, 2013, http://www.washingtonpost.com/opinions /slowing-the-decline-in-the-size-of-the-labor-force/2013/09/07/92b27b50-1734 -11e3-804b-d3a1a3a18f2c_story.html.

2. John Wancheck and Robert Greenstein, "Earned Income Tax Credit Overpayment and Error Issues," Center on Budget and Policy Priorities (2011).

3. "Chart Book: The Earned Income Tax Credit and Child Tax Credit," Center on Budget and Policy Priorities (2015), http://www.cbpp.org/research/federal-tax /chart-book-the-earned-income-tax-credit-and-child-tax-credit.

4. Ibid.

5. "Refundable Tax Credits," Congressional Budget Office, Publication no. 4152 (2013): 2.

6. Ibid., 15.

7. Jackie Calmes, "Obama Budget Would Expand Low-Income Tax Break," *New York Times*, March 3, 2014, http://www.nytimes.com/2014/03/04/us/politics /obama-budget-would-expand-low-income-tax-break.html?_r=0.

8. Kyle Pomerleau, "Overview of the Earned Income Tax Credit on EITC Awareness Day," Tax Foundation (2014).

9. Ibid.

10. Erica Williams and Michael Leachman, "States Can Adopt or Expand Earned Income Tax Credits to Build a Stronger Future Economy," Center on Budget and Policy Priorities (2015).

11. Ibid., 3.

12. Ibid., 3.

13. "Earned Income Tax Credit: Do I Qualify?" Internal Revenue Service, FS-2014-4 (2014).

14. Williams and Leachman, "States Can Adopt or Expand Earned Income Tax Credits," 2–3.

15. "The Tax Policy Briefing Book: A Citizens' Guide to the 2012 Election and Beyond," Tax Policy Center (2012): II-1-25.

16. Hilary Hoynes, "Proposal 11: Building on the Success of the Earned Income Tax Credit," Hamilton Project, Brookings Institution (2014).

17. Michael Tanner, personal communication, August 14, 2014.

18. Chuck Marr, Chye-Ching Huang, and Arloc Sherman, "Earned Income Tax Credit Promotes Work, Encourages Children's Success at School, Research Finds," Center on Budget and Policy Priorities (2014).

19. Ibid., 1.

20. Ibid., 7.

21. Ibid., 6.

22. Gordon B. Dahl and Lance Lochner, "The Impact of Family Income on Child Achievement: Evidence from the Earned Income Tax Credit," *American Economic Review* 102, no. 5 (2012): 1927–1956.

23. Marr, Huang, and Sherman, "Earned Income Tax Credit Promotes Work," 8.

24. Ibid., 4.

25. Molly Dahl, Thomas DeLeire, and Jonathan Schwabish, "Stepping Stone or Stone Dead? The Effects of the EITC on Earnings Growth," Institute for the Study of Labor, DP no. 4146.

26. Chuck Marr and Chye-Ching Huang, "Strengthening the EITC for Childless Workers Would Promote Work and Reduce Poverty," Center on Budget and Policy Priorities (2015).

27. "Tax Policy Briefing Book," II-2-7.

28. Ibid.

29. "Expansion of Controls over Refundable Credits Could Help Reduce the Billions of Dollars of Improperly Paid Claims," Treasury Inspector General for Tax Administration, no. 2012-40-105 (2012).

30. "The Internal Revenue Service Is Not in Compliance with All Improper Payments Eliminations and Recovery Act Requirements," Treasury Inspector General for Tax Administration, no. 2012-40-028 (2012).

31. Bonnie Lee, "Cutting Down on Tax Fraud: Understanding the EITC," *Fox Business*, May 29, 2014, http://www.foxbusiness.com/personal-finance/2014/05/29/cutting-down-on-tax-fraud-understanding-eitc/.

32. Ibid.

CHAPTER 12: PATTERNS OF DEPENDENCE AND INDEPENDENCE

1. Tina Norris, Paul L. Vines, and Elizabeth M. Hoeffel, "The American Indian and Alaska Native Population: 2010," U.S. Census Bureau, 2010 Census Briefs (2012).

2. Ibid.

3. "Attorney General Holder and Secretary Salazar Announce $1 Billion Settlement of Tribal Trust Accounting and Management Lawsuits Filed by More Than 40 Tribes," Department of Justice (2014), http://www.justice.gov/opa/pr/attorney-general-holder-and-secretary-salazar-announce-1-billion-settlement-tribal-trust.

4. "American Indian and Alaska Native Death Rates Nearly 50 Percent Greater Than Those of Non-Hispanic Whites," Centers for Disease Control and Prevention, Press Release (2014).

5. John H. Barnhill, "Substance Abuse," *Encyclopedia of American Indian Issues Today* (Santa Barbara, CA: ABC-CLIO, 2013), 252.

6. "Disparities," Indian Health Service, http://www.ihs.gov/newsroom/factsheets/disparities/.

7. Paloma Esquivel, "Liquor Stores Divide a Dry Reservation," *Los Angeles Times*, February 2, 2013, http://articles.latimes.com/2013/feb/02/nation/la-na-hometown-pine-ridge-20130203.

8. Timothy Williams, "At Tribe's Door, A Hub of Beer and Heartache," *New York Times*, March 5, 2012, http://www.nytimes.com/2012/03/06/us/next-to-tribe-with-alcohol-ban-a-hub-of-beer.html?pagewanted=all.

9. Ibid.

10. Michele C. Black, Kathleen C. Basile, Matthew J. Breiding, Sharon G. Smith, Mikel L. Walters, Melissa T. Merrick, Jieru Chen, and Mark R. Stevens, "The National Intimate Partner and Sexual Violence Survey: 2010 Summary Report," Centers for Disease Control and Prevention (2011): 20.

11. Ibid., 3.

12. Timothy Williams, "For Native American Women, Scourge of Rape, Rare Justice," *New York Times*, May 22, 2012, http://www.nytimes.com/2012/05/23/us/native-americans-struggle-with-high-rate-of-rape.html?pagewanted=all.

13. Norris, Vines, and Hoeffel, "American Indian and Alaska Native Population: 2010."

14. Robin N. Nazzaro, "Indian Issues: Timeliness of the Tribal Recognition Process Has Improved, but It Will Take Years to Clear the Existing Backlog of Petitions," U.S. Government Accountability Office, GAO-05-347T (2005): 1.

15. Beth Ward, *Dying in Indian Country: A Family Journey from Self-Destruction to Opposing Tribal Sovereignty* (Bloomington, IN: WestBow Press, 2000): 280–281.

16. Russell M. Lawson, ed., *Encyclopedia of American Issues Today*, 2 vols. (Santa Barbara, CA: ABC-CLIO, 2013).

17. Zack Colman, "Stakes Are High in Fracking Debate on Indian Reservations," *Washington Examiner*, August 7, 2014, http://www.washingtonexaminer.com/stakes-are-high-in-fracking-debate-on-indian-reservations/article/2551746.

18. Saleem Ali, "Methane and the Transformation of an Indigenous Community in Colorado," *National Geographic*, June 16, 2014, http://voices.nationalgeographic.com/2014/06/16/methane-and-the-transformation-of-an-indigenous-community-in-colorado/.

19. "Scholarships," Southern Ute Indian Tribe (2015), https://www.southernute-nsn.gov/education/scholarships/.

20. Michaela D. Platzer, "Remote Gambling: Industry Trends and Federal Policy," Congressional Research Service, no. R42820 (2012): 1; 14.

21. Timothy Williams, "$1 Million Each Year for All, as Long as Tribe's Luck Holds," *Washington Post* (2012), http://www.nytimes.com/2012/08/09/us/more-casinos-and-internet-gambling-threaten-shakopee-tribe.html?pagewanted=2&ref=us&src=me.

22. "Inside the Richest Native American Tribe in the U.S. Where Casino Profits Pay $1m a Year to EVERY Member," *Daily Mail* (2012), http://www.dailymail.co.uk/news/article-2187456/Shakopee-Mdewakanton-Tribe-Casino-revenue-pays-member-1million-year.html.

23. Steve Date, "Flood of Casino Money Brings Challenges—and Opportunities—for Reservation Schools," *Minnesota Post* (2012), https://www.minnpost.com/politics-policy/2012/12/flood-casino-money-brings-challenges-and-opportunities-reservation-schools.

24. Ibid.

25. "Yakama Tribal Enterprises and Programs," *Yakama Nation,* http://www.yakamanation-nsn.gov/enterprise.php.

26. Carol Alexander, "Backgrounder," University of Tennessee at Martin, https://www.google.com/webhp?sourceid=chrome-instant&ion=1&espv=2&ie=UTF-8#q=Carol+Alexander+%22Backgrounder%22%2C+University+of+Tennessee+at+Martin.

27. E. Jane Costello et al., "Association of Family Income Supplements in Adolescence with Development of Psychiatric and Substance Use Disorders in Adulthood among an American Indian Population," *Journal of the American Medical Association* 303, no. 19 (2010): 1954–1960.

28. Scott McKie, "CHS Improves Graduation, Dropout Rates," *Cherokee One Feather* (2011), http://www.nc-cherokee.com/theonefeather/files/2011/01/July-28.pdf.

29. Charles Murray, *Coming Apart: The State of White America 1960–2010* (New York: Crown Forum, 2012), 16.

30. Justin Abernathy, "Famous Dave Reflects on a Life of Success," *Native Sun News* (2012), http://www.indianz.com/News/2012/004652.asp.

31. Calvin Helin, *The Economic Dependency Trap* (Cubbie Blue Publishing, 2010), https://books.google.com/books?id=VBjJAwAAQBAJ&pg=PT118&dq=look+what+native+americans+have+traded+for+their+welfare+crumbs+Helin&hl=en&sa=X&ved=0CB4Q6AEwAGoVChMIqqfIy8bUxwIVDpuICh2SvggJ#v=onepage&q=look%20what%20native%20americans%20have%20traded%20for%20their%20welfare%20crumbs%20Helin&f=false.

32. "Did You Know," North American Association of State and Provincial Lotteries (2015), http://www.naspl.org/index.cfm?fuseaction=content&menuid=14&pageid=1020.

33. Ibid.

34. Peter Kuhn, Peter Kooreman, Adriaan R. Soetevent, and Arie Kapteyn, "The Own and Social Effects of an Unexpected Income Shock: Evidence from the Dutch Postcode Lottery," University of California–Santa Barbara, Department of Economics (2008).

35. Arthur C. Brooks, *The Battle: How the Fight Between Free Enterprise and Big Government Will Shape America's Future* (New York: Basic Books, 2010), 75.

36. Arthur C. Brooks, *The Road to Freedom: How to Win the Fight for Free Enterprise* (New York: Basic Books, 2012).

37. Jason DeParle, *American Dream: Three Women, Ten Kids, and a Nation's Drive to End Welfare* (New York: Penguin Group, 2004).

38. "The Fate of Families after Welfare," *PBS Newshour*, February 14, 2005, http://www.pbs.org/newshour/bb/government_programs-jan-june05-welfare _2–14/.

39. Charles A. S. Hynam, "The Dysfunctionality of Unrequited Giving," *Human Organization* 25, no. 1 (1966).

40. Krissy Clark, "The Secret Life of a Food Stamp," *National Public Radio: Marketplace and Slate Magazine* (2014), http://www.marketplace.org/topics /wealth-poverty/secret-life-food-stamp/anti-hunger-movements-strange -bedfellows.

41. Eli Saslow, "Hard Work: A Florida Republican Pushing to Overhaul the Food Stamp System Toils to Win Over a Divided Congress," *Washington Post*, September 24, 2013, http://www.washingtonpost.com/sf/national/2013/09/24 /hard-work/.

42. Marianne Bitler and Hilary W. Hoynes, "Immigrants, Welfare Reform, and the U.S. Safety Net," National Bureau of Economic Research, Working Paper no. 17667. http://dx.doi.org/10.3386/w17667

43. Michael Tanner, personal communication, February 27, 2015.

44. Sudhir Alladi Venkatesh, *Off the Books: The Underground Economy of the Urban Poor* (Boston: Harvard University Press, 2009): xix.

45. Ibid., 210.

46. Ibid., 385.

47. Joe Weisenthal, "Look How the Unemployment Rate Is Plunging in the One State That Already Canceled Long-Term Unemployment Benefits," *Business Insider*, January 18, 2014, http://www.businessinsider.com/north-carolina-unemployment -rate-2014-1.

48. Craig Garthwaite, Tal Gross, and Matthew J. Notowidigdo, "Public Health Insurance, Labor Supply, and Employment Lock," National Bureau of Economic Research, Working Paper no. 19220 (2013).

49. Marcus Hagedorn, Iourii Manovskii, and Kurt Mitman, "The Impact of Unemployment Benefit Extensions on Employment: The 2014 Employment Miracle?" National Bureau of Economic Research, Working Paper no. 20884, January 2015, http://dx.doi.org/10.3386/w20884

50. Barbara Blouin, *Labors of Love: The Legacy of Inherited Wealth, Book II* (Canada: The Inheritance Project, 2002), 13.

51. Michael Tanner, "When Welfare Undermines Work Ethic," *New York Times,* May 5, 2013, http://www.nytimes.com/roomfordebate/2013/05/05/denmarks-work -life-balance/when-welfare-undermines-work-ethic.

CHAPTER 13: WHAT SHOULD BE DONE

1. "A Memo to Obama," *The Economist*, March 1, 2014, http://www.economist.com/news/united-states/21597925-want-make-america-less-unequal-here-are-some-suggestions-memo-obama.

2. James Surowiecki, "A Fair Day's Wage," *The New Yorker*, February 9, 2015, http://www.newyorker.com/magazine/2015/02/09/fair-days-wage.

3. Ibid.

4. "Topic 751—Social Security and Medicare Withholding Rates," Internal Revenue Service, http://www.irs.gov/taxtopics/tc751.html.

5. "Tax Reform Act of 2014 Discussion Draft: Section-by-Section Summary," Committee on Ways and Means (2014).

6. Lawrence Summers, "How to Avoid a Lost Decade," *Washington Post*, June 12, 2011, http://www.washingtonpost.com/opinions/how-to-avoid-a-lost-decade/2011/06/12/AGjnG8RH_story.html.

7. Ross Douthat, "Our Enemy, the Payroll Tax," *New York Times*, November 24, 2012, http://www.nytimes.com/2012/11/25/opinion/sunday/douthat-our-enemy-the-payroll-tax.html?_r=0.

8. "Policy Basics: Federal Payroll Taxes," Center on Budget and Policy Priorities (2014).

9. George F. Will, "George Will: Democrats' Policies Make Income Inequality Worse," *Washington Post*, March 14, 2014, http://www.washingtonpost.com/opinions/george-will-democrats-policies-make-income-inequality-worse/2014/03/14/97d5074e-aada-11e3-adbc-888c8010c799_story.html.

10. Melissa M. Favreault, "Why Do Some Workers Have Low Social Security Benefits?" Urban Institute, Discussion Paper 10-03 (2010): 8.

11. Milton Friedman, *Capitalism and Freedom* (Chicago: University of Chicago Press, 2002), 184.

12. "Payroll Tax Cut Temporarily Extended into 2012," Internal Revenue Service, IR-2011-124, December 23, 2011, http://www.irs.gov/uac/Payroll-Tax-Cut-Temporarily-Extended-into-2012/.

13. Edmund S. Phelps, *Rewarding Work: How to Restore Participation and Self-Support to Free Enterprise* (Boston: Harvard University Press, 2007), 7.

14. Tax Policy Center, "Tax Units with Zero or Negative Tax Liability, Current Law, 2004–2011 (T11-0173)," June 14, 2011, http://www.taxpolicycenter.org/numbers/displayatab.cfm?DocID=3054.

15. Krissy Clark, "The Secret Life of a Food Stamp," *National Public Radio: Marketplace and Slate Magazine* (2014), http://www.marketplace.org/topics/wealth-poverty/secret-life-food-stamp/anti-hunger-movements-strange-bedfellows.

16. Franklin D. Roosevelt, "Annual Message to Congress, January 4, 1935," http://www.presidency.ucsb.edu/ws/?pid=14890.

17. Michael D. Tanner and Charles Hughes, "The Work versus Welfare Trade-off: 2013," Cato Institute (2013): 34.

18. David H. Autor and Mark Duggan, "Supporting Work: A Proposal for Modernizing the U.S. Disability Insurance System," Center for American Progress and The Hamilton Project (2010).

19. Stuart Eizenstat and Robert I. Lerman, "Apprenticeships Could Help U.S. Workers Gain a Competitive Edge," Urban Institute (May 9, 2013).

20. Ibid.

21. Paul Ryan, "Expanding Opportunity in America: A Discussion Draft from the House Budget Committee," U.S. House of Representatives (July 24, 2014), http://budget.house.gov/uploadedfiles/expanding_opportunity_in_america.pdf.

22. James Gwartney, Robert Lawson, and Joshua Hall, "Economic Freedom of the World: 2013 Annual Report," Fraser Institute (2013).

23. White House, "2013 Draft Report to Congress on the Benefits and Costs of Federal Regulations and Agency Compliance with the Unfunded Mandates Reform Act," https://www.whitehouse.gov/sites/default/files/omb/inforeg/2013_cb/draft_2013_cost_benefit_report.pdf.

24. Ibid.

25. Philip K. Howard, *The Death of Common Sense: How Law Is Suffocating America* (New York: Random House, 2011), 12–13.

26. David Fahrenholdt, "Watch Him Pull a USDA-Mandated Rabbit Disaster Plan out of His Hat," *Washington Post*, http://www.washingtonpost.com/politics/watch-him-pull-a-usda-mandated-rabbit-disaster-plan-out-of-his-hat/2013/07/16/816f2f66-ed66-11e2-8163-2c7021381a75_story.html.

27. Nicole V. Crain and W. Mark Crain, "The Cost of Federal Regulation to the U.S. Economy, Manufacturing, and Small Business," National Association of Manufacturers (2014).

28. Ibid.

29. Elvina Nawaguna, "U.S. Manufacturers Cry Foul over Cost of Federal Regulations," *Reuters*, September 10, 2014, http://www.reuters.com/article/2014/09/10/us-usa-economy-regulations-idUSKBN0H520E20140910.

30. Dick M. Carpenter, Lisa Knepper, Angela C. Erickson, and John K. Ross, "License to Work: A National Study of Burdens from Occupational Licensing," Institute for Justice (2012).

31. Morris M. Kleiner, "Occupational Licensing: Protecting the Public Interest or Protectionism?" W. E. Upjohn Institute, Policy Paper no. 2011-009 (2011).

32. Dan Mangan, "Employers Face Tax Hit in States with No Medicaid Expansion," http://www.cnbc.com/2014/01/22/onundrum-employers-face-tax-hit-in-states-with-no-medicaid-expansion.html.

33. Tyler Cowen, *Average Is Over: Powering America Beyond the Age of the Great Stagnation* (New York: Penguin Group, 2013): 60.

34. Laurence J. Kotlikoff, "Abolish the Corporate Income Tax," *New York Times*, January 5, 2014, http://www.nytimes.com/2014/01/06/opinion/abolish-the-corporate-income-tax.html.

35. Arthur C. Brooks, "Be Open-Handed Toward Your Brothers," American Enterprise Institute (January 30, 2014).

36. Annie Lowrey, "Government Giving Nonprofits Angst," *New York Times*, November 7, 2013, http://www.nytimes.com/2013/11/08/giving/government-giving-nonprofits-angst.html?pagewanted=all.

37. John C. Goodman and Michael D. Stroup, "Privatizing the Welfare State," National Center for Policy Analysis, NCPA Policy Report no. 123 (1986): 11.

38. Michael Tanner, "Ending Welfare as We Know It," *Toward Liberty: The Idea That Is Changing the World* (Washington, DC: Cato Institute, 2002), 114.

39. Goodman and Stroup, "Privatizing the Welfare State," 34.

40. Ibid., 23.

41. Tanner, "Ending Welfare as We Know It," 117.

42. Jason L. Riley, "A Black Conservative's War on Poverty," *Wall Street Journal*, April 18, 2014, http://www.wsj.com/articles/SB10001424052702304441304579481593325577488.

43. Morley Safer, "Jobs Program Aids Fortune 500 and Underprivileged Youth," *CBS News*, January 26, 2014, http://www.cbsnews.com/news/jobs-program-aids-fortune-500-underprivileged-youth/.

44. Robert Doar, "The Path to Responsibility Can Start with a Broom and a Paycheck," *Wall Street Journal*, February 28, 2014, http://www.wsj.com/articles/SB10001424052702304255604579406943150652398.

45. Charles Murray, "The Happiness of the People," *Culture & Civilization Volume 2: Beyond Positivism and Historicism* (New Jersey: Transaction, 2010), 4.

46. Thomas More, *Utopia* (New York: Washington Square Press, 1975 [1516]).

47. Ibid.

48. "About the Alaska Permanent Fund Corporation (APFC)," Alaska Permanent Fund Corporation, http://www.apfc.org/home/Content/aboutAPFC/aboutAPFC.cfm.

49. Charles Murray, *In Our Hands: A Plan to Replace the Welfare State* (Washington, DC: AEI Press, 2006), 8–9.

50. Rutger Bregman, "Free Money Might Be the Best Way to End Poverty," *Washington Post*, December 29, 2013, http://www.washingtonpost.com/opinions/free-money-might-be-the-best-way-to-end-poverty/2013/12/29/679c8344-5ec8-11e3-95c2-13623eb2b0e1_story.html.

51. Sendhil Mullainathan and Eldar Shafir, "Scarcity: The New Science of Having Less and How It Defines Our Lives" (Picador, 2014).

52. Cara Fineberg, "The Science of Scarcity: A Behavioral Economist's Fresh Perspectives on Poverty," *Harvard Magazine*, May–June 2015, http://harvardmagazine.com/2015/05/the-science-of-scarcity.

53. Anna Edwards, "Streets of Basel Paved with Gold: 15 Tons of Five Cent Coins Are Dumped on City's Streets as Protesters Demand a Basic Minimum Income for Every Swiss Household," *Daily Mail*, October 4, 2013, http://www.dailymail.co.uk/news/article-2443812/Streets-Basel-paved-gold-15-TONS-cent-coins-dumped-citys-streets-protesters-demand-increased-minimum-wage.html.

54. Murray, *In Our Hands*.

55. David J. Armor and Sonia Sousa, "Restoring a True Safety Net," *National Affairs* no. 13 (2012): 27.

56. Editorial Board, "End Mass Incarceration Now," *New York Times*, May 24, 2014, http://www.nytimes.com/2014/05/25/opinion/sunday/end-mass-incarceration-now.html.

57. Tina Rosenberg, "Playing the Odds on Saving," *New York Times*, January 15, 2014, http://opinionator.blogs.nytimes.com/2014/01/15/playing-the-odds-on-saving/?hp&rref=opinion&_r=0.

58. Nicholas Kristof, "Where the G.O.P. Gets It Right," *New York Times*, April 9, 2014, http://www.nytimes.com/2014/04/10/opinion/kristof-where-the-gop-gets-it-right.html.

59. Pamela K. Kohler, Lisa E. Manhart, and William E. Lafferty, "Abstinence-Only and Comprehensive Sex Education and the Initiation of Sexual Activity and Teen Pregnancy," *Journal of Adolescent Health* no. 42 (2008): 344–351.

60. Heather D. Boonstra, "Leveling the Playing Field: The Promise of Long-Acting Reversible Contraceptives for Adolescents," *Guttmacher Policy Review* 16, no. 4 (Fall 2013).

61. Isabel V. Sawhill, *Generation Unbound: Drifting into Sex and Parenthood without Marriage* (Washington, DC: Brookings Institution Press, 2014).

62. Katherine Suellentrop, Jane Brown, and Rebecca Ortiz, "Science Says #45: Evaluating the Impact of MTV's *16 and Pregnant* on Teen Viewers' Attitudes About Teen Pregnancy," National Campaign to Prevent Teen and Unplanned Pregnancy (2010).

63. Melissa S. Kearney and Phillip B. Levine, "Media Influences on Social Outcomes: The Impact of MTV's *16 and Pregnant* on Teen Childbearing," National Bureau of Economic Research, Working Paper no. 19795 (2014).

64. Kathryn Edin and Maria Kefalas, *Promises I Can Keep: Why Women Put Motherhood Before Marriage* (Berkeley: University of California Press, 2011), 3.

65. Sawhill, *Generation Unbound*, 124–126.

66. Ibid., 82.

67. James Pethokoukis, "Can Anything Really Be Done about Family Breakdown and American Poverty? A Q&A with Brad Wilcox," American Enterprise Institute (2014).

Bibliography

Angeles, January. "How Health Reform's Medicaid Expansion Will Impact State Budgets." Center on Budget and Policy Priorities (2012).

Armor, David J., and Sonia Sousa. "Restoring a True Safety Net." *National Affairs* 13 (2012).

Aussenberg, Randy Alison, and Libby Perl. "The 2014 Farm Bill: Changing the Treatment of LIHEAP Receipt in the Calculation of SNAP Benefits." Congressional Research Service, no. R42591.

Autor, David H. "The Unsustainable Rise of the Disability Rolls in the United States: Causes, Consequences, and Policy Options." National Bureau of Economic Research, Working Paper no. 17697 (2011).

Autor, David H., and Mark G. Duggan. "The Growth in the Social Security Disability Rolls: A Fiscal Crisis Unfolding." *Journal of Economic Perspectives* 20, no. 3 (2006).

Autor, David H., and Mark Duggan. "Supporting Work: A Proposal for Modernizing the U.S. Disability Insurance System." Center for American Progress and The Hamilton Project (2010).

Barnhill, John H. "Substance Abuse." *Encyclopedia of American Indian Issues Today.* Santa Barbara, CA: ABC-CLIO, 2013.

Besharov, Douglas J., and Peter Germanis. "Evaluating WIC." *Evaluation Review* 24, no. 2 (2000).

Bitler, Marianne, and Hilary W. Hoynes. "Immigrants, Welfare Reform, and the U.S. Safety Net." National Bureau of Economic Research, Working Paper no. 17667.

Boonstra, Heather D. "Leveling the Playing Field: The Promise of Long-Acting Reversible Contraceptives for Adolescents." *Guttmacher Policy Review* 16, no. 4 (Fall 2013).

Brooks, Arthur C. *The Battle: How the Fight Between Free Enterprise and Big Government Will Shape America's Future.* New York: Basic Books, 2010, 75.

Brooks, Arthur C. *Gross National Happiness: Why Happiness Matters for America—and How We Can Get More of It.* New York: Basic Books, 2008.

Brown, Susan L. "Marriage and Child Well-Being: Research and Policy Perspectives." *Journal of Marriage and the Family* 72, no. 5 (2010).

Carpenter, Dick M., Lisa Knepper, Angela C. Erickson, and John K. Ross. "License to Work: A National Study of Burdens from Occupational Licensing." Institute for Justice (2012).

Collins, Jane L., and Victoria Mayer. *Both Hands Tied: Welfare Reform and the Race to the Bottom in the Low-Wage Labor Market.* Chicago: University of Chicago Press, 2010.

Costello, Jane E., et al. "Association of Family Income Supplements in Adolescence with Development of Psychiatric and Substance Use Disorders in Adulthood among an American Indian Population." *Journal of the American Medical Association* 303, no. 19 (2010).

Cowen, Tyler. *Average Is Over: Powering America Beyond the Age of the Great Stagnation.* New York: Penguin Group, 2013.

Dahl, Gordon B., and Lance Lochner. "The Impact of Family Income on Child Achievement: Evidence from the Earned Income Tax Credit." *American Economic Review* 102, no. 5 (2012).

Dahl, Molly, Thomas DeLeire, and Jonathan Schwabish. "Stepping Stone or Stone Dead? The Effects of the EITC on Earnings Growth." Institute for the Study of Labor, Discussion Paper no. 4146.

Deaven, Paul O., and William H. Andrews. *Social Security: New Issues and Developments.* New York: Nova Science, 2008.

Decker, Sandra L. "In 2011 Nearly One-Third of Physicians Said They Would Not Accept New Medicaid Patients, But Rising Fees May Help." *Health Affairs* 31, no. 8 (2012).

DeNavas-Walt, Carmen, and Bernadette D. Proctor. "Income and Poverty in the United States: 2013." U.S. Census Bureau, *Current Population Reports* (2014).

DeParle, Jason. *American Dream: Three Women, Ten Kids, and a Nation's Drive to End Welfare.* New York: Penguin Group, 2004.

Eberstadt, Nicholas. *The Poverty of "The Poverty Rate": Measure and Mismeasure of Want in Modern America.* Washington, DC: AEI Press, 2008.

Edin, Kathryn and Maria Kefalas. *Promises I Can Keep: Why Poor Women Put Motherhood Before Marriage.* Berkeley: University of California Press, 2007.

Eizenstat, Stuart, and Robert I. Lerman. "Apprenticeships Could Help U.S. Workers Gain a Competitive Edge." Urban Institute (May 9, 2013).

Favreault, Melissa M. "Why Do Some Workers Have Low Social Security Benefits?" Urban Institute, Discussion Paper no. 10-03 (2010).

Fichtner, Jason F., and Jacob Feldman. "Taxing Marriage: Microeconomic Behavioral Responses to the Marriage Penalty and Reforms for the 21st Century." Mercatus Center, Working Paper no. 12–24 (2012).

Fischer, Will. "Expanding Rental Assistance Demonstration Would Help Low-Income Families, Seniors, and People with Disabilities." Center on Budget and Policy Priorities (2014).

Floyd, Ife, and Liz Schott. "TANF Cash Benefits Continued to Lose Value in 2013." Center on Budget and Policy Priorities (2013).

Garthwaite, Craig, Tal Gross, and Matthew J. Notowidigdo. "Public Health Insurance, Labor Supply, and Employment Lock." National Bureau of Economic Research, Working Paper no. 19220 (2013).

Gettings, Robert, Charles Moseley, and Nancy Thaler. "Medicaid Managed Care for People with Disabilities: Policy and Implementation Considerations for State and Federal Policymakers." National Council on Disability (2013).

Goodman, John C., and Michael D. Stroup. "Privatizing the Welfare State." National Center for Policy Analysis, NCPA Policy Report no. 123 (1986).

Gwartney, James, Robert Lawson, and Joshua Hall. "Economic Freedom of the World: 2013 Annual Report." Fraser Institute (2013).

Hawkins, Alan J., Paul R. Amato, and Andrea Kinghorn. "Are Government-Supported Healthy Marriage Initiatives Affecting Family Demographics? A State-Level Analysis." *Family Relations* 62, no. 3 (2013).

Helin, Calvin. *The Economic Dependency Trap*. Cubie Blue Publishing, 2010.

Herbst, Chris. "Welfare Reform and the Subjective Well-Being of Single Mothers." *Journal of Population Economics* 26, no. 1 (2013).

Howard, Philip K. *The Death of Common Sense: How Law Is Suffocating America.* New York: Random House Group, 2011.

Hynam, Charles A. S. "The Dysfunctionality of Unrequited Giving." *Human Organization* 25, no. 1 (1966).

Ifcher, John. "The Happiness of Single Mothers after Welfare Reform." *B. E. Journal of Economic Analysis & Policy* 11, no. 1 (2011).

Joyce, Ted, Robert Kaestner, Sanders Korenman, and Stanley Henshaw. "Family Cap Provisions and Changes in Births and Abortions." National Bureau of Economic Research, Working Paper no. 10214 (2004).

Kearney, Melissa S., and Phillip B. Levine. "Media Influences on Social Outcomes: The Impact of MTV's *16 and Pregnant* on Teen Childbearing." National Bureau of Economic Research, Working Paper no. 19795 (2014).

Kleiner, Morris M. "Occupational Licensing: Protecting the Public Interest or Protectionism?" W. E. Upjohn Institute, Policy Paper no. 2011-009 (2011).

Kohler, Pamela K., Lisa E. Manhart, and William E. Lafferty. "Abstinence-Only and Comprehensive Sex Education and the Initiation of Sexual Activity and Teen Pregnancy." *Journal of Adolescent Health* no. 42 (2008).

Korenman, Sanders, Ted Joyce, Robert Kaestner, and Jennifer Walper. "What Did the 'Illegitimacy Bonus' Reward?" National Bureau of Economic Research, Working Paper no. 10699 (2004).

Kuhn, Peter, Peter Kooreman, Adriaan R. Soetevent, and Arie Kapteyn. "The Own and Social Effects of an Unexpected Income Shock: Evidence from the

Dutch Postcode Lottery." University of California–Santa Barbara, Department of Economics (2008).

Lawson, Russell M., ed. *Encyclopedia of American Issues Today*, 2 vols. Santa Barbara, CA: ABC-CLIO, 2013.

Layard, Richard, Andrew Clark, and Claudia Senik. "Chapter 3: The Causes of Happiness and Misery." *World Happiness Report 2013*. New York: Columbia Earth Institute, 2013.

Malbi, James, Stephen Tordella, Laura Castner, Thomas Godfrey, and Priscilla Foran. "Dynamics of Supplemental Nutrition Assistance Program Participation in the Mid-2000s." U.S. Department of Agriculture Food and Nutrition Service (2011).

Marr, Chuck, Chye-Ching Huang, and Arloc Sherman. "Earned Income Tax Credit Promotes Work, Encourages Children's Success at School, Research Finds." Center on Budget and Policy Priorities (2014).

Martinez-Schiferl, Michael. "WIC Participants and Their Growing Need for Coverage." Urban Institute (2012).

Mauldon, Jane G., Rebecca A. London, David J. Fein, and Steven J. Bliss. "What Do They Think? Welfare Recipients' Attitudes Towards Marriage and Childbearing." Welfare Reform and Family Formation Project, Research Brief no. 2 (2002).

Moffit, Robert A. "The Effect of Welfare on Marriage and Fertility: What Do We Know and What Do We Need to Know?" Institute for Research on Poverty, Discussion Paper no. 1153–97. Johns Hopkins University, 1997.

More, Thomas. *Utopia*. New York: Washington Square Press, 1975.

Moulta-Ali, Umar. "Primer on Disability Insurance (SSDI) and Supplemental Security Income (SSI)." Congressional Research Service, no. RL32279 (2014).

Mullainthan, Sendhil, and Eldar Shafir. *Scarcity: The New Science of Having Less and How It Defines Our Lives*. Picador, 2014.

Murray, Charles. *Coming Apart: The State of White America, 1960–2010*. New York: Crown Forum, 2012.

Murray, Charles. "The Happiness of the People." *Culture & Civilization Volume 2: Beyond Positivism and Historicism*. New Jersey: Transaction, 2010.

Murray, Charles. *In Our Hands: A Plan to Replace the Welfare State*. Washington, DC: AEI Press, 2006.

Murray, Charles. *Losing Ground: American Social Policy, 1950–1980*. New York: Basic Books, 1984.

Nazzaro, Robin N. "Indian Issues: Timeliness of the Tribal Recognition Process Has Improved, but It Will Take Years to Clear the Existing Backlog of Petitions." U.S. Government Accountability Office, GAO-05-347T (2005).

Oliviera, Victor, Elizabeth Frazao, and David Smallwood. "Rising Infant Formula Costs to the WIC Program: Recent Trends in Rebates and Wholesale Prices." U.S. Department of Agriculture, Economic Research Report no. 93 (2010).

Phelps, Edmund S. *Rewarding Work: How to Restore Participation and Self-Support to Free Enterprise*. Boston: Harvard University Press, 2007.

Pirog, Maureen A., and Kathleen M. Ziol-Guest. "Child Support Enforcement: Programs and Policies, Impacts and Questions." *Journal of Policy Analysis and Management* 25, no. 4 (2006).

Rector, Robert, and Katherine Bradley. "Reforming the Food Stamp Program." Heritage Foundation, no. 2708 (2012).

Reeves, Aaron, Martin McKee, and David Stuckler. "Economic Suicides in the Great Recession in Europe and North America." *British Journal of Psychiatry* 205, no. 3 (2014).

Sawhill, Isabel V. *Generation Unbound: Drifting into Sex and Parenthood without Marriage.* Washington, DC: Brookings Institution Press, 2014.

Schott, Liz. "Policy Basics: An Introduction to TANF." Center on Budget and Policy Priorities (2012).

Schott, Liz, LaDonna Pavetti, and Ife Finch. "How States Have Spent Federal and State Funds under the TANF Block Grant." Center on Budget and Policy Priorities (2012).

Tanner, Michael D. "Ending Welfare as We Know It." *Toward Liberty: The Idea That Is Changing the World.* Washington, DC: Cato Institute, 2002.

Tanner, Michael D. "SNAP Failure: The Food Stamp Program Needs Reform." Cato Institute, Policy Analysis no. 738 (2013).

Tanner, Michael D., and Charles Hughes. "The Work versus Welfare Trade-off: 2013." Cato Institute (2013).

Taubman, Sarah L., Heidi L. Allen, Bill J. Wright, Katherine Baicker, and Amy N. Finkelstein. "Medicaid Increases Emergency-Department Use: Evidence from Oregon's Health Insurance Experiment." *Science* 343, no. 6168 (2014).

Terkel, Studs. *Working: People Talk about What They Do All Day and How They Feel about What They Do.* New York: New Press, 2013.

Venkatesh, Sudhir Alladi. *Off the Books: The Underground Economy of the Urban Poor.* Boston: Harvard University Press, 2009.

Voegeli, William. *Never Enough: America's Limitless Welfare State.* New York: Encounter Books, 2013.

Waller, Maureen, and Robert Plotnick. "Child Support and Low-Income Families: Perceptions, Practices, and Policy." Public Policy Institute of California (1999).

Ward, Beth. *Dying in Indian Country: A Family Journey from Self-Destruction to Opposing Tribal Sovereignty.* Bloomington, IN: WestBow Press, 2000.

White, Chapin. "A Comparison of Two Approaches to Increasing Access to Care: Expanding Coverage versus Increasing Physician Fees." *Health Services Research* 47, no. 3. pt1 (2012).

Williams, Erica, and Michael Leachman. "States Can Adopt or Expand Earned Income Tax Credits to Build a Stronger Future Economy." *Center on Budget and Policy Priorities* (2015).

Zedlewski, Sheila, Thomas Callan, and Gregory Acs. "TANF at 16: What Do We Know?" *Urban Institute* (2012).

Index

Additional Child Credit (ACC), 114

Aetna insurance, 147

Affordable Care Act, 32, 93, 156. *See also* Medicaid and the Affordable Care Act

Aid to Families with Dependent Children (AFDC), xi, 4, 41

Alaska Permanent Fund, 161

Aldrin, Buzz, 65

Altvater, Darlene, 76

amenities in poor households, 22 (fig.), 23

American Dream—Three Women, Ten Kids, and a Nation's Drive to End Welfare (DeParle), 138

American Economic Review on EITC, 116, 184n22

American Indians and dependence, 128–136; attraction of "the rez," 130, 131; the future of tribes, 135–136; Indian gaming, 132, 133–134; Pine Ridge reservation, 129–130, 131; Ute Mountain Ute reservation, 131, 133; Yakama Nation of eastern Washington, 134–135

American Recovery and Reinvestment Act, xviii, 20–21, 61, 75, 169nn1–2, 171n5

Americans with Disabilities Act (1990), 84, 152

Anderson, Dave, 136

Anderson, Keith, 134

Angelou, Maya, xvii

apprenticeships, 151, 153, 188n19

Argus Leader (newspaper), 59

Armor, David J., 21, 43, 75, 164, 169n3, 171n7, 174n4, 178n17, 190n55

asset depletion, 9–10

Atlantic magazine, 35

autism, 85

Autor, David, 81, 152, 179n25, 188n18

Barnhill, John, 129, 185n5

barterers, 141–143

The Battle (Brooks), 137

benefits, require work for, 151

Besharov, Douglas J., 69, 177n5

Binder, Charles (Binder group), 78

birth control, 30, 31–32, 165–166

block grants, 42, 44

Blovin, Barbara, 143, 187n50

boredom and depression, 6–7

Box, Matthew, 132
Bregman, Rutger, 162, 190n50
British Journal of Psychiatry on suicide
 rates, 6
Brookings Institution, xii, 114
Brooks, Arthur, 6, 137, 157, 170n10,
 186nn35–36, 189n35
Brooks, David, 83, 179nn31–32
Bucholtz, Debra, 132
Burning Man event, 142

Camp, Dave, 147
cash assistance programs, 72–73
*The Center for Neighborhood
 Enterprise*, 159–160
Center for Public Integrity, 102
Center on Budget and Policy
 Priorities (CBPP): on the childless
 worker, 114; on educational
 outcomes of young children
 in low-income families,
 115–116
Centesimus Annus (papal encyclical,
 John Paul II), 158–159
child poverty rates, 26
child poverty rates by living
 arrangement: 1975–2009, 26 (fig.)
child support and welfare benefits, 36,
 173nn37–41
Child Tax Credit (CTC), xix;
 Additional Child Credit (ACC),
 114; availability of, 113–114; link to
 the EITC, 110
childbirth and marriage, decoupling
 of, 35
Coburn, Tom, 82
cohabitation and fiscal penalization,
 35, 173n32
Collins, Jane, 15, 170n12
condom use, 31
Congressional Budget Office (CBO)
 report on: the Disability Insurance
 Trust Fund (2012), 82, 179nn29–30;
 on Earned Income Tax Credit
 (EITC), 110–111

contraception, the promise of
 long-acting reversible, 31–32. *See
 also* birth control
corporate income tax, elimination or
 reduction of, 157
cost of Medicaid fraud, 102, 103,
 182n25
Costello, Jane, 135
costs of regulation on U.S.
 employers, 155
Cowen, Tyler, 83, 179nn33
Craigslist, 69, 75
Crain, W. Mark, 156
credit unions, 164–165

Dahl, Molly, 116, 184n25
Daily Mail (London), 134
DeParle, Jason, 138
destitution, 20
diagnostic causes of new SSDI awards,
 74 (fig.)
disability: Americans with Disabilities
 Act (1990), 84; "The Disability-
 Industrial Complex," 78, 178n20;
 medical qualifications for disability
 benefits, 92; number of working-
 age Americans now qualified for
 disability, 84; payments to VRAs
 and ENs, 80, 89–90; Social Security
 Disability Insurance (SSDI), 73–75,
 88. *See also* disability for veterans;
 dis-abling children
disability for veterans, 86–88
Disability Insurance Trust Fund, CBO
 report on, 82
dis-abling children, 85–86
doctor shortages, 101, 103
Dodd-Frank law, 155
Doe Fund, 160
Douthat, Ross, 147, 188n7
drug testing, 62
Duggan, Mark, 87, 152, 153, 179n25,
 188n18
dysfunctionality of unrequited
 giving, 139

earned income, 79 (table), 152

earned income and welfare package, hypothetical, 11–12, 170n5

Earned Income Tax Credit (EITC), xix, 109–124; Child Tax Credit (CTC), 110, 113–114; FICA taxes and, 110; Obama, Barack, on, 111, 183n7; original idea for, 109; state EITCs, 112

earned success, 137

earned welfare, 151

earnings in the underground economy, 22

Eastern Band of Cherokee Indians, North Carolina, 135

Eberstadt, Nicholas, 24, 171nn10 and 13

The Economic Dependency Trap (Helin), 136

Edin, Kathryn, 30, 31, 35, 167, 172nn14–16, 191n64

efforts to encourage work: Ticket to Work and Work Incentives Improvement Act, 84, 85; Trial Work Period, 84

Einstein, Albert, 143

EITC and CTC calculations: married taxpayers, 122–124 (table)

EITC and CTC calculations: single taxpayers, 119–121 (table)

Emergency Medical Treatment and Labor Act (EMTALA), 101, 182n

emergency room visits, 101–102

employer mandates, easing up on, 156–157

Employment Networks (ENs), 80, 89–90

The Encyclopedia of American Indian Issues Today, 129

"Family Cap Provisions and Changes in Births and Abortions" (working paper), 34, 173n29

family caps, 34, 46

family structure and the alleviation of poverty, 166–167

Fatherhood, Marriage, and Families Innovation Fund, 33

federal welfare budget, amount of, 21

FICA (Federal Insurance Contributions Act), overall deduction of, 74

FICA taxes, elimination or reduction of, 147–148

financial incentives for remaining single, 34–35

food stamp trading, 69

food stamp trap, 12–13

food stamps, 53–64; cash for, 60; cost of, 53; expansion of the SNAP program, 54; as a gateway to other welfare programs, 61; misuse and abuse of, 60–62; the nonpoor and, 57; recruiting SNAP beneficiaries, 56

"free phone" program, 61

Friedman, Milton: on negative income tax, 161; on the Social Security system, 148

Frontline, 102

Gabriel, Debra, 84, 179n37

Gade, Lt. Col. Daniel, 86, 87–88

Galbraith, John Kenneth, 161

Generation Unbound: Drifting into Sex and Parenthood without Marriage (Sawhill), 167, 191n65

German Socio-Economic Panel, 5, 169n7

Goike, Ken, 62

Goodman, John C., 158, 189n37

Greitens, Eric, 86

Hamilton Project, xii

happiness, 3–7; current welfare system and, 7; earned accomplishment, 167; work and, 4–7

Hawaii, welfare benefits of, 21, 151

health professional–shortage areas in the U.S., number of, 101
Health Resources and Services Administration, 101
Healthy Marriages Initiatives (HMI) program, 33, 34
Helin, Calvin, 136, 186n31
Herbst, Chris, 5, 169n3
high marginal tax rate, 150
housing assistance in 2012 dollars, 51 (fig.)
housing system, 49–52; Center on Budget and Policy Priorities (CBPP) on, 50; noncompliant participants in, 50–52
"How Anti-Poverty Programs Marginalize Fathers" (Stuart), 35
Hynam, Charles, 139, 187n39

Ifcher, John, 5, 169n2
"Illegitimacy Bonus" experiment, 34
illiteracy income, 85
immigrants, 140–141
incarceration, 35, 164
incentives for VRAs and ENs, 90
income inequality, 20
income level defining poverty, 20
income limits, 10–12; the welfare cliff, 11
independence (and aversion to handouts), 137–140
independence, importance of, 7
inherited wealth, 143
In Our Hands (Murray), 163–164

James, Ann, 30
job creation, 154–155
Joffe-Walt, Chana, 78, 80, 81–82, 85–86, 178n20
Journal of Adolescent Health study, 165–166, 191n59
Journal of Family Relations study, 34

Kahneman, Daniel, 162
Kearney, Melissa S., 166, 191n63

Kefalas, Maria, 30, 31, 35, 167, 172nn14–16, 191n64
Kleiner, Morris, 156, 189n31
Kotlikoff, Laurence, 157, 189n34
Kristof, Nicholas, 28, 71, 85, 165, 172n8, 179n42, 191n58
Krugman, Paul, 56, 176n10

labor force participation rate, 82–83, 83 (fig.)
Lapid, Yair, 143
Law of Unintended Rewards, 9, 170n1
LePage, Paul, 55
Levine, Phillip B., 166, 191n63
licensing requirements, elimination of dysfunctional, 156
living standards of the poor, 20
long-acting reversible contraceptives (LARCs), 31–32, 166, 172n20
lottery savings accounts, 164–165
lottery winnings, 137
Low Income Home Energy Assistance Program (LIHEAP) loophole, 58–59
Lowery, Annie, 30, 172n12
low-income childless people, discrimination against, 114
low-income workers, subsidize wages on a sliding scale for: administration of, 150; suggested scale for supplementing the wages of low-income workers, 149 (table)

Malcolm X, 71
marginal tax rate, high, 150
marriage, childbearing, and teen pregnancy, 25–37; correlation between one-parent families and persistent poverty, 28; decline of marriage, 34; financial incentives for remaining single, 34–35; percentage of total births to unmarried women, 1940–2013,

27 (fig.); poverty rate among mothers-only families, 26; teen pregnancy rates, 26. *See also* welfare and childbirth
marriage, decline of, 34–37
marriageable men, declining pool of, 35
Massachusetts SNAP calculations, 151
Maximus Inc. case, 15–16, 170n12
Mayer, Victoria, 15, 170n12
Mead, Lawrence, 27–28
median asking rent, 1998–2013, 50 (fig.)
median monthly rental rates for the U.S., 49
Medicaid and the Affordable Care Act, 93–107; cost of serving Medicaid enrollee varies widely across the states, 107; costs, rising, 97–99; eligibility requirements, 95; emergency room visits, 101–102; federal, state, and local Medicaid expenditures (1980–2010), 99 (fig.); Medicaid benefits under the ACA, 100 (table); prisoner enrollment, 104; state exchanges, 93, 98
Medicaid dental care, substandard, 102, 182n26
Medicaid fraud, cost of, 102, 103, 182n25
medical coverage, 85, 93, 96
medical qualifications for disability benefits, 92
medical review, 81, 85
Medicare, xii; disability and, 72, 84; FICA payroll taxes, 110, 147
Michigan Credit Union League, 164–165
minimum basic income, 161
Minnesota Post, 134
The Mission Continues nonprofit, 86
MOE and block grant spending (in nominal dollars), 43 (fig.)
money and property, 161–163

Morris, Roland Sr., 127
Morrison, S. Kayla, 132
Moynihan, Daniel Patrick, 9, 27, 172n6
Mullainathan, Sendhil, 162, 190n51
Murray, Charles, 9, 72–73, 93, 135, 160, 163–164, 170n1, 178n6

National Affairs magazine, 21
National Bureau of Economic Research (NBER): on cutoff of unemployment benefits, 143; on family caps, 34, 173n29
National Health Service Corps Loan Repayment program, 104
National Public Radio (NPR) interviews with single mothers who had left welfare, 4, 169n1
Native Sun News, 136
negative income tax, 161
negative value of a gift: Ryan's income, 14 (table)
New York Post, 61
New York Times, 23, 35, 58, 62, 164, 171n11, 175nn12–13
nine-month rule, 76–78
noncustodial parents, 36

Obama, Barack, 111, 146, 183n7
Obama administration on the housing system, 51
obesity/overweight, 62–63
Occupational Safety and Health Administration, 155
Off the Books: The Underground Economy of the Urban Poor (Venkatesh), 142
Opportunity Grants, 151, 153–154
opt-in and opt-out states and the District of Columbia, 2014, 105–106 (table)
Organisation for Economic Co-operation and Development (OECD) countries, 19–20
over-the-counter medications, 101

paid employment, 6, 92, 140
patterns of dependence and
    independence: American Indians
    on reservations, barterers, and
    immigrants, 127–144. *See also
    specific entries*
payment by barter and trade, 22
payments to the nonpoor, 20–23
payments to VRAs and ENs, 80, 89–90
payroll taxes, 93, 110, 147. *See also*
    FICA taxes, elimination or
    reduction of
percentage of total births to
    unmarried women (1940–2013),
    27 (fig.)
Personal Responsibility and Work
    Opportunity Reform Act, 42
phase out government-funded
    welfare, 150, 160
Phelps, Edmund S., 150, 188n13
Pine Ridge reservation, 129–130,
    131
Planned Parenthood, 30
Plotnick, Robert, 36, 173n40
Pondiscio, Robert, 30
poverty, what counts as, 19–23;
    amenities in poor households, 22
    (fig.), 23; Armor, David, on, 171n7;
    definitions of, 19, 20; income
    inequality concern, 20; U.S. official
    poverty level, 19
Poverty in America (Wilcox), 167
poverty rate among mothers-only
    families, 26
primary care providers, 101, 103–104
private disability coverage, 153
private sector, sample programs in,
    159–160
privatized welfare, 158–159
*Promises I Can Keep: Why Women Put
    Motherhood before Marriage* (Edin
    & Kefalas), 30–31, 35, 167
Public Consulting Group (PCG), 80
public social expenditures growth,
    xix, 20

Reagan, Ronald, 109
recession of 2008: cash assistance
    programs and, 72; expansion of
    welfare programs, xviii–xix; FICA
    elimination, 148
recruiting, 56, 152
Red Book calculation of SSI payment,
    79 (table)
relative poverty, 20
rent (median asking) 1998–2013,
    50 (fig.)
rental rates for the U.S. (median
    monthly), 49
return-to-work pattern, erosion of, 26
Rewarding Work (Phelps), 150
Rhode Island Food Bank, 56
Rigsby, Dustin, 58
The Road to Freedom (Brooks), 137
Roosevelt, Franklin Delano, 19
Roosevelt, Theodore, 53
Rosenberg, Tina, 164–165, 190n57
rules relating to the five-year lifetime
    TANF limit, 46
Ryan, Paul, 109, 153–154, 188n21

Sanger, Margaret, 41
Santa Clara University's Center for
    Applied Ethics (2012), 4, 169n2
"Save to Win," an imaginative lottery/
    savings scheme, 165
Sawhill, Isabel, 166, 167, 191n61
self respect, 6
Shakopee tribe of Minnesota, 134
single parenthood: as financially
    viable, 35; and poverty rates,
    26, 166
16 and Pregnant (MTV reality-style
    show), 166, 191n63
60 Minutes, 82
Smith, Gary, on hypothetical earned
    income and welfare package, 11,
    170n5
Smith, Patty, 143
Social Security Administration's Red
    Book, 78, 79 (table)

Social Security Disability Insurance
(SSDI), 73–75; analysis of, 152, 153,
188n18; Autor, David, on, 81,
179n25, 188n18; diagnostic causes
of new SSDI awards, 74 (fig.);
eligibility for, 88
Sousa, Sonia, 21, 43, 75, 164, 169n3,
171n7, 174n4, 178n17, 190n55
Southerland, Steve, 140
Southern Ute tribe reservation,
132–133
SSDI and SSI recipients, by year,
73 (fig.)
SSDI eligibility, 88
SSDI/SSI programs, adjudication
for, 81
SSI eligibility, 88
SSI Red Book calculation of SSI
payment, 79 (table)
state family cap provisions, 34, 46
State University's School of Public Aff
airs (2011), 4, 169n3
stop incarcerating people for
nonviolent "no-complaint" crimes,
164
Stroup, Michael D., 158, 189n37
Stuart, Elizabeth, 35, 173n33
subjective well-being (SWB), 4, 5
subsistence living and welfare,
80–81
substandard dental care to Medicaid
participant, 102, 182n26
Substantial Gainful Activity (SGA),
80, 81, 90, 92
suicide, 6
Summers, Lawrence, 147
Supplemental Nutrition Assistance
Program (SNAP), xx–xxi, 43, 53, 58,
58–59. See also food stamps
Supplemental Security Income
(SSI), 75–76; benefits in, 75;
eligibility, 75, 88–89; nine-month
rule and, 76–78
support networks, 142
Surowiecki, James, 147

TANF: the changing face of cash
assistance, 41–49; estimated
number of TANF recipients by
poverty status (2010), 44 (fig.);
federal workforce requirement, 45;
pregnant women and, 46; TANF
eligibility, 43. See also Temporary
Assistance for Needy Families
(TANF) program
TANF total number of recipients and
percent change, 1996–2011, 47
(table)
Tanner, Michael, 60, 115, 141, 144, 158
tax rates for the poor, 110
Temporary Assistance for Needy
Families (TANF) program:
American Recovery and
Reinvestment Act, 20–21, 171n5;
benefits, limit of, 4–5; family caps,
34, 46. See also TANF: the changing
face of cash assistance
Terkel, Studs, 5, 170n9
tests for disability, 81–82
Ticket to Work and Work Incentives
Improvement Act, 84–85, 89
Tobin, James, 161
Tyler, Anne, 25

underground economy, 142–143
United States: babies born out of
wedlock, percentage of, 27; federal
welfare budget, amount of, 21;
poverty threshold amount in, 23
unmarried mothers, 27–28
unmarried women, percentage of
total births to (1940–2013), 27 (fig.)
USDA survey questions to assess
household food security, 63–64
Ute Mountain Ute reservation, 131,
133
Utopia (More), 161

Venkatesh, Sudhir Alladi, on the
underground economy, 142–143,
187n44

Vig, Charlie, 134
Vocational Rehabilitation Agencies
 (VRAs), 80, 89–90
Voegeli, William, 19, 171n3
VRAs and ENs, payments to, 80,
 89–90

wage subsidies, xii, xiii, 150
Waller, Maureen, 36, 173nn40
Washington Post, 56, 98, 109, 140,
 175n6
Washington Times on, 59, 176nn19–20
welfare and childbirth, 28–31; analysis
 of early childbearing by poor
 women, 30; Women, Infants and
 Children (WIC) program, 28
welfare and work, the war between,
 9–16; asset depletion, 9–10; food
 stamp trap, 12–13
welfare benefits and pay for low-wage
 work, 151
welfare benefits from state to state, 21
welfare budget (federal), amount
 of, 21
welfare inertia, 33, 157

welfare: make welfare pay less than
 work, 151
welfare programs, raising the earnings
 caps for all, 152
welfare reforms (1996): Herbst, Chris,
 on, 5, 169n3; significance of, xi
welfare state, expansion of, 20
wheelchair scam, 102
White Clay, Nebraska, 129–130
WIC: missteps with women and
 children, 65–69; antibreastfeeding
 bias, 68; requirement to receive, 28
Wilcox, W. Bradford, 167, 191n67
Will, George, 27, 172n7
Woodson, Bob, 159
work and happiness, 4–7
"workfare" reforms, 4–5
Working (Terkel), 5, 170n9
working-class men's flight from
 work, xii
World Happiness Report 2013, 5,
 169n8
worldwide poverty line, 19

Year Up program, 160

About the Authors

PHIL HARVEY writes for the *Huffington Post, Forbes,* and other publications, and is the author of three nonfiction books: *The Government vs. Erotica*, which was praised by *Publishers Weekly* and *Booklist* and nominated by the ALA Intellectual Freedom Roundtable as a best book on intellectual freedom for 2001; *Let Every Child Be Wanted*, which drew praise from former president Jimmy Carter; and *Government Creep*, which Media Coalition called "a frightening, enlightening story." *Show Time*, his first novel, was published in 2012.

Harvey is president of the DKT Liberty Project, which raises awareness about liberty and freedom in the United States, promotes civil liberties, and supports legal cases that advance individual rights. He is also the chairman of DKT International, a Washington, DC–based charity that provides family planning and HIV/AIDS prevention programs in eighteen nations. He is chairman and founder of the mail-order firm Adam & Eve.

LISA CONYERS is Director of Policy Studies for the DKT Liberty Project, where she works on topics including welfare, inequality, and civil liberties. Also a consultant and ghostwriter who focuses on economics, sociology, and public policy issues, she has contributed to *The New York Times*, *Los Angeles Times*, and *Huffington Post*. She recently served on the Kemp Foundation's Advisory Council for the *Forum on Expanding Opportunity*. She is a contributing author for *Self-Control vs. Government Control*, an Atlas Network anthology of essays on the subject of self-governance.

She divides her time between the East and West Coasts, living in Seattle, Washington, in Washington, DC, and in Sarasota, Florida, where she considers her sailboat a second home.